MY GRANDMOTHER'S
FAMILY COOKBOOK

MY GRANDMOTHER'S FAMILY COOKBOOK

200 RECIPES FROM A TRADITIONAL KITCHEN

OLD-FASHIONED COOKING AT ITS BEST, WITH MUCH-LOVED
DISHES THAT STAND THE TEST OF TIME, SHOWN
STEP BY STEP IN OVER 640 PHOTOGRAPHS

EDITOR: CATHERINE BEST

LORENZ BOOKS

This edition is published by Lorenz Books, an imprint of
Anness Publishing Ltd, Hermes House, 88–89 Blackfriars Road,
London SE1 8HA; tel. 020 7401 2077; fax 020 7633 9499

www.lorenzbooks.com; www.annesspublishing.com

If you like the images in this book and would like to investigate using
them for publishing, promotions or advertising, please visit our website
www.practicalpictures.com for more information.

UK distributor: Book Trade Services; tel. 0116 2759086;
fax 0116 2759090; uksales@booktradeservices.com;
exportsales@booktradeservices.com
North American distributor: National Book Network;
tel. 301 459 3366; fax 301 429 5746; www.nbnbooks.com
Australian distributor: Pan Macmillan Australia;
tel. 1300 135 113; fax 1300 135 103;
customer.service@macmillan.com.au
New Zealand distributor: David Bateman Ltd;
tel. (09) 415 7664; fax (09) 415 8892

Publisher: Joanna Lorenz
Editorial Director: Helen Sudell
Executive Editor: Joanne Rippin
Designer: Adelle Morris
Editorial reader: Barbara Toft
Production controller: Mai-Ling Collyer
For recipe writers and photographers, see p256

ETHICAL TRADING POLICY
Because of our ongoing ecological investment programme, you, as our
customer, can have the pleasure and reassurance of knowing that a tree
is being cultivated on your behalf to naturally replace the materials used
to make the book you are holding. For further information about this
scheme, go to www.annesspublishing.com/trees.

NOTES
Bracketed terms are intended for American readers.
For all recipes, quantities are given in both metric and imperial measures
and, where appropriate, in standard cups and spoons. Follow one set of
measures, but not a mixture, because they are not interchangeable.
Standard spoon and cup measures are level. 1 tsp = 5ml, 1 tbsp = 15ml,
1 cup = 250ml/8fl oz.
Australian standard tablespoons are 20ml. Australian readers should use
3 tsp in place of 1 tbsp for measuring small quantities.
American pints are 16fl oz/2 cups. American readers should use 20fl oz/
2.5 cups in place of 1 pint when measuring liquids.
Electric oven temperatures in this book are for conventional ovens. When
using a fan oven, the temperature will probably need to be reduced by
about 10–20°C/20–40°F. Since ovens vary, you should check with your
manufacturer's instruction book for guidance.
The nutritional analysis given for each recipe is calculated per portion
(i.e. serving or item), unless otherwise stated. If the recipe gives a range,
such as Serves 4–6, then the nutritional analysis will be for the smaller
portion size, i.e. 6 servings. The analysis does not include optional
ingredients, such as salt added to taste.
Medium (US large) eggs are used unless otherwise stated.

Main front cover image shows Game Pie – for recipe, see page 90.

PUBLISHER'S NOTE
Although the advice and information in this book are believed to be accurate
and true at the time of going to press, neither the authors nor the publisher
can accept any legal responsibility or liability for any errors or omissions that
may have been made nor for any inaccuracies nor for any loss, harm or
injury that comes about from following instructions or advice in this book.

CONTENTS

INTRODUCTION

The meals our grandmothers made are often the ones that helped to define our childhood, and they are also the ones we should hand on to the next generation. The variety of ingredients we can call upon in cooking has expanded hugely in the last few generations, but that's no reason to lose the best of the past. The next few pages celebrate and continue that tradition, and help to recreate our own grandmother's kitchen.

TRADITIONAL COOKING

THE WORDS 'GRANDMOTHER'S KITCHEN' SUMMON UP A VISION OF A WARM, FRIENDLY PLACE SUFFUSED WITH THE AROMA OF BREAD AND CAKES, WHERE THERE'S ALWAYS A COSY WELCOME AND PLENTY OF GOODIES TO EAT. BUT THIS PLEASANT SNAPSHOT OF THE KITCHENS OF THE PAST DOES NOT TELL THE WHOLE STORY. THE COOKING OF PREVIOUS GENERATIONS ALSO HAS PLENTY TO TEACH US IN TERMS OF EATING SEASONAL, LOCAL FOOD AND PRESERVING INGREDIENTS WISELY, REDISCOVERING THE JOY OF CULINARY TRADITIONS THAT HAVE BEEN PASSED DOWN THROUGH THE DECADES.

Historically, the kitchen was the hub of the house. The extended family of grandparents, parents and children often lived together and everyone had a role to play in the household. No wonder the kitchen was the favourite place to be, with a warm stove in the winter, fresh produce in the summer and a seemingly endless supply of edible treats. The kitchen was also often the largest room in the house in a time of larders and ranges rather than the neat, streamlined cupboard units and electrical appliances of today.

SEASONAL FOOD

Before the days of supermarkets and food miles, with out-of-season products flown around the world, everyone relied on good quality, freshly picked food, often sourced nearby. The flavour and texture of fresh, local ingredients more

Below: The traditional garden is a practical resource, not a merely ornamental one, where fresh herbs are grown close to the back door.

Above: In the past, families usually stayed in one place, and grandparents played a vital part in children's care and upbringing.

than make up for their transient nature. The first new potatoes and asparagus, with butter, are really worth waiting for. And of course, these foods are pure and natural, with no preservatives.

The downside of using seasonal ingredients is that it could make for boredom in the kitchen, when there are few fresh vegetables in the winter, or nothing but lettuce and tomatoes for weeks on end in the summer; however, cooks knew all sorts of tricks to deal with this. Our grandmothers would have used gluts of ingredients in exciting new ways, such as potato pancakes for breakfast, a spicy root vegetable soup for lunch, or a shepherd's pie made with leftover meat from a joint for tea.

GROWING YOUR OWN

The back gardens of many houses were once divided into flower garden and vegetable plot, where neat rows of potatoes, carrots, onions and other

TRADITIONAL GARDENING

The delicate balance of nature in our grandparents' gardens was helped by careful planting – for example, growing flowers to attract birds and beneficial insects, which then ate the pests that might attack precious vegetables. These organic gardening techniques are being revived, as chemicals fall out of fashion. Our grandparents often followed the traditional planting routines that are now also coming back into fashion; these are often linked to the calendar or religious festivals, and even sometimes to the cycle of the moon.

vegetables vied with fruit cages for whatever space was available. Where a house had no back garden, in crowded towns and cities, people often had an allotment to grow vegetables and fruit, and this tradition continues today.

Many a backyard also contained livestock, which were vital to the family's meals. People kept chickens for their eggs and for the pot, plus a pig or two if they had the space. These useful animals consumed all sorts of kitchen scraps and then provided good protein to eat during the winter. There might

also be a beehive at the end of the garden, providing honey for desserts, cakes, and home remedies.

PRESERVING AND STORING

The old ways of preserving and storing food were passed on within families long before the advent of chilling, freezing and preservatives, and these techniques survived for hundreds of years. Many people are now concerned about chemicals and want to experience the delights of making their own pickles, jams and other preserves; you

will find plenty of these recipes in this book. Our grandmothers also knew how to bottle fruit so that a delicious sweet concoction of apricots or peaches could be enjoyed in midwinter. They dried apple rings in a warm corner of the kitchen to be soaked and used in winter pies and crumbles or biscuits (cookies). Some even preserved their own meat or fish at home. For instance, a joint of salted pork would often be hung in the kitchen chimney and smoked to make ham and bacon.

GOOD HOUSEKEEPING

Grandmother's kitchen was a place of abundance; however, this was not because of a surfeit of food, but rather because traditional cooks used every part of any food available. They would have known by learning from their own grandmothers how to cook windfall apples, wild food such as blackberries, and every part of a home-reared animals. Even scraps that could not be eaten by the family were consumed by the pig or the chickens, or composted for feeding next year's vegetable crop.

A joint of beef may have been a luxury, but once it had been served on Sunday, with Yorkshire pudding and plenty of vegetables, it would then make several more meals. Cold beef and salad, shepherd's pie, rissoles, and finally a rich beef broth could all be made from one joint. Dripping from the joint was saved for cooking or spreading on bread. Nothing was wasted in the old-fashioned kitchen.

Below: Kitchen waste was either fed to the chickens, or composted in the garden.

Below: Vegetables as well as fruit were preserved in the efficient kitchen of the past.

Below: A magnificent Sunday joint would be expected to last well into the week.

THE WELL-STOCKED KITCHEN

THE FILLING MEALS MADE AT HOME WERE VITAL TO THE HEALTH OF PREVIOUS GENERATIONS. MANY ADULTS WERE INVOLVED IN HARD PHYSICAL LABOUR, WHICH MEANT THAT THEY NEEDED PLENTY OF CALORIES, WHILE CHILDREN TENDED TO PLAY PHYSICAL GAMES OUTSIDE AND USED UP LOTS OF ENERGY. FEW CONVENIENCE FOODS OR READY MEALS WERE AVAILABLE, SO ALL MEALS WERE MADE FROM FRESH, SEASONAL INGREDIENTS OR PRESERVES FROM THE STORE CUPBOARD.

Our grandmothers knew how to use the foods that were in season and made for best value. Certain ingredients were available all year round, such as milk, meat, cheese and butter, but other vegetables and fruit were to be treasured in their freshest form – the concept of eating strawberries in mid-winter was unknown – and meats such as spring lamb also had their season.

MEAT, POULTRY AND GAME
In the early to mid-20th century, young chickens for roasting were expensive and tended to be cooked for celebration meals. Joints of beef, lamb or pork were far more common on the Sunday lunch table. Chickens were mainly seen as providers of eggs, and once their laying days were over, they might be eaten in a slow-cooked casserole, as their meat was too tough for roasting. Pork was the cheapest meat, and made meltingly delicious roasts and stews with the addition of homely vegetables such as cabbage and potatoes. A joint of ham or bacon could last a family for a long time, and even the tiniest scraps of

Below: Fresh game is a real treat, and a good cook would have known how to prepare it.

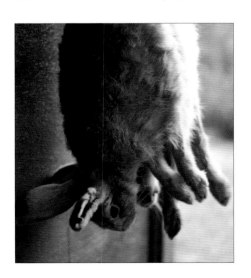

Above: The food prepared in an old-fashioned kitchen is free from preserves and additives.

meat and bones flavoured soup. Game birds such as pheasant or pigeon might be available at certain times of year, particularly in the countryside, as were mild, sweet rabbit and dark, rich venison. These tasty meats are best served in a well-flavoured sauce using herbs from the garden and juniper berries from the hedgerows.

FISH
Inland areas rarely saw fresh seafish in the days before chilled transport containers. Around the coast, however, cooks knew hundreds of recipes for the common fish such as cod or mackerel, while anyone who lived near a fast-flowing river might have access to the occasional freshwater trout or salmon. The freshest fish only needs frying gently and quickly in butter, while a small amount can be eked out for even a large family in a fish pie with hardboiled eggs and potato topping, or made into herby fishcakes.

DAIRY PRODUCTS
The larder was the place to keep milk, cream, cheese, eggs and butter. Most of these ingredients retain their flavour better in a cool place rather than in a refrigerator. They did have to be used up quickly in hot weather, hence the many traditional recipes for egg dishes, cakes and pancakes. Desserts such as gooseberry fool or strawberry snow used cream or egg whites for thickening and helped to stretch a bowlful of summer fruit to feed a whole family.

VEGETABLES
Spring and summer vegetables such as peas, asparagus, runner beans, spring cabbage and broad (fava) beans all had their season and were enjoyed at the peak of tender perfection. Hardier root vegetables could be stored carefully for winter use, and worked well in tasty combinations such as celeriac and potato mash or carrot and parsnip bake. The classic winter vegetables – leeks, parsnips, cabbage and turnips – are not harmed by a sharp frost; in fact it often enhances their flavour.

Above: Some vegetables can be picked as needed, others need storing or preserving.

FRUITS

Soft fruits such as cherries, peaches, apricots and plums need to be eaten in the summer when they are just ripe, or preserved in sugar syrup, either whole or in the form of a full-flavoured jam. Apples and pears last a little longer in storage and can make a delicious winter fruit crumble or a moist cake. Berries such as blackberries and elderberries were often gathered from the hedgerows, and traditional cooks used this free produce in pies and crumbles, or in jams and pickles that go so well with meat or cheese.

Below: Bottling or drying fruits means that they can be enjoyed all year round.

THE STORE CUPBOARD

Because most baking was done at home, the pantry or store cupboard of a grandmother's kitchen would always be stocked with constant supplies of basic ingredients: flour, yeast, lard and butter, salt, sugar, tea, cocoa powder, dried herbs and spices.

Split peas, dried beans, oats and other grains such as rice or pearl barley were economical ingredients often used in breakfast dishes or to add bulk and nutritional value to soups. Cans of food such as sardines and pilchards, corned beef, fruit in syrup and vegetables in brine were all excellent standby products to be used when fresh food was unavailable in the depths of winter.

Below: Trimming gooseberries or stoning (pitting) plums can be a sociable occasion.

KEEPING FOOD FRESH

One aspect of the kitchen that has now largely disappeared is the separate cool larder, a generously sized walk-in cupboard with a door, where dry goods and stored vegetables were neatly arranged, and jars of chutney, jam and bottled fruit gleamed on the top shelf. Many a larder used to contain a meat safe with a fine mesh to keep the meat cool and away from flies. Some even had marble shelves to keep the temperature down and make sure that milk and cheese stayed fresh, even in the hottest summer. Refrigerators and freezers may have superseded most functions of larders, but the storage space in a larder is hard to beat.

GRANDMOTHER'S HERITAGE

EVEN THOUGH FOR MANY GRANDPARENTS THE FOCUS IS NOW PERHAPS LESS ON THE KITCHEN AND MORE ON THE WORLD OUTSIDE, MANY GRANDMOTHERS ARE STILL INVOLVED IN CARING FOR THE NEXT GENERATION AND HOSTING FAMILY EVENTS AND CELEBRATIONS. COOKING HAS BECOME A POPULAR HOBBY, AND TAKING CARE OVER MEALS HAS BECOME AN ENJOYABLE LUXURY RATHER THAN A CHORE FOR THOSE WHO HAVE THE TIME TO PLAN, SHOP AND SPEND TIME IN THE KITCHEN.

The basic cookery techniques and the unbroken heritage of recipes that our grandmothers learned from their mothers are as important today as they ever were, and we should play our part in passing them on to the next generation. From using seasonal food, to baking celebration cakes, to cherishing kitchen equipment that lasted a lifetime – our ancestors knew how important these things were for the well-being of the whole family.

PATTERNS OF EATING
Perhaps the most important meal of the day in past years was breakfast. Wherever possible, a family would eat breakfast together, and this was not just a matter of a hurried slice of toast and cup of tea, but a proper meal with porridge, eggs, meat, pancakes and bread. There is a whole chapter on these delightful dishes in this book, and even if people are too busy these days to cook this kind of breakfast every day, the recipes are ideal for a special occasion or on holiday.

Right: Many families have recipe collections that have been handed down.

The midday meal needed to be another sustaining affair, with plenty of protein and vegetables to keep people going throughout the afternoon's work. High tea or supper after the working day was over was, for many people, more of a light meal of bread, cheese, ham and pickles, and maybe a slice of cake. The kind of cooked meal that many people would have eaten at lunchtime has now been superseded by a quick sandwich or salad, while the main meal today is usually in the evening. Eating patterns are usually defined by work and school; in the past people were able to come home for lunch, but now this is impractical, and most of us are out until the evening.

Family meals are often hurried affairs, but they should still be the focus of the day. Making casseroles in advance, or choosing easy main dishes that can be cooked in minutes, means the family can still eat together.

To fill the hunger gap between meals, there are plenty of recipes in this book for healthy snacks, like fruit-filled cakes, sweet breads and cookies that would once have been served for afternoon tea. Teatime may not be quite

Below: As the most important meal of the day, breakfast was a proper sit-down meal.

Below: What could be more sustaining at lunch time than a bowl of soup?

Below: Afternoon tea is an old tradition that is well worth reviving.

Above: Baking cakes and biscuits with children is a favourite family activity.

the institution it was, but the recipes remain and are universally popular, particularly with children.

The highlight of the normal working week was a special Sunday roast, which provided plenty of leftovers. The thrifty cook might make rissoles, shepherd's pie, a cold platter, and soup from one joint of meat. These days we are used to having more variety in our weekday meals, but a return to the simplicity and frugal habits of the past is returning to favour in our busy lives. Efficient refrigeration and freezing means that we can construct wonderful dishes out of leftovers that will keep for months.

Meat on Sundays, leftovers on Mondays, fish on Fridays. These homely traditions have become less important in the 21st century, but the dishes that

families enjoyed day after day are just as tempting, even if they are only made at weekends when there is more time.

FAMILY TRADITIONS

In many families, a folder or box of handwritten recipes exists, handed down from one generation to the next. Splashed with gravy, worn at the corners and annotated by the cook, these recipe books hold the memories of each family's traditions.

Celebration dishes are the most evocative element of a family's traditions. At Christmas, Easter or Thanksgiving, and for birthdays, weddings or christenings, families gradually create their own favourite dishes and rituals that are called for each year. The centrepiece might be a succulent roast joint or a special cake or dessert – made the same way each time to continue the tradition.

ABOUT THIS BOOK

The welcoming warmth and bounty of a grandmother's kitchen is re-created here in this collection of recipes. The book begins with a chapter on breakfasts, including such traditional dishes as pancakes with bacon, scrambled eggs, or porridge topped with plums. Next comes the soup chapter, packed with ideas on using seasonal vegetables to feed your family. Further chapters on fish and meat give examples of the recipes used both for daily meals and for special occasions.

Left: The evening meal is usually the time when the family sits down to eat together.

GRANDMOTHER'S UTENSILS

Along with your family recipe book, you may be lucky enough to have an antique utensil too. The tools of the kitchen were ingenious and long-lasting, and many of them are still used today. They often perform a single specific function – for example, a curved fruit knife that makes short work of peeling and coring piles of fruit for a pie, a cherry stoner (pitter) to pop the kernel out of the fruit in one movement for bottling, or a basting spoon with a long handle to baste meat without taking it out of the oven and burning the fingers.

Many of us possess a pretty glass lemon squeezer and spring-clip tins (pans) to make turning out large cakes easy. In an antique shop you may find a little china bird whose beak peeks out of an apple pie while holding up the top crust, a melon baller or a nutmeg grater with a little drawer for the whole nutmeg. Treasure these just as you do your favourite recipes.

Grandmothers are especially renowned for their baking, and the chapters here on mouthwatering traditional desserts, cakes, biscuits and cookies give recipes from the lightest sponge cake to a rib-sticking tea loaf, while the last chapter holds all you need to make wonderful chutneys and jams. With such a wealth of well-loved traditional recipes, you will be able to make the kitchen the heart of your own home.

BREAKFASTS

Everyone knows that a good breakfast makes an excellent start to the morning. These traditional recipes will inspire you with all kinds of fresh ideas based on the homely, nourishing ingredients that grandmothers would have kept in their larder or store cupboard.

PORRIDGE WITH PLUMS

ON COLD MORNINGS THERE IS NOTHING BETTER THAN BOWLS OF DELICIOUS, CREAMY PORRIDGE TO WARM UP THE WHOLE FAMILY. THE PLUMS CAN BE COOKED IN ADVANCE AND IF YOU USE ROLLED OATS, THE WHOLE DISH IS READY IN FIVE MINUTES.

SERVES 4

INGREDIENTS
- 300ml/½ pint/1¼ cups fruity red wine
- 75g/3oz/scant ½ cup caster (superfine) sugar
- 1 cinnamon stick
- 1 star anise
- 450g/1lb red or purple plums
- 115g/4oz/1 cup medium oatmeal
- salt
- cold milk, single (light) or double (heavy) cream, to serve

VARIATION
Rolled oats can be used instead, in the proportion of 115g/4oz/generous 1 cup to 750ml/1¼ pints/3 cups water, plus a pinch of salt. This cooks more quickly than pinhead oatmeal. Simmer, stirring to prevent sticking, for about 5 minutes.

1 To make the poached plums, pour the wine into a pan and stir in the sugar. Add the cinnamon stick and the star anise. Bring to the boil and boil for about 1 minute.

2 Halve and stone (pit) the plums. Add the plums to the wine syrup and barely simmer for about 10 minutes until just beginning to soften. Allow the plums to cool in the liquid.

3 Put the water, pinhead oatmeal and salt into a heavy pan and bring to the boil over a medium heat, stirring with a wooden spatula.

4 When the porridge is smooth and beginning to thicken, reduce the heat to a simmer.

5 Cook gently for about 25 minutes, stirring occasionally, until the oatmeal is cooked and the consistency even.

6 Serve hot with cold milk and extra salt, if required. It is frequently served with chopped fresh fruit.

7 Try eating porridge in a traditional way. Pour it into deep, warmed bowls and serve the plums alongside, with really cold cream in a separate bowl. Take a spoonful of porridge and dip it into the cream. Eat this, then take a spoonful of plums. Savour the contrast – this is not a dish to be hurried.

Energy 268Kcal/1136kJ; Protein 4g; Carbohydrate 44g, of which sugars 25g; Fat 2.5g, of which saturates 0.5g; Cholesterol 0mg; Calcium 31mg; Fibre 3g; Sodium 171mg.

GRILLED KIPPERS WITH MARMALADE TOAST

WONDERFUL KIPPERS ARE PRODUCED AROUND THE COAST OF BRITAIN, WHERE HERRINGS ARE STILL CURED IN SMOKEHOUSES DATING FROM THE 19TH CENTURY. KIPPERS HAVE BEEN ENJOYED FOR BREAKFAST SINCE VICTORIAN TIMES, AND HERE THEY ARE PAIRED WITH MARMALADE.

SERVES 2

INGREDIENTS

    melted butter, for greasing
    2 kippers (smoked herrings)
    2 slices of bread
    soft butter, for spreading
    orange marmalade, for spreading

1 Line the grill (broiling) pan with foil and brush with melted butter.

2 Preheat the grill (broiler). If you prefer your fish opened flat, use kitchen scissors, or a knife, to cut the heads and tails off the kippers.

3 Lay the fish, skin side up, on the buttered foil. Put under the hot grill and cook for 1 minute. Turn the kippers over, brush the uppermost (fleshy) side with melted butter, put them under the grill and cook for 4–5 minutes.

4 Toast the bread and spread it first with butter and then with marmalade. Serve the sizzling hot kippers immediately with the marmalade toast.

VARIATION
Omit the marmalade and cook the kippers sprinkled with a little cayenne pepper. Serve with a knob of butter melting over the top of the hot kippers, and lemon wedges for squeezing.

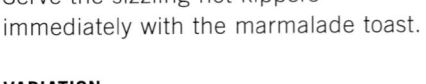

Energy 518kcal/2155kJ; Protein 33.9g; Carbohydrate 17.6g, of which sugars 5.9g; Fat 35.1g, of which saturates 7.6g; Cholesterol 121mg; Calcium 126mg; Fibre 0.4g; Sodium 1640mg.

POTATO CAKES

THIS IS A TRADITIONAL RECIPE FOR POTATO CAKES, MADE ON AN IRON GRIDDLE OR IN A HEAVY FRYING PAN. THESE LITTLE CAKES ARE IDEAL SERVED WARM, WITH A FULL COOKED BREAKFAST. POTATO CAKES WERE TRADITIONALLY BUTTERED AND EATEN HOT WITH SUGAR, RATHER LIKE PANCAKES.

MAKES ABOUT 12

INGREDIENTS
   675g/1½lb potatoes, peeled
   25g/1oz/2 tbsp unsalted
      butter
   about 175g/6oz/1½ cups plain
      (all-purpose) flour
   salt

1 Boil the potatoes in a large pan over a medium heat until tender, then drain thoroughly, replacing in the pan over a low heat for a few minutes to allow any moisture to evaporate completely.

VARIATION
Try serving potato cakes like pancakes, buttered and sprinkled with sugar.

2 Mash the potatoes with plenty of salt, then mix in the butter and cool.

3 Turn out on to a floured work surface and knead in about one-third of the mixture's volume in flour, or as much as is needed to make a pliable dough.

4 Roll out to a thickness of about 1cm/½in and cut into triangles.

5 Heat a dry griddle (grill) or heavy frying pan over a low heat and cook the potato cakes on it for about 3 minutes on each side until browned. Serve hot.

Per batch: Energy 1276kcal/5392kJ; Protein 30.4g; Carbohydrate 249.1g, of which sugars 6.7g; Fat 24.1g, of which saturates 13.4g; Cholesterol 53mg; Calcium 282mg; Fibre 14g; Sodium 203mg.

ENGLISH BREAKFAST

FOR MOST OF US, A COOKED BREAKFAST IS A SPECIAL TREAT, AND IT IS DEFINITELY WORTH MAKING ON DAYS WHEN THERE IS NO RUSH TO GET TO WORK. PREVIOUS GENERATIONS ADDED SMOKED FISH, KIDNEYS, EARTHY FIELD MUSHROOMS OR LEFTOVERS FROM THE LARDER TO THIS SPLENDID PLATEFUL.

SERVES 4

INGREDIENTS
225–250g/8–9oz small potatoes
oil, for grilling or frying
butter, for grilling and frying
4 large or 8 small good-quality
    sausages
8 rashers (strips) of back or streaky
    (fatty) bacon, preferably dry-cured
4 tomatoes
4 small slices of bread, crusts
    removed
4 eggs

COOK'S TIP
For the best flavour, fry the bread and tomatoes in any fatty juices remaining in the pan from the sausages and bacon.

1 Thinly slice the potatoes. Heat 15ml/1 tbsp oil with a knob of butter in a large, preferably non-stick frying pan, add the potatoes and cook over a medium heat for 10–15 minutes, turning them occasionally until they are crisp, golden, and cooked through.

2 Using a slotted spoon, lift the potatoes out of the pan and keep them warm on a plate in a low oven.

GRANDMOTHER'S TIP
This is a good way to use up cold potatoes of any size from the night before. Just chop or slice them up and fry on a high heat until they are crisp and golden. You can even cook leftover mashed potato this way.

3 Meanwhile, grill or fry the sausages in a little oil until golden brown all over and cooked through (test by inserting a skewer in the centre – the juices should run clear). Keep warm.

4 Grill the bacon or fry it in a little oil in the non-stick pan. Keep warm.

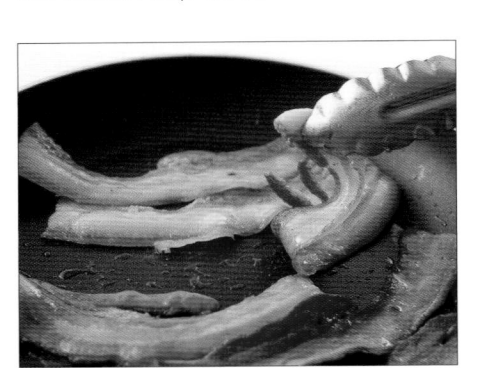

5 Halve the tomatoes and top each half with a tiny piece of butter, salt and pepper, and grill until they are soft and bubbling, or fry in a little oil in the frying pan. Keep warm.

6 Fry the bread in a little oil and butter over a medium-high heat until crisp and golden brown. Keep warm.

7 Add extra oil if necessary to the hot frying pan. As soon as the oil is hot, crack the eggs into the pan, leaving space between them.

8 Cook the eggs over a medium heat, until the yolks are set.

9 As soon as the eggs are cooked to your liking, arrange the bacon, sausage, potatoes and tomatoes on warmed plates, top each with an egg, and serve immediately.

VARIATIONS
English hotels and cafés often serve breakfast in a roll, which is easy to do at home; simply warm long crusty rolls or baguettes in the oven, then cut them in half vertically without slicing through the bottom crust. Fill each roll with the hot breakfast ingredients, draping the fried egg over the top. Serve with a serrated knife for cutting.
• If you like black pudding (blood sausage), a few slices can be gently fried or grilled and served in place of the sausages.
• A few field mushrooms grilled together with the tomatoes make a delicious addition to a traditional English breakfast.
• Serve a spoonful of Bubble and Squeak, (see page27), in place of the fried potatoes.

Energy 731kcal/3046kJ; Protein 32.7g; Carbohydrate 35.3g, of which sugars 7.6g; Fat 52.2g, of which saturates 16.5g; Cholesterol 288mg; Calcium 185mg; Fibre 3.1g; Sodium 2049mg.

OATMEAL PANCAKES WITH BACON

THESE OATY PANCAKES MADE WITH BUTTERMILK HAVE A SPECIAL AFFINITY WITH OLD-FASHIONED DRY-CURED BACON. THEY CAN ALSO BE SERVED WITH TRADITIONAL OR HOME-MADE SAUSAGES, POACHED EGGS OR GRILLED TOMATOES FRESH FROM THE GARDEN FOR A REAL TASTE OF SUMMER.

MAKES 8 PANCAKES

INGREDIENTS
   115g/4oz/1 cup fine wholemeal
      (whole-wheat) flour
   25g/1oz/¼ cup fine pinhead oatmeal
   pinch of salt
   2 eggs
   about 300ml/½ pint/1¼ cups
      buttermilk
   butter or oil, for greasing
   8 bacon rashers (strips)

GRANDMOTHER'S TIP
When whole oats are chopped into pieces they are called pinhead or coarse oatmeal. They take longer to cook than rolled oats and have a chewier texture.

1 Mix the flour, oatmeal and salt in a bowl or food processor, beat in the eggs and add enough buttermilk to make a creamy batter of the same consistency as ordinary pancakes.

2 Thoroughly heat a griddle (grill) or frying pan over a medium heat. When very hot, grease lightly with butter or oil.

3 Pour in a ladleful of batter and tilt the pan to spread the batter. Cook for about 2 minutes until the underside is browned. Turn over and cook the other side for 1 minute until browned.

4 Keep the pancakes warm while you cook the others. Fry the bacon. Roll the pancakes with a cooked rasher to serve.

Per pancake: Energy 202Kcal/845kJ; Protein 11.9g; Carbohydrate 13.1g, of which sugars 2g; Fat 11.8g, of which saturates 4.8g; Cholesterol 87mg; Calcium 59mg; Fibre 1.5g; Sodium 654mg.

PANCAKES <u>WITH</u> GRILLED BACON

THESE SMALL, THICK, BUTTERY PANCAKES WILL BE EATEN IN SECONDS, SO MAKE PLENTY. MAPLE SYRUP AND BACON IS THE TRADITIONAL ACCOMPANIMENT, BUT ALL SORTS OF TOPPINGS WOULD WORK WELL, SUCH AS MUSHROOMS FROM THE FIELDS OR WILD BERRIES FROM THE HEDGEROWS.

MAKES ABOUT TWENTY

INGREDIENTS
175g/6oz/1½ cups plain (all-purpose)
   flour, sifted
pinch of salt
15ml/1 tbsp caster (superfine) sugar
2 large eggs
150ml/¼ pint/⅔ cup milk
5ml/1 tsp bicarbonate of soda
   (baking soda)
10ml/2 tsp cream of tartar
oil, for cooking
butter, maple syrup and crisply
   grilled bacon, to serve

1 To make the batter, mix together the flour, salt and sugar. In a separate bowl, beat the eggs and milk together, then gradually stir into the flour, beating to a smooth, thick consistency. Add the bicarbonate of soda and cream of tartar, mix well, then cover and chill for 30 minutes.

2 When you are ready to cook the pancakes, beat the batter again. Heat a little oil in a heavy-based frying pan or griddle. Drop dessertspoonfuls of the mixture into the pan, spaced well apart, and cook over a fairly high heat until bubbles appear on the surface of the pancakes and the undersides become golden brown.

3 Turn the pancakes over and cook briefly until golden underneath, then transfer them to a heated serving dish. Top each pancake with a little butter and drizzle with maple syrup. Serve with grilled bacon.

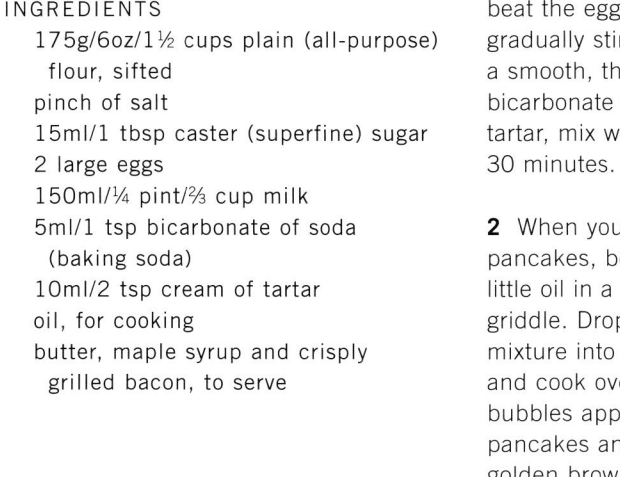

Energy 46Kcal/196kJ; Protein 1.8g; Carbohydrate 7.9g, of which sugars 1.3g; Fat 1.1g, of which saturates 0.3g; Cholesterol 23mg; Calcium 25mg; Fibre 0.3g; Sodium 12mg.

EGGS BENEDICT

THE DELICATE FLAVOURS OF THE EGGS AND HOLLANDAISE SAUCE, SPRINKLED WITH CHIVES FRESHLY PICKED FROM A KITCHEN WINDOWSILL OR A HERB GARDEN IN SPRING AND SUMMER, MAKE A SPECIAL BREAKFAST. USE GOOD COUNTRY HAM AND REALLY FRESH BUTTER FOR THE BEST TASTE.

SERVES 4

INGREDIENTS
    4 eggs
    2 English muffins or 4 slices
     of bread
    butter, for spreading
    4 thick slices cooked ham, cut
     to fit the muffins
    fresh chives, to garnish
For the sauce
    3 egg yolks
    30ml/2 tbsp fresh lemon juice
    1.5ml/¼ tsp salt
    115g/4oz/½ cup butter
    30ml/2 tbsp single (light) cream
    ground black pepper

GRANDMOTHER'S TIP
Use only very fresh eggs for poaching, because they keep their shape better in the water.

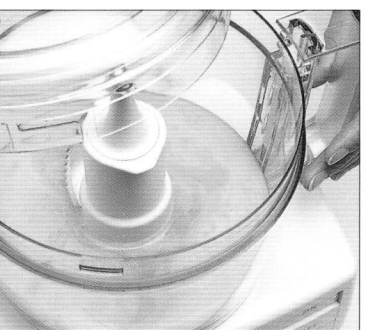

1 To make the sauce, blend the egg yolks, lemon juice and salt in a food processor or blender for 15 seconds.

2 Melt the butter in a small saucepan. With the motor running, slowly pour the hot butter into the food processor or blender through the feed tube in a slow, steady stream. Turn off the machine as soon as all the butter has been added.

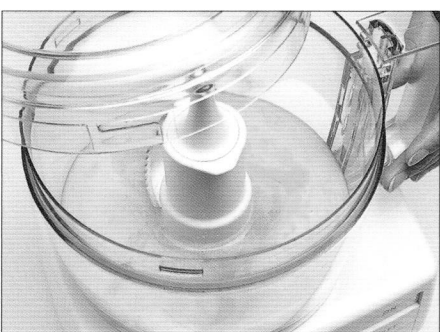

3 Pour the sauce into a bowl, placed over a pan of simmering water. Stir for 2–3 minutes, until thickened. If the sauce begins to curdle, whisk in 15ml/ 1 tbsp boiling water. Stir in the cream and season with pepper. Remove from the heat and keep warm over the pan.

4 Bring a shallow pan of lightly salted water to the boil. Break each egg into a cup, then slide it carefully into the water. Delicately turn the white around the yolk with a spoon. Cook for about 4 minutes until the white is set. Remove the eggs from the pan, one at a time, using a slotted spoon, and drain on kitchen paper.

5 While the eggs are poaching, split and toast the muffins or toast the slices of bread. Spread with butter while still warm.

6 Place a piece of ham on each muffin half or slice of toast, then place an egg on each ham-topped muffin. Spoon the warm sauce over the eggs, garnish with chives and serve.

Energy 478Kcal/1985kJ; Protein 17g; Carbohydrate 13g, of which sugars 1.7g; Fat 40g, of which saturates 21g; Cholesterol 474mg; Calcium 100mg; Fibre 0.6g; Sodium 760mg.

BOILED EGG

SOFT-BOILED EGGS ARE JUST MADE FOR DIPPING TOAST 'SOLDIERS' MADE OF CRISP BUTTERED TOAST CUT INTO FINGERS. THIS NURSERY TREAT IS HARD TO BEAT FIRST THING IN THE MORNING. FOR BOILED EGGS, USE THE FRESHEST POSSIBLE EGGS, WHICH WILL GIVE THE BEST TASTE AND TEXTURE.

SERVES 2

INGREDIENTS
    2–4 eggs
    hot buttered toast, to serve

1 Put the eggs into a pan just large enough to hold them in a single layer and cover with cold water.

2 Bring to the boil, then simmer for 3 minutes for soft-boiled, 4 minutes for a just-set yolk, or 8 minutes for hard-boiled. Drain and serve immediately with hot buttered toast.

GRANDMOTHER'S TIP
To ensure the eggs do not crack during cooking, prick a tiny hole in the round end (where there is a pocket of air).

CODDLED EGGS

THIS METHOD OF SOFT-COOKING EGGS BECAME VERY POPULAR IN THE VICTORIAN ERA. SPECIAL DECORATIVE POTS WITH LIDS WERE PRODUCED BY ROYAL WORCESTER FROM THE 1890s, BUT RAMEKINS WORK JUST AS WELL. GENTLE, SLOW COOKING IS THE KEY TO SUCCESS.

SERVES 2

INGREDIENTS
    butter, for greasing
    2 large eggs
    60ml/4 tbsp single (light) cream
      (optional)
    chopped fresh chives, to garnish
    hot buttered toast, to serve

1 Butter two small ramekin dishes or cups and break an egg into each. Top with a spoonful of cream, if using, and a knob of butter. Cover with foil.

2 Put a wide, shallow pan over medium heat. Stand the covered dishes in the pan. Add boiling water to come halfway up the sides of the dishes.

3 Heat until the water just comes to the boil, then cover the pan with a lid and simmer gently for 1 minute.

4 Remove from the heat and leave to stand, still covered, for 10 minutes. Serve sprinkled with chives.

Boiled egg: Energy 74kcal/306kJ; Protein 6.3g; Carbohydrate 0g, of which sugars 0g; Fat 5.6g, of which saturates 1.6g; Cholesterol 190mg; Calcium 29mg; Fibre 0g; Sodium 70mg.
Coddled egg: Energy 92kcal/383kJ; Protein 6.3g; Carbohydrate 0g, of which sugars 0g; Fat 7.6g, of which saturates 2.9g; Cholesterol 196mg; Calcium 29mg; Fibre 0g; Sodium 85mg.

SAVOURY SCRAMBLED EGGS

THESE SCRAMBLED EGGS ARE FLAVOURED WITH A HINT OF ANCHOVY FROM THE GENTLEMAN'S RELISH, A POPULAR SPREAD FROM EDWARDIAN TIMES, WHICH ADDS AN INTRIGUING SALTINESS TO THESE SMOOTH, RICH EGGS. ADD EXTRA ANCHOVIES AS A GARNISH IF YOU LIKE.

SERVES 4

INGREDIENTS
  2 slices bread
  40g/1½oz/3 tbsp butter, plus
    extra for spreading
  anchovy paste, such as
    Gentleman's Relish, for spreading
  2 eggs and 2 egg yolks, beaten
  60–90ml/4–6 tbsp single (light)
    cream or milk
  salt and ground black pepper
  anchovy fillets, cut into strips
    (optional),
    and paprika, to garnish

GRANDMOTHER'S TIP
These creamy scrambled eggs make a great brunch dish. Serve with a glass of crisp white wine and follow with a fresh fruit salad.

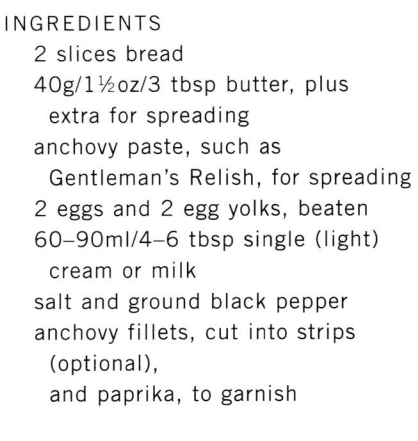

1 Toast the bread, spread with butter and anchovy paste, cut off the crusts, cut into triangles and keep warm.

2 Melt the rest of the butter in a medium pan, then stir in the beaten eggs, cream or milk. Season, then heat very gently, stirring constantly, until the mixture begins to thicken.

3 Remove the saucepan from the heat and continue to stir until the mixture is creamy, but do not allow it to harden.

4 Divide the scrambled eggs among the triangles of toast and garnish each one with strips of anchovy fillet and a generous sprinkling of paprika. Serve immediately, while still hot.

Energy 410Kcal/170kJ; Protein 13.8g; Carbohydrate 11.3g, of which sugars 1.3g; Fat 35g, of which saturates 17.5g; Cholesterol 489g; Calcium 104mg; Fibre 1.5g; Sodium 358mg.

BUBBLE AND SQUEAK

THE NAME OF THIS DISH IS DERIVED FROM THE BUBBLING AND SQUEAKING NOISES THE VEGETABLES MAKE IN THE PAN. IT IS A TYPICAL THRIFTY RECIPE, MADE WITH LEFTOVERS, FROM THE DAYS WHEN NOTHING WAS WASTED. IT MAKES AN EXCELLENT BREAKFAST WITH A FRIED EGG ON TOP.

SERVES 4

INGREDIENTS
    60ml/4 tbsp oil
    1 onion, finely chopped
    450g/1lb cooked, mashed potatoes
    225g/8oz cooked cabbage
    salt and ground black pepper

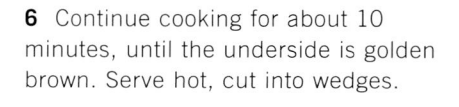

1 Heat half the oil in a heavy, preferably non-stick frying pan. Add the onion and cook, stirring frequently, until softened but not browned.

2 Mix together the mashed potatoes and cabbage and season to taste with salt and plenty of pepper.

GRANDMOTHER'S TIP
Though cabbage is traditional, other cooked vegetables could be added too.

3 Add the vegetable mixture to the pan, stir well to incorporate the cooked onions, then flatten the mixture out over the base of the pan to form a large, even cake.

4 Cook over a medium heat for about 15 minutes, until the cake is nicely browned underneath.

5 Hold a large plate over the pan, then invert the cake onto it. Add the remaining oil to the pan and, when hot, slip the cake back into the pan, browned side uppermost.

6 Continue cooking for about 10 minutes, until the underside is golden brown. Serve hot, cut into wedges.

Energy 219kcal/908kJ; Protein 2.5g; Carbohydrate 17.2g, of which sugars 2.5g; Fat 15.9g, of which saturates 1.9g; Cholesterol 0mg; Calcium 33mg; Fibre 2.6g; Sodium 14mg.

SODA BREAKFAST SCONES

THESE LIGHT SCONES ARE VIRTUALLY FAT-FREE, SO THEY ARE AT THEIR BEST EATEN VERY FRESH, STILL WARM FROM THE OVEN. SERVE WITH THE BEST QUALITY BUTTER AND SOME HOME-MADE JAM OR SPRINKLE THEM WITH FARMHOUSE CHEESE FOR A PERFECT START TO THE DAY.

MAKES ABOUT SIXTEEN

INGREDIENTS
- 225g/8oz/2 cups plain (all-purpose) flour
- 2.5ml/½ tsp bicarbonate of soda (baking soda)
- 2.5ml/½ tsp salt
- 225g/8oz/2 cups wholemeal (wholewheat) flour
- about 350ml/12fl oz/1½ cups buttermilk or sour cream and milk mixed
- 1 egg, beaten, or a little grated cheese (optional)

1 Preheat the oven to 220°C/425°F/Gas 7. Oil and flour a baking tray. Sift the flour, bicarbonate of soda and salt in a bowl, add the flour and mix. Make a well in the centre, pour in almost all the liquid and mix, adding the remaining liquid as needed to make a soft, moist dough. Do not overmix.

2 Turn the dough out on to a floured surface and dust the top with flour; press out evenly to a thickness of 4cm/1½in. Cut out about 16 scones with a 5cm/2in fluted pastry (cookie) cutter. Place on the baking tray and brush the tops with beaten egg, or sprinkle with a little grated cheese, if using.

3 Bake for about 12 minutes until well risen and golden brown; serve warm.

VARIATION
For a more traditional scone mixture that keeps longer, rub 50g/2oz/¼ cup butter into the dry ingredients. Increase the proportion of the soda to 5ml/1 tsp if you like, as the scones will not be as light.

Per scone: Energy 117Kcal/493kJ; Protein 3.8g; Carbohydrate 20.9g, of which sugars 1.5g; Fat 2.6g, of which saturates 1.4g; Cholesterol 6mg; Calcium 49mg; Fibre 1.7g; Sodium 72mg.

BAGELS

THIS TRADITIONAL JEWISH RECIPE ORIGINATED IN EASTERN EUROPE, BUT NOW BAGELS ARE SERVED ALL OVER THE WORLD. THE BASIC RECIPE GIVEN HERE USES AN EGG-ENRICHED DOUGH WHICH IS FIRST BOILED AND THEN BAKED. SERVE WARM, SPREAD WITH BUTTER AND FRUIT PRESERVES.

MAKES ABOUT TWELVE

INGREDIENTS
175ml/6fl oz/¾ cup lukewarm water
1 packet active dried yeast or
  25g/1oz fresh yeast
60ml/4 tbsp caster (superfine) sugar
60ml/4 tbsp vegetable oil
2 eggs, plus beaten egg to glaze
5ml/1 tsp salt
450g/1lb/4 cups strong white
  bread flour

GRANDMOTHER'S TIP
Some varieties of flour absorb more liquid than others, so don't worry if you cannot work in all the flour or need an extra spoonful.

1 Put the water, yeast and 1.5ml/¼ tsp sugar in a large bowl and blend together, then leave for stand for 10 minutes, until bubbles form.

2 Add a further 15ml/1 tbsp of the sugar to the bowl, along with the oil and eggs and stir together. Stir in the salt and half the flour, then slowly add the remaining flour.

3 Using your hands, work in the remaining flour to form a dough. Turn the dough on to a lightly floured surface and knead for 10 minutes, until smooth. Cover, then leave in a warm place for about 1 hour, until doubled in size.

4 Knead the dough again by knocking back and kneading several times, then divide the dough into 12 balls and knead each ball until smooth.

5 Form the dough into rolls, the thickness of a cigar, loop them into rings and press the ends together to join. Alternatively, roll out the dough balls and poke a hole in the centre using your finger or the handle of a wooden spoon. Place the rings on a baking sheet and leave to rise in a warm place for 15 minutes.

6 Preheat the oven to 200°C/400°F/ Gas 6. Put about 2 litres/3½ pints/ 8 cups water in a large pan and bring to the boil. Add the remaining sugar.

7 Drop 2 bagels at a time into the water, boil for 1 minute, turning over half way through, then, using a slotted spoon, remove them from the water.

8 Transfer to a baking sheet and brush with beaten egg. Bake for 20 minutes, then leave to cool on a wire rack.

GRANDMOTHER'S TIP
The hole in the middle of the bagels tend to close as they are boiled. Use the handle of a wooden spoon or something similar to keep the centre open.

Per bagel: Energy 179kcal/754kJ; Protein 4.2g; Carbohydrate 31.1g, of which sugars 5.7g; Fat 5g, of which saturates 0.8g; Cholesterol 32mg; Calcium 54mg; Fibre 1g; Sodium 177mg.

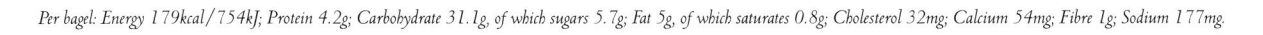

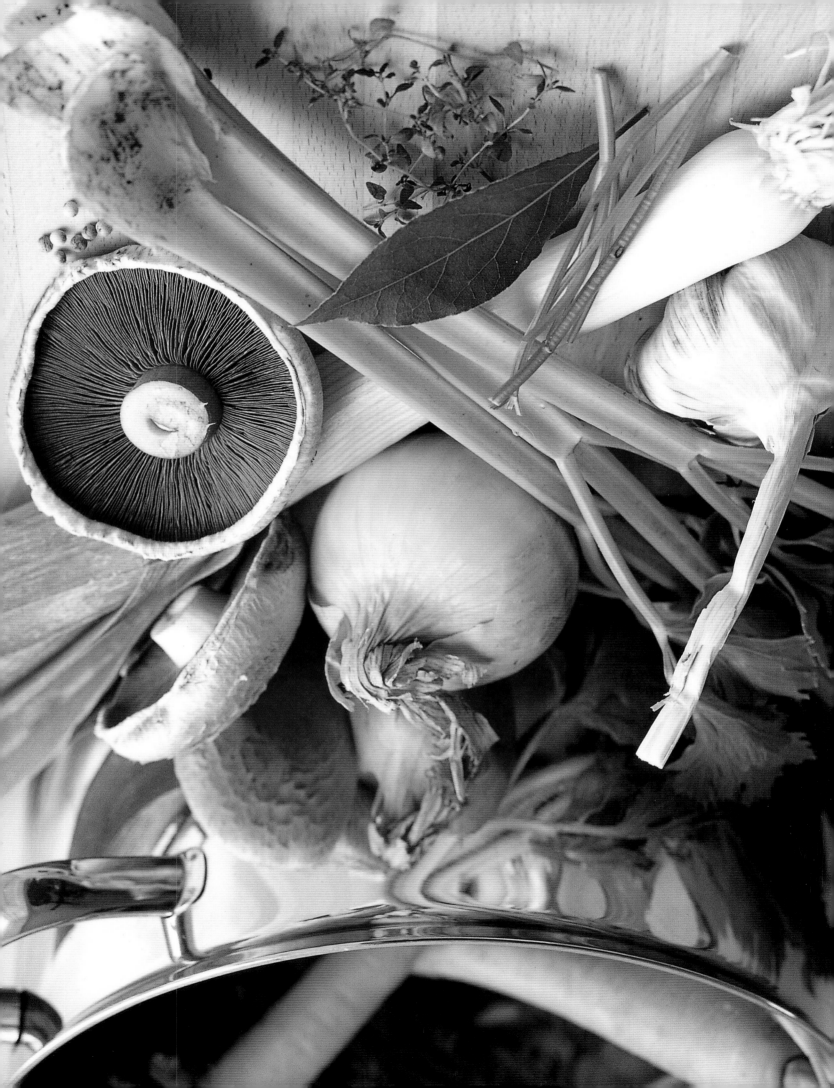

SOUPS

Soup is the ideal comfort food and has been a staple dish for centuries. It can be quite frugal, made with leftovers or a glut of vegetables from the garden, or more elaborate for a special occasion. It is always warming, hearty and packed full of goodness — a perfect family lunch served with a crusty loaf and butter.

CULLEN SKINK

SCOTTISH FISHERMEN TRADITIONALLY SMOKED THE SMALLER FISH IN THEIR CATCH, SUCH AS HADDOCK, FOR HOME CONSUMPTION. THIS SOUP BLENDS FISH, ONION, POTATOES AND FRESH MILK TO CREATE A REALLY CREAMY BROTH THAT IS FULL OF GOODNESS.

SERVES 4

INGREDIENTS

1 smoked haddock, about 350g/12oz in weight
1 onion, chopped
1 bouquet garni
900ml/1½ pints/3¾ cups water
500g/1¼lb potatoes, quartered
600ml/1 pint/2½ cups milk
40g/1½oz/3 tbsp butter
salt and pepper
chopped chives, to garnish

1 Put the haddock, onion, bouquet garni and water into a large pan and bring to the boil. Skim the surface with a slotted spoon, discarding any fish skin, then cover the pan. Reduce the heat and gently poach for 10–15 minutes, until the fish flakes easily.

GRANDMOTHER'S TIP
When you buy your smoked haddock make sure it is naturally smoked, and not the type that has been dyed yellow.

2 Lift the fish from the pan and remove the skin and any bones. Return the skin and bones to the pan and simmer, uncovered, for 30 minutes. Flake the cooked fish flesh and leave to cool.

3 Strain the stock and return to the pan, add the potatoes and simmer for 25 minutes. Remove the potatoes from the pan, add the milk and heat.

4 Mash the potatoes with the butter, then whisk them into the soup a little at a time. Add the fish, season to taste, sprinkle with chives and serve.

Energy 205kcal/864kJ; Protein 16.1g; Carbohydrate 19g, of which sugars 6.4g; Fat 7.8g, of which saturates 4.7g; Cholesterol 41mg; Calcium 137mg; Fibre 1g; Sodium 132mg.

OXTAIL SOUP

THIS HEARTY SOUP IS AN ENGLISH CLASSIC, STEMMING FROM THE DAYS WHEN IT WAS NATURAL TO MAKE FULL USE OF EVERY PART OF AN ANIMAL, INCLUDING THE TAIL. OXTAIL MAY NEED LONG, SLOW COOKING, BUT IT HAS A FLAVOUR THAT IS RICH AND DELICIOUS.

SERVES FOUR TO SIX

INGREDIENTS
  1 oxtail joints, about 1.3kg/3lb,
    washed and trimmed of fat
  25g/1oz/2 tbsp butter
  2 medium onions, chopped
  2 medium carrots, chopped
  2 celery sticks, sliced
  1 bacon rasher (strip), chopped
  2 litres/3½ pints/8 cups beef stock
  1 bouquet garni
  2 bay leaves
  30ml/2 tbsp plain (all-purpose) flour
  squeeze of fresh lemon juice
  60ml/4 tbsp port, sherry or Madeira
  salt and ground black pepper

1 Melt the butter in a large pan, and when foaming, add the oxtail a few pieces at a time. Brown them quickly on all sides. Lift the meat out onto a plate.

2 To the same pan, add the onions, carrots, celery and bacon. Cook over a medium heat for 5–10 minutes, stirring occasionally, until the vegetables are softened and golden brown.

3 Return the oxtail to the pan and add the stock, bouquet garni, bay leaves and seasoning. Bring just to the boil and skim off any foam. Cover and simmer gently for about 3 hours or until the meat is falling from the bones.

4 Strain the mixture, discard the vegetables, bouquet garni and bay leaves, and leave to stand.

5 When the oxtail has cooled sufficiently to handle, pick all the meat off the bones and cut it into small pieces.

6 Skim off any fat that has risen to the surface of the stock, then tip the stock into a large pan. Add the pieces of meat and reheat.

7 Whisk the flour with a little cold water to make a smooth paste. Stir in a little of the hot stock, then stir the mixture into the pan. Bring to the boil, stirring, until the soup thickens slightly.

8 Reduce the heat and simmer gently for about 5 minutes. Season with salt, pepper and lemon juice, stir in the port, sherry or Madeira, and serve.

Energy 459kcal/1914kJ; Protein 45.4g; Carbohydrate 6.5g, of which sugars 2.6g; Fat 26.8g, of which saturates 11.8g; Cholesterol 176mg; Calcium 36mg; Fibre 0.7g; Sodium 403mg.

CHICKEN, LEEK AND CELERY SOUP

THIS SOUP MAKES FULL USE OF ALL THE INGREDIENTS THAT GROW IN A KITCHEN GARDEN. THE WHOLE CHICKEN MAKES AN EXCELLENT, RICH STOCK AND THE VEGETABLES AND HERBS ADD DEPTH TO THE FLAVOUR. SERVE WITH FRESHLY BAKED BREAD AND BUTTER TO MAKE A SUSTAINING MEAL.

SERVES FOUR TO SIX

INGREDIENTS

   1.4kg/3lb free-range chicken
   1 small head of celery, trimmed
   1 onion, coarsely chopped
   1 fresh bay leaf
   a few fresh parsley stalks
   a few fresh tarragon sprigs
   2.4 litres/4 pints/10 cups cold water
   3 large leeks
   65g/2½oz/5 tbsp butter
   2 potatoes, cut into chunks
   150ml/¼ pint/⅔ cup dry white wine
   30–45ml/2–3 tbsp single (light)
     cream (optional)
   salt and ground black pepper
   6 bacon rashers (strips), grilled
     (broiled) until crisp, to garnish

1 Cut the breasts off the chicken and set aside. Joint the rest of the chicken carcass and place in a large pan.

2 Chop 4–5 of the outer sticks of the celery and add them to the pan with the onion. Tie the bay leaf, parsley and tarragon together and add to the pan. Pour in the cold water to cover the ingredients and bring to the boil. Reduce the heat and cover the pan, then simmer for 1½ hours.

3 Remove the chicken, cut off and reserve the meat. Strain the stock, then return to the pan and boil rapidly until reduced to 1.5 litres/2½ pints/6¼ cups.

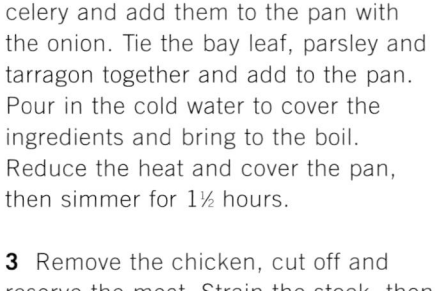

4 Slice about 150g/5oz of the leeks and set aside. Slice the remaining leeks and the remaining celery, together with the celery leaves.

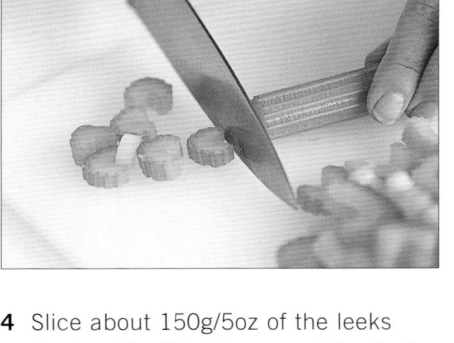

5 Melt half the butter in a large, heavy-based pan. Add the sliced leeks and celery, cover and cook over a low heat for about 10 minutes, or until softened but not browned. Add the potatoes, wine and 1.2 litres/2 pints/ 5 cups of the stock.

6 Season well with salt and pepper, bring to the boil and reduce the heat. Partially cover the pan and simmer the soup for 15–20 minutes, or until the potatoes are cooked.

7 Meanwhile, skin the reserved chicken breasts and cut the flesh into small pieces. Melt the remaining butter in a frying pan, add the chicken pieces and fry for 5–7 minutes, until cooked.

8 Add the set-aside leeks to the pan and cook, stirring occasionally, for a further 3–4 minutes, until just cooked.

9 Process the soup with the cooked chicken from the stock in a blender or food processor. Taste and adjust the seasoning, add more stock if too thick.

10 Stir in the cream, if using. Reheat the soup gently. Pour the soup in to warmed bowls, sprinkle the chicken and leek mixture on top, and crumble the grilled bacon rashers (strips) over before serving.

PEA AND HAM SOUP

COMFORTING AND WARMING, THIS PEA AND HAM SOUP IS A GOOD
DEFENCE AGAINST THE COLD ON A WINTER'S DAY. OUR THRIFTY
ANCESTORS USED EVERY PART OF A PIG, INCLUDING THE TROTTERS,
AND HERE A TROTTER IS USED TO GIVE A BEAUTIFULLY RICH
FLAVOUR AND TEXTURE TO THE FINISHED DISH.

SERVES 4

INGREDIENTS
200g/7oz dried peas
1.5 litres/2½ pints/6¼ cups water
1 pig's trotter (foot), split lengthways
200g/7oz smoked bacon, diced
1 onion, chopped
1 carrot, chopped
1 leek, chopped
2.5ml/½ tsp ground allspice
2.5ml/½ tsp dried marjoram
30ml/2 tbsp German or Dijon
  mustard
salt and ground black pepper

1 Soak the peas overnight in plenty of cold water. The next day, rinse and put the peas in a pan with the pig's trotter, bacon, onion, carrot, leek and allspice. Add the water.

2 Bring the liquid to the boil. Skim away any foam that rises, then lower the heat, cover and simmer for about 2 hours, until the meat and vegetables are tender. If the soup has thickened too much to your taste, dilute it with a little extra water.

GRANDMOTHER'S TIP
Pig's trotters are a rich source of gelatine, and when cooked slowly for long enough they can create a tasty jelly. Here enough of the gelatinous properties are released to thicken the soup.

3 Lift out the trotter and cut away the meat, discarding the bones and gristle. Chop the meat into small pieces and return to the soup. Stir in the dried marjoram and mustard.

4 Taste for seasoning and add salt if needed. Pour into individual serving bowls and serve hot.

VARIATION
If your butcher is unable to let you have a pig's trotter then you can substitute it with some pork belly instead. The fat from this cut will render out to give a similar rich, tasty soup.

Energy 306kcal/1287kJ; Protein 26.8g; Carbohydrate 27.3g, of which sugars 2.8g; Fat 10.7g, of which saturates 3.6g; Cholesterol 42mg; Calcium 57mg; Fibre 5.7g; Sodium 869mg.

ONION SOUP

THIS IS A MARVELLOUS RECIPE FOR USING UP A GLUT OF ONIONS. SIMPLY CHOPPED AND TURNED IN MELTED BUTTER UNTIL THEY ARE SOFT AND GOLDEN, THEY ARE TRANSFORMED INTO A TASTY SOUP.

SERVES 4-6

INGREDIENTS

50g/2oz/¼ cup butter
4 medium onions (total weight about 800g/1¾lb), chopped
4 garlic cloves, finely chopped
1 medium potato (about 200g/7oz), peeled and chopped
45ml/3 tbsp sherry (if not using beer, see below)
1 litre/1¾ pints/4 cups vegetable, chicken or beef stock, or half stock and half beer (preferably Rodenbach)
1–2 sprigs fresh thyme
1 bay leaf
salt and ground black pepper, to taste
45ml/3 tbsp freshly chopped parsley, to garnish
freshly grated Gruyère cheese (optional)
bread or croûtons, to serve

VARIATION

For cheesy onion soup, place a generous amount of grated Gruyère in each soup bowl and top with a thin slice of toast before pouring in the hot soup. Sprinkle with a little more Gruyère and place under the grill (broiler) for 5–10 minutes, until lightly browned.

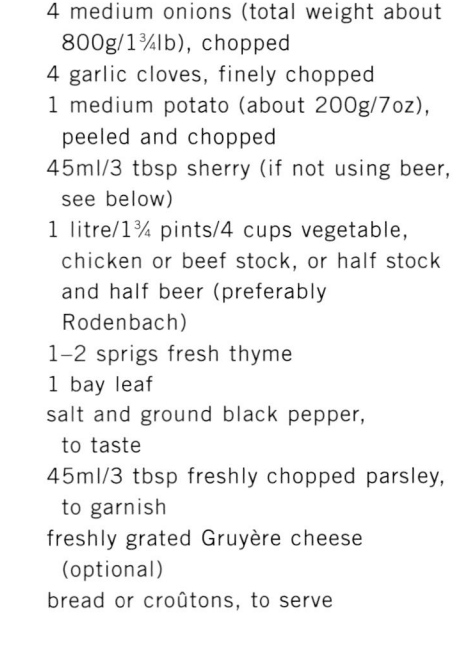

1 Melt the butter in a large, heavy pan and sauté the onions over medium heat for about 10 minutes until caramelized. Add the garlic and sauté for 1 minute.

2 Add the potato to the onions and stir well. If you are using sherry instead of beer, add it to the pan at this point and let the mixture simmer for 3 minutes.

3 Pour in the stock (or stock and beer if using) and add the thyme and bay leaf. Bring to the boil, reduce the heat and simmer for 35 minutes.

4 Remove the herbs and purée with a hand-held blender or in a food processor, until it reaches the desired consistency. Season with salt and ground black pepper to taste. Reheat the soup if necessary, then ladle into warmed bowls.

5 Top each serving with freshly chopped parsley and add grated cheese if you like. Serve immediately with crusty country bread or croûtons.

Energy 146kcal/608kJ; Protein 2.5g; Carbohydrate 16.3g, of which sugars 8.1g; Fat 7.5g, of which saturates 4.4g; Cholesterol 18mg; Calcium 38mg; Fibre 2.2g; Sodium 339mg.
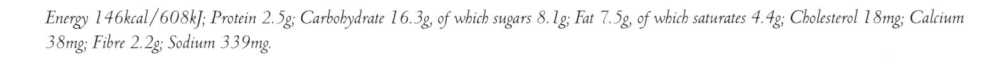

SPICED CREAMED PARSNIP SOUP WITH SHERRY

SOME OF THE BEST SOUP RECIPES ARE MADE WITH SIMPLE, EARTHY INGREDIENTS SUCH AS THESE WINTER STAPLES, PARSNIPS AND ONIONS. A DASH OF SHERRY AND CURRY POWDER TRANSFORMS THIS VELVETY SOUP INTO A DISH WORTHY OF THE BEST VICTORIAN COUNTRY HOUSE KITCHEN.

2 Cut the parsnips into even-sized pieces, add to the pan and stir to coat them with butter. Add the curry powder and stir through.

3 Pour in the sherry and cover with a cartouche (see Grandmother's Tip) and then the pan lid. Cook over a low heat for 10 minutes or until the parsnips are softened, making sure they do not colour.

4 Add the stock and season to taste. Bring to the boil then simmer for about 15 minutes or until the parsnips are soft. Remove from the heat. Allow to cool for a while then purée in a blender.

5 When ready to serve, reheat the soup and check the seasoning. Add a swirl of cream, if you like.

SERVES 4

INGREDIENTS
  115g/4oz/½ cup butter
  2 onions, sliced
  1kg /2¼lb parsnips, peeled
  10ml/2 tsp curry powder
  30ml/2 tbsp medium sherry
  1.2 litres/2 pints/5 cups chicken or
    vegetable stock
  salt and ground black pepper
  single cream, to serve (optional)

1 Melt the butter in a pan, add the onions and sweat gently without allowing them to colour.

GRANDMOTHER'S TIP
A cartouche is a circle of greaseproof (waxed) paper that helps to keep in the moisture, so the vegetables cook in their own juices along with the sherry.

Energy 437kcal/1820kJ; Protein 5.9g; Carbohydrate 39.5g, of which sugars 20.2g; Fat 28.7g, of which saturates 16.8g; Cholesterol 67mg; Calcium 134mg; Fibre 12.9g; Sodium 218mg.

JERUSALEM ARTICHOKE SOUP

THESE STRANGE-LOOKING, KNOBBLY VEGETABLES WERE FIRST INTRODUCED TO THE ENGLISH KITCHEN GARDEN IN THE 1600S. THEY BLEND WELL WITH OTHER BETTER-KNOWN VEGETABLES SUCH AS CARROTS, ONIONS AND CELERY, AND MAKE A LOVELY SMOOTH, SUBTLY FLAVOURED SOUP.

SERVES 4-6

INGREDIENTS

500g/1¼lb Jerusalem artichokes
1 onion, roughly chopped
4 celery sticks, roughly chopped
2 carrots, roughly chopped
4 garlic cloves
45ml/3 tbsp olive oil
1.2 litre/2 pints/5 cups vegetable
 or chicken stock
60ml/4 tbsp double (heavy) cream
salt and ground black pepper

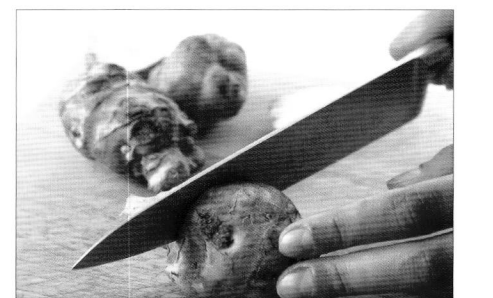

1 Preheat the oven to 200°C/400°F/ Gas 6. Scrub the artichokes well and halve them lengthways.

2 Toss all the vegetables in the olive oil and spread them in a roasting pan.

3 Put the vegetables into the hot oven and roast for 30–40 minutes until they are soft and golden brown. Stir them once during cooking so that the edges brown evenly. Transfer the roasted vegetables to a large pan.

4 Add the stock, bring to the boil and simmer for 15 minutes. Process or blend until smooth, return to the pan, add the cream, season, and reheat.

GRANDMOTHER'S TIP
Peel the Jerusalem artichokes before roasting, if preferred, dropping them into water with a good squeeze of lemon to prevent them discolouring once peeled.

Energy 310kcal/1277kJ; Protein 2.7g; Carbohydrate 4.7g, of which sugars 4.3g; Fat 31.3g, of which saturates 19.4g; Cholesterol 80mg; Calcium 116mg; Fibre 1.5g; Sodium 168mg.

STILTON AND WATERCRESS SOUP

A GOOD CREAMY STILTON AND PLENTY OF PEPPERY WATERCRESS BRING MAXIMUM FLAVOUR TO THIS RICH, SMOOTH SOUP. WATERCRESS, WHICH GROWS WILD IN RIVER BEDS AS WELL AS BEING CULTIVATED, IS AN EXCELLENT SOURCE OF IRON, AND THIS IS A GOOD RECIPE FOR WHEN IT IS IN SEASON.

SERVES 4

INGREDIENTS
  600ml/1 pint/
    2½ cups chicken or vegetable stock
  225g/8oz watercress
  150g/5oz Stilton or other
    blue cheese
  150ml/¼ pint/⅔ cup single (light)
    cream

1 Pour the stock into a pan and bring almost to the boil. Remove and discard any very large stalks from the watercress, reserving a few leaves to garnish. Add the watercress to the pan and simmer gently for 2–3 minutes, until tender.

2 Crumble the cheese into the pan and simmer for 1 minute more, until the cheese has started to melt. Process the soup in a blender or food processor, in batches if necessary, until very smooth. Return the soup to the pan.

3 Stir in the cream and check the seasoning, don't add too much salt, as the cheese is salty. Reheat the soup, without boiling and serve, garnished with snipped watercress leaves.

Energy 159Kcal/659kJ; Protein 7.9g; Carbohydrate 0.7g, of which sugars 0.7g; Fat 13.7g, of which saturates 8.9g; Cholesterol 38mg; Calcium 168mg; Fibre 0.6g; Sodium 223mg.

CELERY AND BLUE CHEESE SOUP

CELERY IS OFTEN EATEN WITH BLUE CHEESE, AND THIS SOUP TAKES ADVANTAGE OF A PERFECT PAIRING IN WHICH THE FRESH, CLEAN TASTE OF THE CELERY SETS OFF THE CREAMY RICH TEXTURE OF THE BLUE CHEESE. STILTON IS USED HERE, BUT YOU COULD ALSO USE SHROPSHIRE BLUE OR DANISH BLUE.

SERVES 6

INGREDIENTS

40g/1½oz/3 tbsp butter
1 large onion, finely chopped
1 medium potato, cut into
  small cubes
1 whole head of celery, thinly
  sliced
900ml/1½ pints/3¾ cups vegetable
  or chicken stock
100g/3¾oz Stilton cheese, crumbled
150ml/¼ pint/⅔ cup single (light)
  cream
salt and ground black pepper

1 Melt the butter in a large pan and add the chopped onion. Cook over a medium heat for 5 minutes, stirring occasionally, until the onions are soft but not browned.

2 Stir in the potato and celery and cook for a further 5 minutes until the vegetables soften and begin to brown.

3 Add the stock to the vegetables, bring to the boil, then cover the pan and simmer gently for about 30 minutes, until all the vegetables are very soft.

4 Process or blend about three-quarters of the mixture until smooth, then return it to the pan with the rest of the soup.

5 Bring the soup just to the boil and season to taste with salt and ground black pepper.

6 Remove the pan from the heat and stir in the cheese, reserving a little for the garnish. Stir in the cream and reheat the soup gently without boiling.

7 Serve topped with the reserved crumbled cheese.

VARIATION
If you would prefer not to use a blue-veined cheese, try using a strong-tasting, mature Cheddar.

Energy 199kcal/826kJ; Protein 5.9g; Carbohydrate 7.5g, of which sugars 2.4g; Fat 16.2g, of which saturates 10.4g; Cholesterol 44mg; Calcium 117mg; Fibre 1.4g; Sodium 233mg

POTATO AND LEEK SOUP

LEEKS ARE INDISPENSABLE AS THE BASIS OF MANY SOUPS. THEY ARE EASY TO GROW AND STORE WELL, AND GROW IN THE WINTER MONTHS, BUT THEY DO NEED CAREFUL CLEANING ONCE THEY ARE LIFTED FROM THE SOIL. THIS RECIPE MAKES A DELICIOUS AND COMFORTING WINTER SOUP.

SERVES 4-6

INGREDIENTS
- 25g/1oz/2 tbsp unsalted butter
- 1 onion, thinly sliced
- 2–3 leeks (white and pale green parts only), thinly sliced and rinsed
- 3 garlic cloves, roughly chopped
- 120ml/4fl oz/½ cup dry white wine
- 3 medium waxy potatoes, peeled and chopped small
- 1.5 litres/2½ pints/6¼ cups chicken or vegetable stock
- 3 sprigs fresh parsley
- 3 sprigs fresh thyme
- 1 bay leaf
- 200ml/7fl oz/scant 1 cup single (light) cream or milk (optional)
- salt and ground white pepper
- 30ml/2 tbsp thinly chopped fresh chives or chopped parsley, to garnish

1 Heat the butter in a large, heavy pan over a medium heat. Add the onion, leeks and garlic to the pan and sauté gently for about 12 minutes, stirring occasionally, until softened but not browned.

2 Increase the heat to high and pour in the wine. Boil vigorously for about 4 minutes, or until the mixture is almost dry. Add the potatoes and stock.

3 Make a bouquet garni by tying the fresh parsley, thyme and bay leaf together with a piece of kitchen string (twine). Add this to the soup.

4 Bring to the boil, lower the heat and cover the pan, leaving the lid slightly ajar to let the excess steam escape. Simmer for 20 minutes, until the potatoes are very tender.

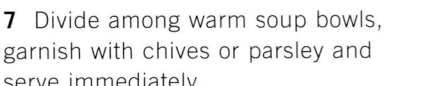
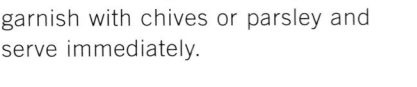

5 Lift out and discard the bouquet garni. With a hand-held blender or in a food processor, purée the soup until the desired consistency is reached.

6 If using the milk or cream, whisk it into the soup. Season and heat through.

7 Divide among warm soup bowls, garnish with chives or parsley and serve immediately.

Energy 127kcal/534kJ; Protein 3.4g; Carbohydrate 19.6g, of which sugars 3.9g; Fat 4.4g, of which saturates 2.4g; Cholesterol 9mg; Calcium 40mg; Fibre 3.2g; Sodium 180mg.

VEGETABLE SOUP

IN THE PAST, EVERY HOUSE OR COTTAGE IN THE COUNTRYSIDE WOULD HAVE HAD ITS KITCHEN GARDEN FOR CONSTANT SEASONAL PRODUCE. THIS RECIPE USES AS MANY DIFFERENT FRESH VEGETABLES AS YOU CAN FIND — IT IS WONDERFULLY ADAPTABLE AND IS BOUND TO BECOME A FAMILY FAVOURITE.

SERVES 4

INGREDIENTS
  1kg/2¼lb mixed fresh vegetables
    in season
  25g/1oz/2 tbsp butter or 30ml/2 tbsp
    vegetable oil
  1 onion, chopped
  115g/4oz/⅔ cup lean smoked
    bacon, diced
  3 potatoes, peeled and grated
  salt and ground black pepper
  30ml/2 tbsp fresh parsley, to garnish
  sour cream, to serve (optional)

VARIATION
For a more substantial main course soup, stir in a 200g/7oz can of drained and rinsed haricot (navy) or black-eyed beans with the potatoes at step 5. This is delicious served with a loaf of freshly baked crusty white bread or rolls.

1 Peel or prepare the vegetables and dice them into small chunks.

2 Melt the butter or heat the oil in a large pan and add the onion. Cook gently, stirring occasionally, for about 10 minutes, until softened.

3 Add the bacon and cook, stirring, for 5 minutes, until both the onion and bacon are lightly browned. Add all the prepared vegetables to the pan.

GRANDMOTHER'S TIP
For a richer soup, use chicken stock instead of water to cook the vegetables.

4 Add enough water to cover. Bring to the boil, then cover and reduce the heat.

5 Simmer for 5–10 minutes, then add the potatoes. Bring the soup back to the boil and simmer for a further 10 minutes, or until all the vegetables are tender.

6 Taste and season the soup with salt and pepper. Finely chop the parsley. Serve in warmed bowls, garnished with a little parsley.

7 Serve each portion with a small spoonful of sour cream, if you like. This creates a delectable contrasting flavour.

Energy 295Kcal/1234kJ; Protein 8.9g; Carbohydrate 41.3g, of which sugars 21.2g; Fat 11.5g, of which saturates 2.8g; Cholesterol 15mg; Calcium 95mg; Fibre 8g; Sodium 523mg.

CREAM OF TOMATO SOUP

THIS TRADITIONAL SOUP CALLS FOR RIPE TOMATOES, GENTLY COOKED WITH FRESH VEGETABLES FROM THE KITCHEN GARDEN, PLUS SOME HERBS, STOCK AND MILK. A LITTLE SUGAR BLENDED IN WILL REALLY BRING OUT THE FLAVOUR OF THE TOMATOES AND CHILDREN WILL LOVE THE SWEETNESS.

SERVES 4–6

INGREDIENTS
    25g/1oz/2 tbsp butter
    1 medium onion, finely chopped
    1 small carrot, finely chopped
    1 celery stick, finely chopped
    1 garlic clove, crushed
    450g/1lb ripe tomatoes, chopped
    400g/14oz can chopped tomatoes
    30ml/2 tbsp tomato purée (paste)
    30ml/2 tbsp sugar
    1 tbsp chopped fresh thyme
    600ml/1 pint/2½ cups chicken or
        vegetable stock
    600ml/1 pint/2½ cups milk
    salt and ground black pepper

1 Melt the butter in a large pan. Add the onion, carrot, celery and garlic and cook for about 5 minutes, stirring.

2 Add the tomatoes, purée, sugar, stock and thyme, reserving some to garnish. Bring to the boil, then cover and simmer gently for about 20 minutes until all the vegetables are very soft.

3 Process or blend the mixture until smooth, then press it through a sieve (strainer) to remove skins and seeds.

4 Return the strained soup to the cleaned pan, place on a medium heat and stir in the milk. Reheat gently, stirring, without allowing it to boil.

5 Season the soup to taste with a little salt and ground black pepper. Serve in warm bowls, garnished with the remaining herbs.

Energy 107kcal/447kJ; Protein 2.3g; Carbohydrate 11.4g, of which sugars 10.9g; Fat 6.1g, of which saturates 3.5g; Cholesterol 13mg; Calcium 50mg; Fibre 3.9g; Sodium 71mg.

CARROT AND APPLE CREAM SOUP

THE SWEETNESS OF FRESHLY-DUG CARROTS COMBINES HERE WITH THE FRUITY TASTE OF APPLES IN A WONDERFUL VELVETY SOUP, WHICH IS AT ITS BEST IN LATE AUTUMN WHEN THE INGREDIENTS ARE OF TOP QUALITY. ROASTED PUMPKIN SEEDS CAN BE SPRINKLED ON TOP FOR A CONTRASTING CRUNCH.

SERVES 4

INGREDIENTS

50g/2oz/4 tbsp butter
1 onion, roughly chopped
1 garlic clove, roughly chopped
500g/1¼lb carrots, roughly chopped
1 large apple, peeled, cored and
  roughly chopped
100ml/3½fl oz/scant ½ cup white
  wine
500ml/17fl oz/generous 2 cups
  vegetable stock
100ml/3½fl oz/scant ½ cup
  apple juice
200ml/7fl oz/scant 1 cup single
  (light) cream
100ml/3½fl oz/scant ½ cup crème
  fraîche
15ml/1 tbsp pumpkin seeds and
  5ml/1 tsp snipped fresh chives,
  to garnish
salt and ground white pepper

1 Melt the butter in a pan over medium heat. Add the onions and cook for 5 minutes until softened. Add the garlic and cook for a few minutes more. Stir in the carrots and the apples.

2 Add the Riesling, followed by the stock and the apple juice. Season with salt and pepper. Bring to the boil, reduce the heat and simmer for 15 minutes.

3 Add the cream and the crème fraîche and bring the soup to the boil. Blend the soup with a hand blender. If it seems too thick, add some more stock.

4 Heat a frying pan over medium heat and roast the pumpkin seeds for 3 minutes until toasted, stirring. Sprinkle with salt. When serving the soup, sprinkle some pumpkin seeds on top and scatter with chives.

Energy 341kcal/1412kJ; Protein 3g; Carbohydrate 18.2g, of which sugars 16.5g; Fat 27.2g, of which saturates 16.8g; Cholesterol 71mg; Calcium 84mg; Fibre 3.7g; Sodium 150mg.

SPICED PUMPKIN SOUP

IN THIS OLD-FASHIONED RECIPE, THE PUMPKIN IS ROASTED WHOLE IN THE OVEN, THEN SCOOPED OUT TO MAKE A DELICIOUS SOUP, TOPPED WITH CRISP FRIED PUMPKIN STRIPS.

SERVES 6–8

INGREDIENTS
   1.5kg/3–3½lb pumpkin
   90ml/6 tbsp olive oil
   2 onions, chopped
   3 garlic cloves, chopped
   7.5cm/3in piece fresh root ginger,
     grated
   5ml/1 tsp ground coriander
   2.5ml/½ tsp ground turmeric
   pinch of cayenne pepper
   1 litre/1¾ pints/4 cups vegetable
     stock
   salt and ground black pepper
   15ml/1 tbsp sesame seeds and
     fresh parsley leaves, to garnish
For the pumpkin crisps
   wedge of fresh pumpkin, seeded
   120ml/4fl oz/½ cup olive oil

GRANDMOTHER'S TIP
If only very large pumpkins are available, simply cut off two or three large wedges weighing 1.5kg/3–3½lb in total. Brush them with oil and roast as above for 20–30 minutes or until tender.

1 Preheat the oven to 200°C/400°F/ Gas 6. Prick the pumpkin around the top several times with a fork. Brush the pumpkin with plenty of the oil and bake for 45 minutes or until tender.

2 Take care when cutting the pumpkin as there may still be a lot of hot steam inside. When cool enough to handle, scoop out and discard the seeds. Scoop out and chop the flesh.

3 Heat about 60ml/4 tbsp of the remaining oil in a large saucepan and add the onions, garlic and ginger, then cook gently for 4–5 minutes. Add the coriander, turmeric and cayenne, and stir in. Add the pumpkin flesh and stock. Bring to the boil, reduce the heat and simmer for 20 minutes.

4 Cool the soup slightly, then purée it in a food processor or blender until smooth. Return the soup to the rinsed-out saucepan and season well.

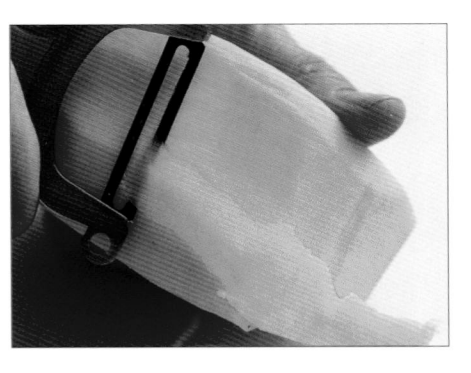

5 Meanwhile, prepare the pumpkin crisps. Using a swivel-blade vegetable peeler, pare long thin strips off the wedge of pumpkin.

6 Heat the oil in a small saucepan and fry the strips in batches for 2 minutes, until crisp. Drain on kitchen paper.

7 Reheat the soup and ladle it into bowls. Top with the pumpkin crisps and garnish each portion with sesame seeds and coriander leaves.

Energy 203Kcal/839kJ; Protein 2.3g; Carbohydrate 8.3g, of which sugars 6.2g; Fat 18.1g, of which saturates 2.7g; Cholesterol 0mg; Calcium 82mg; Fibre 2.8g; Sodium 2mg.

FISH DISHES

Fish and shellfish are wonderfully nutritious,
packed full of protein and vitamins, and ideal
for family meals. In past times, sea fish such as
cod and haddock would only have been available
near the coast, but further inland, freshwater
fish such as trout and salmon could be caught
from rivers and lakes.

SOUSED HERRINGS

MANY FISHING VILLAGES AROUND THE NORTH OF BRITAIN MAKE VARIATIONS OF THIS RECIPE, SOME INVOLVING BRINE (SALT WATER) RATHER THAN VINEGAR. THIS IS A VERY GOOD WAY TO PRESERVE HERRINGS FOR A FEW DAYS, AND THEY CAN THEN BE EATEN HOT OR COLD.

2 Preheat the oven to 150°C/300°F/ Gas 2. Slice the onion horizontally and separate into thin rings. Cover the bottom of a shallow ovenproof dish with a layer of onion rings, arrange the rolled herrings on top and scatter the remaining onion rings over them.

3 Mix the vinegar with 200ml/7fl oz/ scant 1 cup water and pour over the herrings. Add the remaining ingredients to the dish and cover securely with a lid or a sheet of foil.

4 Put into the preheated oven and cook for 1–1¼ hours until the herrings are cooked and the onion soft. Leave the herrings to cool completely in the cooking liquid before serving with watercress.

VARIATIONS
• Use 7.5–10ml/1½–2 tsp ready-made pickling spice in place of the final six ingredients.
• Replace the vinegar and water with 400ml/14fl oz/1⅔ cups dry (hard) cider for a fruitier, less sharp flavour.

SERVES 4

INGREDIENTS
4 large or 8 small herrings, boned and filleted
1 medium onion
200ml/7fl oz/scant 1 cup malt vinegar
5ml/1 tsp sugar
6 black peppercorns
2 bay leaves
2.5ml/½ tsp mustard seeds
2.5ml/½ tsp coriander seeds
pinch of ground ginger
1 small dried chilli
salt and ground black pepper
watercress sprigs, to serve

1 Lay out the herring fillets skin side down, and sprinkle with salt and pepper. Roll up the fillets, beginning at the head end, and secure each with a wooden cocktail stick or toothpick.

SEA TROUT MOUSSE

THIS DELICIOUSLY CREAMY MOUSSE MAKES A LITTLE SEA TROUT GO A LONG WAY, IN THE FRUGAL FASHION OF THE GOOD HOUSEKEEPER. IT ALSO LOOKS IMPRESSIVE, SET IN A PRETTY OLD-FASHIONED RAMEKIN DISH, WITH A FROND OF FEATHERY DILL ON TOP AND DELICATE SLICES OF CUCUMBER.

SERVES 4

INGREDIENTS
    250g/9oz sea trout fillet
    120ml/4fl oz/½ cup fish stock
    2 gelatine leaves or 15ml/1 tbsp
      powdered gelatine
    juice of ½ lemon
    30ml/2 tbsp dry sherry or dry
      vermouth
    30ml/2 tbsp freshly grated Parmesan
    300ml/½ pint/1¼ cups whipping
      cream
    2 egg whites
    15ml/1 tbsp sunflower oil
    salt and ground white pepper
For the garnish
    5cm/2in piece cucumber, with peel,
      thinly sliced
    6 small sprigs fresh dill or chervil,
      plus extra, chopped

4 When the trout is cool enough to handle, remove the skin and flake the flesh. Pour the stock into a food processor, then add the flaked trout, lemon juice, sherry or vermouth and Parmesan through the feeder tube, continuing to process the mixture until smooth. Scrape into a large bowl and leave to cool completely.

5 Lightly whip the cream then fold it into the cold trout mixture. Season to taste, then cover with clear film (plastic wrap) and chill until the mousse is beginning to set.

6 Beat the egg whites with a pinch of salt until softly peaking. Stir one-third into the trout mixture to lighten it, then fold in the rest.

7 Lightly grease six ramekin dishes with the sunflower oil. Divide the mousse among the ramekins and level the surface. Place in the refrigerator for 2–3 hours, until set.

8 Just before serving, arrange a few slices of cucumber and a small sprig of dill or chervil on each mousse.

1 Place the trout fillet in a shallow pan. Pour in the fish stock and heat to simmering point. Poach the fish for about 3–4 minutes, until lightly cooked.

2 Lift the trout out of the pan and set it aside to cool slightly. Strain the stock into a jug (pitcher), then add the gelatine to the hot stock and stir until dissolved completely. Set aside to cool.

3 While the trout is still warm, remove the skin from the fillets and discard.

VARIATION
You can replace the trout with the same quantity of salmon if you wish.

Per portion Energy 286kcal/1181kJ; Protein 12g; Carbohydrate 1.5g, of which sugars 1.5g; Fat 25.2g, of which saturates 13.9g; Cholesterol 58mg; Calcium 94mg; Fibre 0g; Sodium 111mg.

SMOKED HADDOCK FLAN

THE CLASSIC COMBINATION OF SMOKED HADDOCK AND POTATOES IS SET IN A BUTTERY HOME-MADE PASTRY SHELL. IT IS IMPORTANT TO BUY TRADITIONAL UNDYED SMOKED HADDOCK RATHER THAN THE BRIGHT YELLOW VARIETY, WHICH HAS PROBABLY BEEN DYED AND MAY NOT BE PROPERLY SMOKED.

SERVES 4

INGREDIENTS
For the pastry
    225g/8oz/2 cups plain
      (all-purpose) flour
    pinch of salt
    115g/4oz/1½ cup cold butter, cut
      into chunks
    cold water, to mix
For the filling
    2 undyed smoked haddock fillets
      (approximately 200g/7oz)
    600ml/1 pint/2½ cups full-fat
      (whole) milk
    3–4 black peppercorns
    sprig of fresh thyme
    150ml/¼ pint/⅔ cup double
      (heavy) cream
    2 eggs
    200g/7oz potatoes, peeled and diced
    ground black pepper

1 Preheat the oven to 200°C/400°F/ Gas 6. Use a food processor to make the pastry. Put the flour, salt and butter into the food processor bowl and process until the mixture resembles fine breadcrumbs. Pour in a little cold water (you will need about 40ml/8 tsp, but see Grandmother's Tip) and continue to process until the mixture forms a ball. If this takes longer than 30 seconds, add a dash or two more water.

2 Take the pastry ball out of the food processor, wrap in clear film (plastic wrap) and leave to rest in a cool place for about 30 minutes.

GRANDMOTHER'S TIP
Different flours absorb water at different rates. When making any kind of pastry a traditional rule of thumb is to use the same number of teaspoons of water as the number of ounces of flour, but some flours will require less water and others more, so add the water gradually. If you add too much water, the pastry will become unworkable and adding more flour can make the cooked result heavy.

3 Roll out the dough and line a 20cm/ 8in tin (pan). Prick the pastry base all over with a fork, then bake blind in the preheated oven for 20 minutes.

4 Put the smoked haddock fillets in a pan with the milk, peppercorns and thyme. Poach the fish for 10 minutes. Remove the fish from the pan and flake into small chunks. Allow the poaching liquor to cool.

5 Whisk the cream and eggs together thoroughly, then whisk in the cooled poaching liquid.

6 Layer the flan case with the flaked fish and diced potato, seasoning with black pepper. You won't need to add any salt, as smoked fish is often salty.

7 Pour the cream mixture over the top. Put the flan in the oven and bake for 40 minutes, until browned and set.

VARIATION
Add 2 hard boiled eggs, cut into eighths, before adding the potatoes.

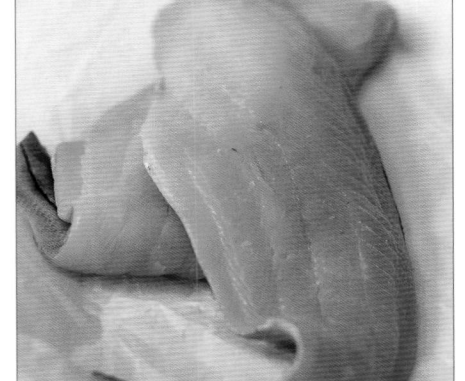

Energy 734kcal/3064kJ; Protein 23.8g; Carbohydrate 58.4g, of which sugars 8.2g; Fat 46.8g, of which saturates 27.9g; Cholesterol 225mg; Calcium 280mg; Fibre 2.3g; Sodium 636mg.

CRAB GRATIN

THIS DISH MAKES A FILLING MAIN COURSE AND IS A REMNANT OF A BYGONE ERA WHEN FRESH CRABS WERE PLENTIFUL, ESPECIALLY IN COASTAL AREAS. THE SKILL INVOLVED IN COOKING AND CUTTING UP CRABS IS WORTH ACQUIRING IF YOU LOVE THE SALTY, FRESH FLAVOUR OF THIS DISH.

SERVES 6

INGREDIENTS
  6 large crabs
  3 litres/2½ pints/6¼ cups water
  350ml/12fl oz beer
  100g/4oz/1 cup coarse sea salt
  2 sugar lumps
  40g/1½oz Cheddar cheese, grated
  mixed salad leaves, to serve
For the sauce
  25g/1oz/2 tbsp butter
  15ml/1 tbsp plain (all-purpose) flour
  475ml/16fl oz/2 cups double (heavy)
    cream
  2 egg yolks
  30ml/2 tbsp brandy
  10ml/2 tsp liquid from a can of
    anchovies, or other fish stock
  salt and ground black pepper
  mixed leaves, to serve

1 Put the crabs in individual, strong plastic bags, seal and place in the freezer for 2 hours to put them to sleep (this is the most humane and least traumatizing way of killing them).

2 Put the water, beer, salt and sugar in a very large pan and bring to the boil. Remove 1–2 crabs, depending upon the size of your pan, from the freezer, unseal the bag and immediately drop the unconscious crab or crabs into the boiling water.

3 Cover the pan, return to the boil and cook for 15 minutes for one crab, 25 minutes for two. Then remove the crab(s) from the water. Add the next one or two crabs to the pan and cook the same way until all of the crabs are cooked. Make sure the water keeps at a rolling boil each time.

GRANDMOTHER'S TIP
Instead of boiling live crabs yourself, you could use 500g/1¼lb fresh crabmeat. You will then also need 300ml/½ pint/ 1¼ cups fish stock to make the sauce.

4 Pour the hot cooking liquid over the crabs, allow to cool in the liquid and then leave in the refrigerator overnight.

5 Remove the crabs from the liquid and reserve 300ml/½ pint/1¼ cups. Put the crab on a chopping board on its back to extract the meat. First, hold a claw firmly in one hand and twist to remove it. Remove the remaining claw and legs in the same way.

6 Break the claws in half by bending them backwards, then crack the shells with a nutcracker or rolling pin and hook out the meat with a skewer.

7 Remove the stomach sac and mouth and discard. Hold the shell firmly, press the body section upwards and gently pull them apart.

8 Remove the grey gills and discard, then cut the body into small pieces and hook out the meat. Finally, scoop the brown meat out of the shell. Preheat the oven to 200°C/400°F/Gas 6.

9 To make the sauce, melt the butter in a pan, add the flour and cook over a low heat for 1 minute, stirring.

10 Slowly stir in the reserved liquid and cook, stirring, for 2–3 minutes until thickened. Remove from the heat, stir in the cream, egg yolks, brandy and anchovy liquid. Season with pepper.

11 Add the crab meat to the sauce and then put the mixture into the shells. Sprinkle the grated cheese on top and bake for 10–15 minutes until golden brown. Serve hot, with mixed leaves.

Energy 544kcal/2244kJ; Protein 10.9g; Carbohydrate 6.1g, of which sugars 4.2g; Fat 51.7g, of which saturates 30.8g; Cholesterol 209mg; Calcium 112mg; Fibre 0.1g; Sodium 216mg.

STUFFED LEMON SOLE <u>WITH</u> GRATIN SAUCE

THIS IS A REALLY GOOD WAY TO SERVE A DELICATE WHITE FISH LIKE LEMON SOLE. FINELY CHOPPED WILD MUSHROOMS AND A LITTLE CHEESE ADD FLAVOUR TO THE LIGHT SAUCE, WITH THE HEADY SCENT OF TARRAGON. SERVE WITH STEAMED VEGETABLES AND POTATOES OR A SALAD.

SERVES 4

INGREDIENTS

4 large lemon sole fillets (or any other white fish fillet), about 200g/7oz each, skinned and bones removed
10g/¼oz/½ tbsp butter
300g/11oz wild mushrooms, finely chopped
5ml/1 tsp finely chopped fresh tarragon
60ml/4 tbsp white wine
60ml/4 tbsp double (heavy) cream
salt and ground black pepper

For the sauce
7.5ml/1½ tsp butter
1 shallot, finely chopped
15ml/1 tbsp cornflour (cornstarch)
200ml/7fl oz/scant 1 cup fish stock
115g/4oz/1¼ cups freshly grated Parmesan cheese
15ml/1 tbsp finely chopped fresh tarragon

1 Season the fillets on both sides, then lay them on your work surface, skin side down.

2 To make the filling, melt the butter in a medium pan over a medium heat and add the mushrooms. Stir for 4–5 minutes, or until soft, then add the tarragon. Season with salt and pepper.

3 Add the wine and cream, and cook for 5–6 minutes more, or until the liquid has evaporated. Remove from the heat and allow to cool.

4 Meanwhile, make the sauce. Melt the butter in a small pan over a medium heat and add the shallot. Sauté for 1–2 minutes, or until softened.

5 Stir the cornflour into the sautéed shallots, then gradually add the stock, stirring continuously. Cook over a low heat for 5 minutes, until thickened, then add the Parmesan and tarragon. Cover and keep warm while you finish preparing the fillet rolls.

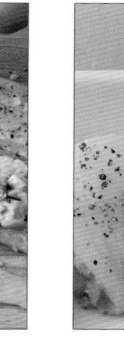

6 Preheat the oven to 180°C/350°F/ Gas 4. Divide the cooled mushroom mixture between the four fillets of fish, spreading it along the fillets. Roll up the fillets, making sure that the mushroom filling remains inside.

7 Secure the rolled fillets with cocktail sticks (toothpicks) and arrange in an ovenproof dish. Pour the sauce over the stuffed sole fillet and bake for 20–25 minutes, or until golden brown. Remove from the oven and serve.

Energy 420kcal/1757kJ; Protein 46g; Carbohydrate 5.1g, of which sugars 1.3g; Fat 23.9g, of which saturates 13.2g; Cholesterol 178mg; Calcium 393mg; Fibre 0.2g; Sodium 545mg.

GRILLED SARDINES WITH PARSLEY

Sardines are easy to cook, good value for money and extremely tasty, and used to be much more popular than they are now. It is well worth searching out these little fish, and simply grilling them with butter and parsley for a nutritious and speedy lunch.

SERVES 4

INGREDIENTS

900g/2lb fresh sardines, gutted
  and scaled
30ml/2 tbsp melted butter or
  vegetable oil
salt and ground black pepper,
  to taste
60ml/4 tbsp chopped fresh parsley,
  to garnish
lemon wedges, to serve

1 Preheat the grill (broiler) to high. Wash the prepared sardines under cold running water and pat them dry on kitchen paper.

2 Brush the fish on both sides with melted butter or oil, then season to taste with salt and pepper.

GRANDMOTHER'S TIP
Sardines can also be fried. Use a heavy-bottomed pan and heat it first, then fry the fish on high a heat for 3–4 minutes on each side.

3 Place the sardines on the grill pan and place under the preheated grill. Cook for about 3–4 minutes on each side, until the skin begins to brown. Don't worry if the skin burns slightly in places, this adds to the flavour.

4 Transfer the sardines to warmed plates, sprinkle with parsley, and serve immediately, while still piping hot, with lemon wedges.

Energy 327kcal/1362kJ; Protein 35g; Carbohydrate 0.3g, of which sugars 0.3g; Fat 20.5g, of which saturates 8g; Cholesterol 16mg; Calcium 192mg; Fibre 0.5g; Sodium 240mg.

FRIED FISH WITH TARTARE SAUCE

THIS RECIPE CALLS FOR PERCH, WHICH IS A FRESHWATER FISH FOUND IN INLAND RIVERS, STREAMS AND LAKES. HOME-MADE TARTARE SAUCE, MADE FROM STORE-CUPBOARD INGREDIENTS, GIVES A LIFT TO THE FINISHED DISH, AND CHILDREN WILL LOVE THE LIGHT, FOAMY BATTER.

SERVES 4

INGREDIENTS

700g/1lb 10oz perch fillet, skinned
  and with bones removed
5ml/1 tsp salt
15ml/1 tbsp fresh lemon juice
115g/4oz/1 cup plain white
  (all-purpose) flour
150ml/¼ pint/⅔ cup light beer
1 egg white
about 1 litre/1¾ pints/4 cups
  rapeseed (canola) oil
lemon wedges, to garnish
green salad, to serve

For the tartare sauce
3 large pickled gherkins
200g/7fl oz/scant 1 cup mayonnaise
15ml/1 tbsp capers
5ml/1 tsp finely chopped fresh dill
15ml/1 tbsp finely chopped fresh
  parsley
2.5ml/½ tsp mustard
1.5ml/¼ tsp salt
1.5ml/¼ tsp ground black pepper

1 To make the tartare sauce, peel and finely chop the gherkins. Put in a bowl with the mayonnaise, capers, dill, parsley and mustard. Mix together. Add salt and pepper to taste, and transfer to a serving bowl.

2 Cut the fish fillets into pieces measuring about 3cm/1¼in and put on a plate. Squeeze the lemon over the fish pieces, then sprinkle with the salt. Mix well so that all the pieces are seasoned, and set aside.

3 Sift the flour into a bowl and add the beer, then whisk together until the mixture forms a smooth batter.

4 In a separate bowl, whisk the egg white until it stands in soft peaks, then fold it into the beer batter.

5 Heat the oil in a deep fryer to 180°C/350°F or until a cube of bread browns in 1 minute. Dip and turn the fish pieces in the batter and then drop into the hot oil.

5 Fry for 1–2 minutes, until golden. Using a slotted spoon, remove from the pan and drain on kitchen paper. Serve the fish hot with lemon wedges and the tartare sauce.

Energy 719kcal/2986kJ; Protein 36.7g; Carbohydrate 24.3g, of which sugars 2.1g; Fat 53.4g, of which saturates 7.6g; Cholesterol 118mg; Calcium 95mg; Fibre 1.8g; Sodium 352mg.

TROUT WITH BACON

IF YOU ARE LUCKY ENOUGH TO OBTAIN SOME WILD TROUT FOR THIS DISH, YOU WILL APPRECIATE JUST HOW WELL THEIR DELICATE FLAVOUR WORKS WITH THE BACON AND LEEK WRAPPING. IF POSSIBLE, USE DRY-CURED BACON, AS ITS TEXTURE AND FLAVOUR IS PERFECT FOR THIS TRADITIONAL DISH.

SERVES 4

INGREDIENTS
 4 trout, each weighing about
   225g/8oz, cleaned
 small parsley sprigs
 4 lemon slices, plus lemon wedges
   to serve
 8 large leek leaves
 8 thinly sliced bacon rashers, rinds
   removed
 salt and ground black pepper

1 Preheat the oven to 180°C/ 350°F/Gas 4. Rinse the trout, inside and out, under cold running water, then pat dry with kitchen paper.

2 Season the cavities of the fish and put a few parsley sprigs and a slice of lemon into each.

3 Wrap two leek leaves, then two bacon rashers, spiral fashion around each fish. It may be helpful to secure the ends with wooden cocktail sticks (toothpicks).

4 Lay the fish in a shallow ovenproof dish, in a single layer and side by side, head next to tail.

5 Bake for about 20 minutes, until the bacon is brown and the leeks are tender. The trout should be cooked through; check by inserting a sharp knife into the thickest part.

6 Sprinkle the remaining parsley over the trout and serve.

GRANDMOTHER'S TIPS
• This dish is nicer to eat if the backbone is removed from the fish before it is cooked – ask your fishmonger to do this. Leave the head and tail on or cut them off, as you prefer.
• Use tender leaves (layers) of leek, rather than the tough outer ones. Alternatively, soften some leaves by pouring boiling water over them and leaving them to stand for a few minutes before draining.

Energy 324kcal/1357kJ; Protein 44.4g; Carbohydrate 0.4g, of which sugars 0.3g; Fat 16.1g, of which saturates 5.1g; Cholesterol 174mg; Calcium 60mg; Fibre 0.3g; Sodium 997mg.

MACKEREL WITH GOOSEBERRY RELISH

THIS OILY FISH IS VERY NUTRITIOUS, AND IS STILL CAUGHT IN LARGE NUMBERS AROUND THE COASTLINE OF THE NORTH SEA. THE ACCOMPANYING SAUCE IS MADE FROM LITTLE TART, HARD GOOSEBERRIES, WHOSE FLAVOUR REALLY SHINES THROUGH AGAINST THE DARK-FLESHED MACKEREL.

3 Preheat the grill (broiler) to high and line the grill (broiling) pan with foil. Using a sharp knife, slash the fish two or three times down each side to help the cooking process, then season and brush with the olive oil.

4 Place the fish in the grill pan and grill (broil) for about 4 minutes on each side until cooked. You may need to cook them for a few minutes longer if they are particularly large. The slashes will open up and the skin should be lightly browned.

5 To check the fish are cooked properly, use a small sharp knife to pierce the skin and check for uncooked flesh. Place the mackerel on warmed plates and spread generous dollops of the gooseberry relish over them.

SERVES 4

INGREDIENTS
    4 whole mackerel
    60ml/4 tbsp olive oil
For the sauce
    250g/9oz gooseberries
    25g/1oz/2 tbsp soft light brown sugar
    5ml/1 tsp wholegrain mustard
    salt and ground black pepper

GRANDMOTHER'S TIPS
• Turn the grill (broiler) on well in advance, as the fish need a very fierce heat so that they cook quickly. If you like the fish but hate the cooking smells, try barbecuing outside.
• The foil lining in the grill (broiling) pan is to catch the smelly drips. Simply roll it up and throw it away afterwards, leaving a nice clean grill pan.

1 For the sauce, wash and trim the gooseberries and then roughly chop them, so there are some pieces larger than others.

2 Cook the gooseberries in a little water with the sugar in a small pan. A thick and chunky purée will form. Add the mustard and season to taste with salt and ground black pepper.

Energy 576kcal/2390kJ; Protein 38.1g; Carbohydrate 8.4g, of which sugars 8.4g; Fat 43.5g, of which saturates 8.2g; Cholesterol 108mg; Calcium 43mg; Fibre 1.5g; Sodium 128mg.

FISH PIE

THIS IS A DELICIOUS FISH PIE, WITH A TEMPTING FLAKY PASTRY TOPPING. IT USES A COMBINATION OF WHITE FISH AND SMOKED HADDOCK, WITH THE ADDITION OF SOME OLD-FASHIONED FRESH SORREL, A WILD HEDGEROW PLANT THAT ADDS AN EXTRA TWIST OF TRADITIONAL FLAVOUR.

SERVES 4

INGREDIENTS

225g/8oz skinless white fish, such as hake, haddock or cod
225g/8oz skinless smoked haddock or cod
425ml/¾ pint/scant 2 cups milk
25g/1oz/2 tbsp butter
25g/1oz/¼ cup plain (all-purpose) flour
good pinch of freshly grated nutmeg
1 leek, thinly sliced
200g/7oz shelled cooked cockles (small clams)
30ml/2 tbsp sorrel (optional)
30ml/2 tbsp finely chopped fresh parsley
1 sheet ready-rolled puff pastry
salt and ground black pepper

4 Stir in the fish flakes and their juices. Add nutmeg and seasoning. Add the leek, cockles, sorrel and parsley and spoon into a 1.2 litre/2 pint dish. Brush the edges of the dish with water. Unroll the pastry and lay it over the top of the dish, trimming it to fit.

5 Use the pastry off-cuts to make decorative fish or leaves for the top, brushing each one with a little water to help them stick. Put into the hot oven and cook for about 30 minutes, or until the pastry is puffed and golden brown. Serve the pie immediately.

1 Preheat the oven to 200°C/400°F/ Gas 6. Put the white and smoked fish in a pan with the milk. Heat until the milk barely comes to the boil, then cover and poach gently for about 8 minutes or until the fish is just cooked.

2 Lift the fish out, reserving the liquid. Break into flakes, discarding any bones.

3 Melt the butter, stir in the flour and cook for 1–2 minutes. Remove and stir in the reserved cooking liquid. Stir over medium heat until the sauce thickens.

GRANDMOTHER'S TIP
If you don't have sorrel growing in the garden, add some finely grated lemon rind instead.

Energy 573kcal/2401kJ; Protein 36.8g; Carbohydrate 41g, of which sugars 7.3g; Fat 31.2g, of which saturates 4.7g; Cholesterol 92mg; Calcium 270mg; Fibre 1.2g; Sodium 1084mg

COD, BASIL, TOMATO AND POTATO PIE

Smoked and white fish mixed together, with a hint of tomato and basil, make a great combination in this pie. It is topped with buttery mashed potatoes and baked in the oven for an ideal family supper dish, served with fresh garden vegetables or a green salad.

SERVES 8

INGREDIENTS

1kg/2¼lb smoked cod
1kg/2¼lb white cod
900ml/1½ pint/3¾ cups milk
1.2 litres/2 pints/5 cups water
2 basil sprigs
1 lemon thyme sprig
150g/5oz/10 tbsp butter
1 onion, chopped
75g/3oz/⅔ cup plain (all purpose)
  flour
30ml/2 tbsp chopped fresh basil
4 firm plum tomatoes, peeled
  and chopped
12 medium-sized floury potatoes
salt and ground black pepper
lettuce leaves and crushed black
  peppercorns, to serve

1 Place both kinds of fish in a roasting tin with 600ml/1 pint/2½ cups milk, the water and the herb sprigs. Bring to a simmer and cook gently for about 3–4 minutes. Leave the fish to cool in the liquid for about 20 minutes. Remove the fish, reserving the liquid. Flake the fish, discarding skin and any bones.

2 Melt 75g/3oz/6 tbsp of the butter in a large pan, add the onion and cook for about 5 minutes until soft. Sprinkle over the flour and half the chopped basil.

3 Gradually add the reserved cooking liquid, stirring constantly, add a little more milk to make a fairly thin sauce. Bring to the boil, season with salt and pepper, and add the remaining basil.

4 Remove the pan from the heat, then add the fish and tomatoes and stir gently to combine. Pour into an ovenproof dish.

5 Preheat the oven to 180°C/350°F/ Gas 4. Cook the potatoes in boiling water until tender. Drain, then add the remaining butter and milk, and mash. Season to taste and spoon over the fish mixture, using a fork to create a pattern. You can freeze it at this stage.

6 Bake for 30 minutes until the top is golden. Sprinkle with the crushed peppercorns and serve with lettuce.

Energy 474Kcal/1989kJ; Protein 49.6g; Carbohydrate 30.7g, of which sugars 4.6g; Fat 17.8g, of which saturates 10.2g; Cholesterol 155mg; Calcium 62mg; Fibre 2.5g; Sodium 1672mg.

SMOKED FISH SOUFFLÉ

SOUFFLÉS ARE NOT DIFFICULT TO MAKE, BUT THERE ARE A FEW TRICKS WORTH REMEMBERING. USE AN OLD-FASHIONED METAL BOWL TO WHISK THE EGG WHITES, AND FOLD THEM INTO THE MIXTURE USING A METAL SPOON. MOST IMPORTANTLY, SERVE THE SOUFFLÉ THE MINUTE IT IS READY.

SERVES 4

INGREDIENTS

225g/8oz skinless smoked haddock
300ml/½ pint/1¼ cups milk
2 bay leaves (optional)
40g/1½oz/3 tbsp butter, plus extra
  for greasing
40g/1½oz/5 tbsp plain (all-purpose)
  flour
55g/2oz mature Cheddar cheese
5ml/1 tsp English (hot) mustard
4 egg yolks
5 egg whites
ground black pepper

1 Put the fish into a pan just large enough to hold it in a single layer, and add the milk and bay leaves (if using). Heat slowly until the milk is very hot, with small bubbles rising to the surface, but not boiling. Cover and simmer very gently for 5–8 minutes until the fish is just cooked.

2 Lift out the fish with a slotted spoon, reserving the cooking liquid, and remove any bones. Discard the bay leaves and break the fish into flakes. Preheat the oven to 190°C/375°F/Gas 5 and butter a 20cm/8in soufflé dish.

3 Melt the butter in a pan, stir in the flour and cook gently for 1 minute, stirring. Remove from the heat and gradually stir in the reserved cooking liquid. Cook the sauce, stirring constantly until it begins to thicken and comes to the boil.

4 Remove from the heat. Stir in the cheese, mustard, pepper and fish.

GRANDMOTHER'S TIPS
Eggs are easier to separate when cold, but whites incorporate more air at room temperature. Separate the eggs direct from the fridge, then allow the whites to warm up for 30 minutes before whisking.

5 Beat in the egg yolks, one at a time. Whisk the egg whites until stiff. Stir a little egg white into the sauce then use a large metal spoon to fold in the rest.

6 Pour the mixture into the prepared dish and cook in the hot oven for about 40 minutes until risen and just firm to the touch. Serve immediately.

Energy 325kcal/1356kJ; Protein 24.4g; Carbohydrate 11.4g, of which sugars 3.8g; Fat 20.3g, of which saturates 10.7g; Cholesterol 272mg; Calcium 247mg; Fibre 0.3g; Sodium 706mg.

SALMON, POTATO AND MUSHROOM BAKE

THIS IS A LOVELY FISH BAKE IN WHICH SALMON IS COOKED WITH MUSHROOMS AND POTATOES, WITH A DELICIOUS HINT OF CARAWAY TO COUNTERACT THE RICH FLAVOUR. THIS DISH MAKES A HEARTY MEAL, WITH JUST A SALAD TO ACCOMPANY IT, SO IT CAN BE MADE IN ADVANCE AND BAKED WHEN NEEDED.

2 Add the butter to the pan and when it has melted, add the mushrooms. Sauté the mushrooms for 4 minutes, or until soft. Season to taste and remove from the pan.

3 Add the remaining oil to the pan and cook the onion rings for 4–5 minutes, or until lightly browned and soft.

4 Line individual serving dishes, or a 20cm/8in square ovenproof dish, with most of the pre-cooked potatoes in a solid layer, overlapping the slices a little. Spoon over the mushrooms, and then top with the onion rings. Sprinkle the ground caraway over the top.

SERVES 4–6

INGREDIENTS
135ml/4½fl oz/scant ⅔ cup
  vegetable oil
4 baking potatoes, peeled and
  thinly sliced
10g/¼oz/½ tbsp butter
300g/11oz/generous 4 cups
  mushrooms, thinly sliced
1 large onion, finely sliced in rings
1.5ml/¼ tsp caraway seeds, ground
  with a mortar and pestle
500g/1¼lb thin salmon fillets, bones
  and skin removed
2 large eggs, beaten
300ml/½ pint/1¼ cups single
  (light) cream
200g/7oz/3½ cups breadcrumbs
salt and ground black pepper

GRANDMOTHER'S TIPS
• Avoid farmed salmon and Atlantic salmon. The most sustainable choice is wild-caught Alaskan salmon.
• When buying salmon, look for moist, translucent flesh. Fresh salmon will give slightly with finger pressure, and then spring back into shape. When you get home, wipe it with a damp cloth, wrap it in plastic wrap and store in the bottom of the refrigerator. Use within two days.

1 Preheat the oven to 180°C/350°F/Gas 4. Heat 75–90ml/5–6 tbsp oil in a large non-stick frying pan over a medium heat. Add the potatoes a few at a time, and cook for 5–8 minutes, or until they are almost tender and lightly browned. Add more oil if needed. Remove from the pan with a slotted spoon and set aside.

5 Top with the salmon fillets and finish with a layer of the remaining potatoes. Combine the eggs and cream in a bowl and pour over the bake. Sprinkle with the breadcrumbs.

6 Bake in the hot oven. Individual dishes will need 20–25 minutes, and the larger dish will need 35–40 minutes, or until golden brown. Serve hot.

Per portion Energy 689kcal/2877kJ; Protein 27.2g; Carbohydrate 57.6g, of which sugars 7.1g; Fat 40.4g, of which saturates 11.2g; Cholesterol 149mg; Calcium 144mg; Fibre 3.4g; Sodium 422mg.

PAN-FRIED DOVER SOLE

FOR MANY, DOVER SOLE IS ONE OF THE FINEST OF THE FLAT FISH, OFTEN CALLED 'THE ENGLISHMAN'S FISH OF CHOICE' BECAUSE IN THE DAYS WHEN TRANSPORT WAS SLOW, ITS FLAVOUR ACTUALLY IMPROVED DURING THE JOURNEY FROM THE KENT COAST. USE HERBS SUCH AS DILL, PARSLEY OR TARRAGON.

SERVES 4

INGREDIENTS

4 small Dover sole, dark skin and fins removed
30–45ml/2–3 tbsp plain (all-purpose) flour, seasoned with salt and pepper
45ml/3 tbsp olive oil
25g/1oz/2 tbsp butter
juice of 1 lemon
15ml/1 tbsp chopped fresh herbs
watercress sprigs and lemon wedges to garnish

3 Add the remaining oil and the butter to the hot pan and heat until the butter has melted. Squeeze in the lemon juice and stir into the hot butter.

4 Add the chopped herbs, then drizzle the pan juices over the fish and serve immediately, garnished with watercress sprigs and extra lemon wedges.

1 Spread the seasoned flour on a plate, and coat each fish, shaking off any excess. Heat a large non-stick frying pan and add the oil.

2 Add one or two fish to the pan and cook over a medium heat for 3–5 minutes on each side until golden brown and cooked through. Lift them out and keep them warm while you cook the remaining fish.

Energy 177kcal/739kJ; Protein 18.6g; Carbohydrate 3g, of which sugars 0.2g; Fat 10.2g, of which saturates 1.2g; Cholesterol 50mg; Calcium 42mg; Fibre 0.3g; Sodium 101mg.

BAKED COD WITH CREAM

THIS STRAIGHTFORWARD RECIPE LETS THE FRESH FLAVOUR AND FIRM TEXTURE OF THE FISH SHINE THROUGH. IT IS SIMPLY GARNISHED WITH LEFTOVER BREADCRUMBS, CREAM AND CHOPPED PARSLEY, WITH LEMON WEDGES TO SQUEEZE OVER. IF YOU CAN'T FIND COD, USE ANOTHER WHITE FISH.

SERVES 4-6

INGREDIENTS

1.3kg/3lb cod steaks
15ml/1 tbsp salt
1 egg, beaten
50g/2oz/½ cup fine breadcrumbs
40g/1½oz/3 tbsp butter, cut into small pieces
300ml/½ pint/1¼ cups single (light) cream
45ml/3 tbsp chopped fresh parsley and 8 lemon wedges to garnish
boiled potatoes and peas, to serve

GRANDMOTHER'S TIP
If you can find a whole cod, bake it in the oven for around 1 hour, adding the cream 20 minutes before the end of the cooking time.

1 Preheat the oven to 190°C/375°F/ Gas 5. Pat the fish steaks dry and rub the salt over the skin.

2 Place the steaks in a lightly greased baking dish, brush the tops with the egg, sprinkle with breadcrumbs and dot with butter.

3 Pour the cream around the steaks. Bake the fish for about 15–20 minutes, depending on thickness, until the topping is browned and the flesh flakes easily with a fork. Serve the fish with potatoes and peas, garnished with parsley and lemon wedges.

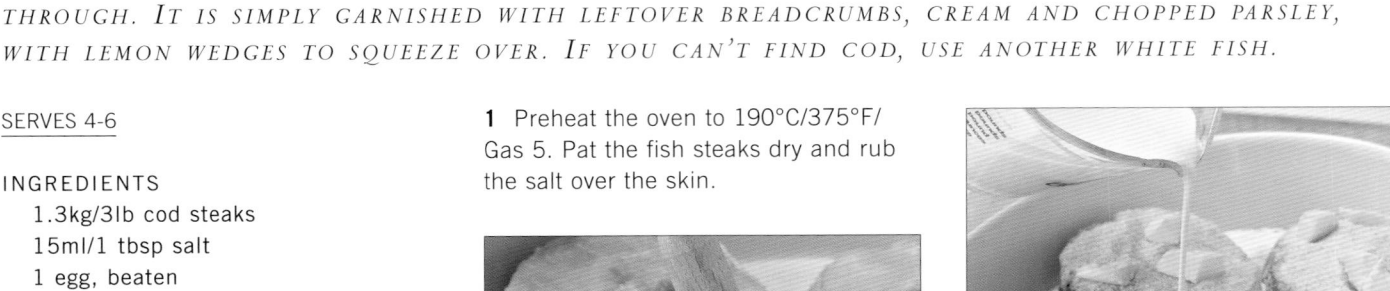

Energy 355kcal/1484kJ; Protein 42.5g; Carbohydrate 8.9g, of which sugars 1.4g; Fat 16.7g, of which saturates 9.8g; Cholesterol 141mg; Calcium 78mg; Fibre 0.2g; Sodium 261mg.

HADDOCK IN CHEESE SAUCE

ANY WHITE FISH CAN BE USED FOR THIS DISH, BUT HADDOCK IS EVERY GENERATION'S FAVOURITE. THE SAUCE IS FLAVOURED WITH STRONG CHEESE AND A DASH OF HOT ENGLISH MUSTARD. IT MAKES AN EASY FAMILY SUPPER, SERVED WITH A SALAD OR STEAMED BROCCOLI FOR A SUMMERY MEAL.

SERVES 4

INGREDIENTS

1kg/2¼lb haddock fillets
300ml/½ pint/1¼ cups milk
1 small onion, thinly sliced
2 bay leaves
a few black peppercorns
25g/1oz/2 tbsp butter
25g/1oz/2 tbsp plain (all-purpose) flour
5ml/1 tsp English (hot) mustard
115g/4oz Cheddar cheese, grated
salt and ground black pepper

VARIATION
This dish can be made with smoked haddock; use fillets that have been mildly smoked. You can also use half smoked and half unsmoked fish.

GRANDMOTHER'S TIP
The fish can be left whole, spoon the sauce over them before grilling.

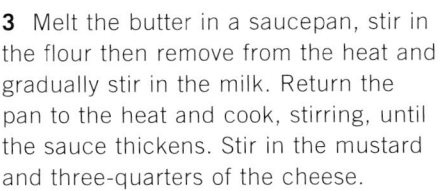

1 Put the fish in a pan large enough to hold it in a single layer. Add the milk, onion, bay leaves and peppercorns and heat slowly until small bubbles are rising to the surface.

2 Cover and simmer very gently on low heat for 5–8 minutes, until the fish is only just cooked. Lift the fillets out with a slotted spoon, and reserve the cooking liquid. Flake the fish, removing any bones.

3 Melt the butter in a saucepan, stir in the flour then remove from the heat and gradually stir in the milk. Return the pan to the heat and cook, stirring, until the sauce thickens. Stir in the mustard and three-quarters of the cheese.

4 Gently stir the fish into the sauce. Spoon into individual flameproof dishes. Sprinkle the remaining cheese over the top. Put under a hot grill (broiler) until bubbling. Serve with crusty bread.

Energy 430kcal/1809kJ; Protein 58.2g; Carbohydrate 9.6g, of which sugars 4.5g; Fat 17.4g, of which saturates 10.6g; Cholesterol 136mg; Calcium 351mg; Fibre 0.4g; Sodium 446mg.

ROASTED SALMON WITH MUSTARD

These salmon fillets really benefit from being left in the marinade for 30 minutes, or longer if you have time. The honey and mustard permeates the salmon flesh and the resulting baked fish is succulent and juicy. Serve with steamed cabbage.

1 To make the marinade, put the oil, honey, mustard and lemon rind in a small bowl and mix together. Season the marinade with salt and pepper to taste.

2 Put the salmon fillets in an ovenproof dish or on a baking sheet lined with baking parchment and spread the marinade over each fillet. Leave to marinate for 30 minutes. Preheat the oven to 200°C/400°F/Gas 6.

3 Roast in the oven for 10–12 minutes, until the flesh flakes easily. Serve hot.

SERVES 4

INGREDIENTS
   30ml/2 tbsp olive oil
   15ml/1 tbsp honey
   30ml/2 tbsp wholegrain French
      mustard
   grated rind ½ lemon
   4 salmon fillets, each about
      150g/5oz
   salt and ground black pepper

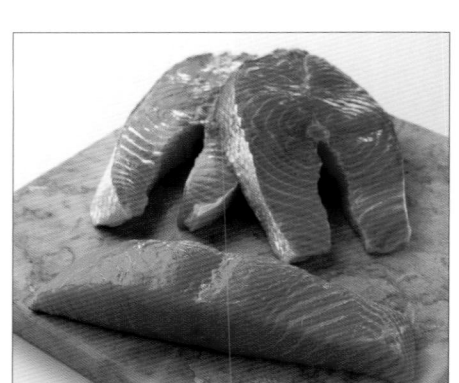

Energy 296kcal/1231kJ; Protein 25.9g; Carbohydrate 3.2g, of which sugars 3.2g; Fat 20g, of which saturates 3.2g; Cholesterol 63mg; Calcium 36mg; Fibre 0.4g; Sodium 178mg.

SALMON FISH CAKES

FISH CAKES CAN BE MADE WITH FRESHLY COOKED FISH AND POTATOES, BUT THIS IS A GREAT WAY TO USE UP LEFTOVERS. IF THE MIXTURE IS DIFFICULT TO SHAPE, TRY THE OLD TRICK OF LEAVING IT TO FIRM UP IN A COOL PLACE FOR HALF AN HOUR TO HELP BIND TOGETHER WELL FOR COOKING.

SERVES 4

INGREDIENTS

    450g/1lb cooked salmon fillet
    450g/1lb freshly cooked potatoes,
      mashed
    25g/1oz/2 tbsp butter, melted
    10ml/2 tsp wholegrain mustard
    15ml/1 tbsp each chopped fresh dill
      and chopped parsley
    grated rind and juice of 1 lemon
    15g/ oz/1 tbsp plain (all-purpose)
      flour
    1 egg, lightly beaten
    150g/5oz/¼ cup dried breadcrumbs
    60ml/4tbsp sunflower oil
    salt and ground black pepper
    rocket (arugula), chives and lemon
      wedges, to serve

5 Heat the oil in a frying pan until it is very hot. Fry the fish cakes in batches until golden brown and crisp all over. As each batch is ready, drain on kitchen paper and keep warm. Serve hot, garnished with rocket leaves and chives and accompanied by lemon wedges.

1 Flake the cooked salmon, discarding any skin and bones. Put the salmon flakes in a bowl with the mashed potato, melted butter and wholegrain mustard, and mix well.

2 Stir the chopped dill, parsley and lemon rind and juice into the salmon and potato mixture. Season to taste.

3 Divide the mixture into 8 portions and shape each into a ball, then flatten into a thick disc.

4 Dip the fish cakes in flour and coat on all sides, then in the egg and finally in breadcrumbs, making sure that they are evenly coated. Leave for 10–15 minutes to help the breadcrumbs stick.

Energy 399Kcal/1670kJ; Protein 27.5g; Carbohydrate 28.2g, of which sugars 2.1g; Fat 20.4g, of which saturates 5.6g; Cholesterol 160mg; Calcium 71mg; Fibre 2g; Sodium 252mg.

POACHED SALMON

CHUNKY SALMON STEAKS NEED VERY GENTLE COOKING, AND THIS METHOD OF POACHING IN STOCK IS IDEAL. THE SAUCE IS SIMPLICITY ITSELF, MADE FROM NOTHING BUT FRESH CREAM, BUTTER AND GARDEN HERBS SIMMERED TOGETHER. CUCUMBER IS THE TRADITIONAL ACCOMPANIMENT.

SERVES 4

INGREDIENTS

4 salmon steaks, each about
    175g/6oz
about 1 litre/1¾ pints/4 cups water
45ml/3 tbsp salt
5ml/1 tsp whole peppercorns
1 lemon slice
1 onion slice
boiled potatoes and cucumber salad,
    to serve
For the butter sauce
100ml/3½ fl oz/scant ½ cup double
    (heavy) cream
225g/8oz/1 cup chilled unsalted
    butter, cut into small cubes
30–45ml/2–3 tbsp chopped fresh
    parsley or chives

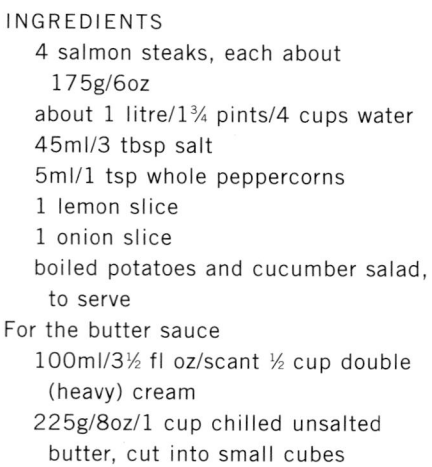

1 Put the fish steaks in a pan and add the water to just cover. Add the salt, peppercorns, lemon and onion slice. Bring to the boil then lower the heat to below simmering point. (The water should just throw up the occasional bubble.) Poach the fish for 6–8 minutes, until the flesh easily loosens from the backbone.

2 To make the butter sauce, pour the cream into a clean pan and slowly bring to the boil. Lower the heat and add the butter, in small pieces, whisking all the time until well incorporated before adding another piece. Do not allow the sauce to boil or it will separate. The sauce can be kept warm by putting it in a bowl standing over a pan of gently simmering water.

3 Just before serving, add the parsley or chives to the sauce. Serve the fish with boiled potatoes and a cucumber salad, accompanied with the sauce.

VARIATIONS
The dish can also be prepared with trout, but you will need eight trout steaks, instead of four salmon steaks, to serve four people.

Energy 771kcal/3184kJ; Protein 26.3g; Carbohydrate 1.1g, of which sugars 1g; Fat 73.6g, of which saturates 40g; Cholesterol 217mg; Calcium 71mg; Fibre 0.6g; Sodium 406mg.

PLAICE FILLETS WITH SORREL BUTTER

SORREL USED TO BE ONLY AVAILABLE IN THE WILD, GROWING ALONG THE HEDGEROWS, BUT CAN NOW BE BOUGHT IN STORES. WHEN ROUGHLY CHOPPED AND STIR-FRIED IN BUTTER, ITS STRONG, RUSTIC FLAVOUR MAKES AN EXCELLENT SAUCE TO POUR OVER THIS SWEET-FLESHED, DELICATE FISH.

SERVES 4

INGREDIENTS
200g/7oz/scant 1 cup butter
500g/1¼lb plaice fillets, skinned
  and patted dry
30ml/2 tbsp fresh sorrel
90ml/6 tbsp dry white wine
a little lemon juice

1 Melt half the butter in a large frying pan and add the fillets, skin side down. Cook briefly, just to firm up, reduce the heat and turn the fish over. The fish will be cooked in less than 5 minutes.

2 Remove the fish fillets from the pan and keep warm between two plates.

3 Chop the sorrel and add it to the pan and stir. Add the wine to the pan, and heat. As the wine bubbles, stir in a little lemon juice. Cut the remaining butter into chunks.

4 Add the butter and when melted, serve the fish with the sauce.

VARIATION
Instead of using sorrel, you could try this recipe with fresh tarragon or parsley.

Energy 494kcal/2047kJ; Protein 25.7g; Carbohydrate 0.5g, of which sugars 0.5g; Fat 43.3g, of which saturates 26.4g; Cholesterol 170mg; Calcium 98mg; Fibre 0.3g; Sodium 501mg.

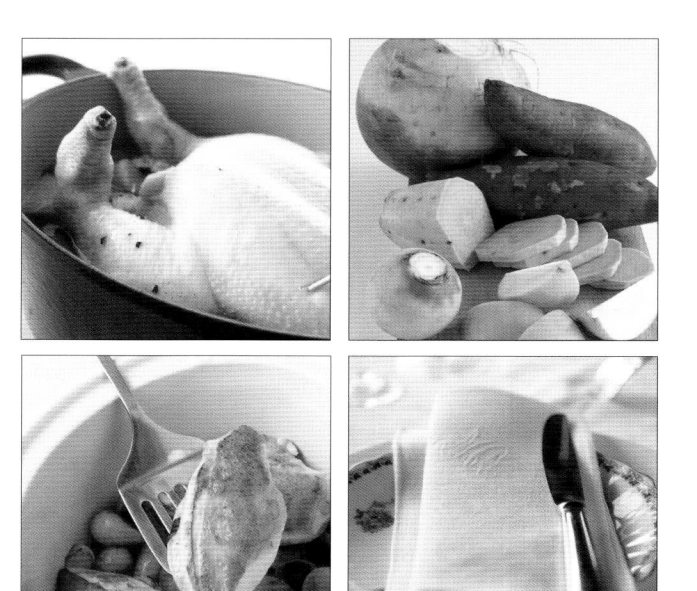

POULTRY
AND GAME

In the past, many country families kept chickens,
geese and ducks, both for their eggs and for their
meat. The tradition arose of eating roasted
poultry and game birds for a special family
meal at Christmas or Easter, and the jointed
pieces cook to tender perfection in casseroles and
stews. Simmer the bones of a roasted bird to
make delicious stock for soup.

ROAST CHICKEN WITH HERB STUFFING

THERE'S NOTHING TO BEAT A TRADITIONAL ROAST CHICKEN STUFFED WITH BREADCRUMBS MIXED WITH FRESH GARDEN HERBS. THE CLASSIC ACCOMPANIMENTS ARE ROAST POTATOES, SAUSAGES, GRAVY, BREAD SAUCE AND A FRUITY ACCOMPANIMENT SUCH AS CRANBERRY OR REDCURRANT JELLY.

SERVES 6

INGREDIENTS
    1 large chicken, about 1.8kg/4lb,
      with giblets and neck if possible
    1 small onion, sliced
    1 small carrot, sliced
    small bunch of parsley and thyme
    15g/½oz/1 tbsp butter
    30ml/2 tbsp chicken fat or oil
    6 rashers (strips) of streaky
      (fatty) bacon
    salt and ground black pepper
For the stuffing
    1 onion, finely chopped
    50g/2oz/¼ cup butter
    150g/5oz/2½ cups fresh
      white breadcrumbs
    15ml/1 tbsp fresh chopped parsley
    15ml/1 tbsp fresh chopped mixed
      herbs, such as thyme, marjoram
      and chives
    finely grated rind and juice
      of ½ lemon
    1 small egg, lightly beaten (optional,
      see step 5)
    15ml/1 tbsp plain (all-purpose) flour

1 Remove the giblets from the chicken. Wipe out the inside of the bird thoroughly. Separate the liver from the rest of the giblets, chop it and set it aside for use in the gravy.

2 Put the rest of the giblets and the neck into a pan with the sliced onion and carrot, the bunch of parsley and thyme and a good sprinkling of salt and pepper.

3 Add enough cold water to cover generously, bring to the boil and leave to simmer gently for about 1 hour. Strain the stock and discard the giblets. Preheat the oven to 200°C/400°F/Gas 6.

4 Meanwhile, make the herb stuffing: fry the onion in the butter in a frying pan over a low heat until the onion is beginning to soften.

5 Remove from the heat, and stir in the breadcrumbs, herbs and lemon rind. Mix in the lemon juice, beaten egg, if using, and a good seasoning of salt and pepper. The egg will bind the stuffing and make it firmer, but it can be omitted if you prefer a lighter, more crumbly texture.

6 Spoon the stuffing into the cavity of the chicken, without packing it in too tightly. Secure the opening with a small skewer or by tying the legs together with kitchen string.

7 Weigh the stuffed chicken and work out the cooking time at 20 minutes per 450g/1lb plus 20 minutes. Spread the butter over the breast, then put the chicken fat or oil into a roasting pan and lay the bird in it. Season, and lay the bacon rashers over the breast.

8 Put into the preheated oven. After 20 minutes, reduce the temperature to 180°C/350°F/Gas 4 for another 45–60 minutes, or until cooked. Test by inserting a sharp knife between the body and thigh: if the juices run clear with no hint of blood, it is cooked.

9 Transfer the cooked chicken to a serving dish and allow it to rest for 20 minutes in a warm place.

10 To make the gravy, pour off the excess fat from the roasting pan, then add the chopped liver and stir over low heat for 1 minute. Sprinkle in just enough flour to absorb the remaining fat and cook gently, stirring to blend, for 1 minute. Gradually add some of the giblet stock, scraping the pan to dissolve the residues and stirring well to make a smooth gravy.

11 Bring to the boil, stirring, gradually adding more stock until the consistency is as you like it. Adjust the seasoning, and then pour into a heated sauce boat to hand round separately.

12 Carve the chicken. Serve on heated plates with the herb stuffing and gravy.

Energy 562Kcal/2342kJ; Protein 40.9g; Carbohydrate 23.2g, of which sugars 2.7g; Fat 34.5g, of which saturates 11.9g; Cholesterol 216mg; Calcium 72mg; Fibre 1.5g; Sodium 381mg.

STOVED CHICKEN

THE WORD 'STOVED' HERE SIMPLY MEANS COOKED IN A COVERED POT. THE DELICIOUS FLAVOURS OF CHICKEN, BACON, HERBS AND ONIONS ARE ABSORBED INTO THE STOCK UNDER A LAYER OF CRISPY POTATO SLICES, AND THE WHOLE DISH IS COOKED IN A LOW OVEN UNTIL IT IS MELTINGLY TENDER.

SERVES 4

INGREDIENTS

900g/2lb potatoes, cut into 5mm/¼in
    slices
2 large onions, thinly sliced
15ml/1 tbsp chopped fresh thyme
25g/1oz/¼ stick butter
15ml/1 tbsp oil
2 large bacon rashers (strips), chopped
4 large chicken joints, halved
1 bay leaf
600ml/1 pint/2½ cups chicken stock
salt and ground black pepper

VARIATION

You can use tarragon instead of the thyme: French tarragon has a superior flavour to the Russian variety.

1 Preheat the oven to 150°C/300°F/ Gas 2. Make a thick layer of half the potato slices in the base of a large, heavy casserole, then cover with half the onion. Sprinkle with half the thyme and salt and ground black pepper.

2 Heat the butter and oil in a large frying pan, then brown the bacon and chicken. Using a slotted spoon, transfer the chicken and bacon to the casserole. Reserve the fat in the pan. When cool, store in the fridge and use another time for roasting potatoes.

3 Tuck the bay leaf in between the chicken pieces. Sprinkle the remaining thyme over, then cover with the remaining onion, followed by a layer of overlapping potato slices. Season.

4 Pour the stock into the casserole. Brush the top layer of the sliced potatoes with the reserved fat from the frying pan, then cover tightly and cook in the preheated oven for about 2 hours, until the chicken is thoroughly cooked and tender.

5 Preheat the grill (broiler) to high. Uncover the casserole, place under the grill and cook until the slices of potato are beginning to brown and crisp. Serve hot.

Energy 630kcal/2653kJ; Protein 69.2g; Carbohydrate 48.2g, of which sugars 8.9g; Fat 19.2g, of which saturates 7.2g; Cholesterol 195mg; Calcium 57mg; Fibre 3.9g; Sodium 574mg.

CHICKEN CASSEROLE

WARMING AND NOURISHING, THIS CASSEROLE IS IDEAL COMFORT FOOD ON A COLD WINTER'S DAY. THE EGG YOLKS IN THE SAUCE LEND IT EXTRA NUTRITIONAL VALUE. THIS DISH CAN BE SERVED WITH ANY KIND OF GRAIN, SUCH AS PLAIN RICE OR BULGUR WHEAT, OR WITH CREAMY MASHED POTATOES.

SERVES 4

INGREDIENTS

50g/2oz dried mushrooms, rinsed
   and soaked in warm water for
   30 minutes
800g/1¾lb chicken pieces
550ml/18fl oz/2½ cups water
2 celery sticks, chopped
1 carrot, chopped
30ml/2 tbsp chopped fresh parsley
25g/1oz/2 tbsp butter
25g/1oz/2 tbsp plain (all-purpose)
   flour
120ml/4fl oz/½ cup dry white wine
2 egg yolks
salt and ground black pepper,
   to taste
brown rice, bulgur wheat or mashed
   potato, to serve

1 Strain the mushrooms, reserving the juices, then chop finely. Put the chicken in a flameproof casserole or a frying pan with a lid, add the water and bring to the boil. Simmer for 10 minutes.

2 Add the mushrooms, celery, carrot, parsley and reserved mushroom juices to the casserole. Season, cover, and simmer for 30–45 minutes. Remove the chicken from the casserole and set aside on a warm plate.

GRANDMOTHER'S TIP
To get the full, authentic flavour of this traditional casserole, it is best to use organic chicken.

3 Meanwhile, make the roux. Melt the butter in a small pan, add the flour and cook, stirring, for 1 minute.

4 Add the roux to the casserole and stir. Add the wine and bring to the boil.

5 Remove the casserole from the heat. Put the egg yolks in a small bowl and add a ladleful of the hot juices, stirring constantly. Add to the casserole and stir to combine.

6 Remove the chicken meat from the bones, and cut into smaller pieces if you wish. Return the chicken to the sauce and heat gently to warm through. Serve the chicken with rice, bulgur wheat or potatoes.

Energy 285kcal/1196kJ; Protein 38.3g; Carbohydrate 6.7g, of which sugars 1.8g; Fat 9.7g, of which saturates 4.5g; Cholesterol 219mg; Calcium 43mg; Fibre 0.8g; Sodium 148mg.

CHICKEN AND HAM PIE

THIS PIE HAS A FILLING OF CHOPPED CHICKEN AND HAM BOUND WITH AROMATIC HERBS AND THICK CREAM, ALL SET WITHIN A DOUBLE CRUST OF HOME-MADE BUTTERY PASTRY. IT WOULD BE IDEAL TO TAKE ON A PICNIC, OR AS THE CENTREPIECE OF A SUMMER LUNCH, SERVED WARM OR COLD.

SERVES 6

INGREDIENTS
For the pastry
   275g/10oz/2½ cups plain (all-
     purpose) flour
   pinch of salt
   150g/5oz/⅔ cup butter, diced
For the filling
   800g/1¾lb chicken breast
   350g/12oz smoked or cured ham
   6 spring onions (scallions), finely
     chopped
   15ml/1 tbsp chopped fresh tarragon
   10ml/2 tsp chopped fresh thyme
   grated rind and juice of ½ lemon
   60ml/4 tbsp double (heavy) cream
   5ml/1 tsp ground mace or nutmeg
   beaten egg, to glaze
   salt and ground black pepper

1 Sift the flour into a bowl with the salt and rub in the butter until the mixture resembles fine crumbs.

2 Mix in just enough cold water to bind the mixture, gathering it together with your fingertips. Chill for 30 minutes.

3 Preheat the oven to 190°C/375°F/ Gas 5. Roll out one-third of the pastry and cut into a round to fit a 20cm/8in pie dish 5cm/2in deep tin.

GRANDMOTHER'S TIP
For a flakier, more traditional pastry, use half butter to half white vegetable fat (shortening), or lard, and add an extra pinch of salt.

4 Line the pie dish (tin) with the pastry. Place on a baking (cookie) sheet.

5 Mince (grind) or process 115g/4oz of the chicken with the ham. Place the meat in a bowl and add the spring onions, tarragon and thyme, lemon rind, 15ml/1 tbsp lemon juice and seasoning. Stir well, adding enough cream to make a soft mixture.

6 Cut the remaining chicken into 1cm/½in pieces and mix with the remaining lemon juice, the mace or nutmeg and seasoning.

7 Put a third of the gammon mixture in the pastry base and cover with half the chopped chicken. Repeat the layers, then top with the remaining gammon.

8 Dampen the edges of the pastry base. Roll out the remaining pastry and cover the pie, sealing the edges firmly.

9 Use the trimmings to decorate the top. Make a small hole in the centre and brush with beaten egg. Cook for 20 minutes then turn the oven down to 160°C/325°F/Gas 3 and cook for a further 1–1¼ hours. Serve hot or chilled.

Energy 431kcal/1804kJ; Protein 34.8g; Carbohydrate 23.8g, of which sugars 0.8g; Fat 22.5g, of which saturates 8.3g; Cholesterol 98mg; Calcium 57mg; Fibre 1.1g; Sodium 648mg.

TARRAGON CHICKEN IN CIDER

AROMATIC TARRAGON HAS A DISTINCTIVE FLAVOUR THAT HAS A SPECIAL AFFINITY WITH BOTH CHICKEN AND CREAM. THIS IS A CLASSIC COMBINATION THAT WOULD BE PERFECT FOR A CELEBRATION MEAL. CHILDREN WILL LOVE THE BABY ONIONS AND THE TENDER CHICKEN IN ITS CREAMY SAUCE.

SERVES 4

INGREDIENTS
    350g/12oz small baby (pearl) onions
    15ml/1 tbsp sunflower oil
    4 garlic cloves, peeled
    4 boneless chicken breast portions,
      skin on
    350ml/12fl oz/1½ cups dry (hard)
      cider
    1 bay leaf
    200g/7oz/scant 1 cup crème fraîche
      or sour cream
    30ml/2 tbsp chopped fresh tarragon
    15ml/1 tbsp chopped fresh parsley
    salt and ground black pepper

1 Put the baby onions in a heatproof bowl and pour over enough boiling water to cover. Leave to stand for at least 10 minutes, then drain and peel.

2 Heat the oil in a frying pan, add the onions and cook gently for 10 minutes, or until lightly browned, turning them frequently. Add the garlic and cook for a further 2–3 minutes. Using a slotted spoon, transfer the onions and garlic to the ceramic cooking pot.

3 Place the chicken breast portions in the frying pan and cook for 3–4 minutes, turning once or twice until lightly browned on both sides. Transfer the chicken to an ovenproof dish.

4 Pour the cider into the frying pan, add the bay leaf and a little salt and pepper, and bring to the boil. Preheat the oven to 200°C/400°F/Gas 6.

GRANDMOTHER'S TIP
When preparing and cooking poultry, always wash utensils, surfaces and hands afterwards to avoid risk of contamination or food poisoning. Use a plastic or glass chopping board when cutting meat or fish because they are easier to wash and more hygienic.

5 Pour the hot cider and bay leaf over the chicken. Cover the pot with the lid and cook in the oven for 30 minutes, or until the chicken and onions are cooked and tender.

6 Lift out the chicken breasts and keep warm while you finish the cider sauce.

7 Stir the crème fraîche or sour cream and the herbs into the sauce, heat through until piping hot then return the chicken breasts to the sauce. Serve immediately, with lightly sautéed potatoes and green vegetables.

VARIATIONS
• Guinea fowl and pheasant portions can also be cooked in this way. Try using white wine in place of the cider, and serve with creamy mashed potatoes and steamed baby carrots drizzled with a little melted butter.
• Try using 1 or 2 sprigs of fresh thyme in place of the tarragon. It gives a very different flavour but is equally good. Serve with rice and roasted tomatoes.

Energy 520Kcal/2167kJ; Protein 36.9g; Carbohydrate 12.1g, of which sugars 9.2g; Fat 33.9g, of which saturates 12.9g; Cholesterol 184mg; Calcium 90mg; Fibre 1.5g; Sodium 138mg.

HUNTER'S CHICKEN

STRIPS OF GREEN PEPPER CAN BE ADDED TO THE SAUCE FOR THIS DISH, BUT LARGE EARTHY MUSHROOMS GIVE A MORE AUTHENTIC FLAVOUR OF THE AUTUMN COUNTRYSIDE. IT IS EXCELLENT SERVED WITH FLOURY MASHED POTATOES OR WITH A CHUNK OF CRUSTY BREAD FOR A SIMPLE SUPPER.

SERVES 4

INGREDIENTS
   30ml/2 tbsp olive oil
   15g/½oz/1 tbsp butter
   4 chicken portions, on the bone
   1 large onion, thinly sliced
   400g/14oz can chopped tomatoes
   150ml/¼ pint/⅔ cup red wine
   1 garlic clove, crushed
   1 rosemary sprig, finely chopped,
    plus extra whole sprigs to garnish
   115g/4oz fresh field (portabello)
    mushrooms, thinly sliced
   salt and ground black pepper

1 Heat the oil and butter in a large, flameproof casserole until foaming. Fry the chicken portions for 5 minutes.

2 Remove the chicken pieces from the pan, cover and keep warm. Add the sliced onion to the pan and cook gently, stirring frequently, for about 3 minutes.

3 When the onion has softened, stir the tomatoes and their juice, and the red wine, into the pan.

4 Add the crushed garlic and chopped rosemary, and season. Bring to the boil, stirring continuously.

5 Return the chicken to the casserole and turn to coat with the sauce. Cover with a tightly fitting lid and simmer gently for 30 minutes.

6 Add the fresh mushrooms to the casserole and stir well to mix into the sauce. Continue simmering gently for 10 minutes, or until the chicken is tender. Taste and add more salt and ground black pepper if necessary.

7 Garnish with the fresh rosemary sprigs. Serve hot, with creamy mashed potatoes and green beans, or crusty white bread and butter, if you like.

Energy 386kcal/1622kJ; Protein 53.6g; Carbohydrate 4.5g, of which sugars 4.1g; Fat 14.5g, of which saturates 4.5g; Cholesterol 155mg; Calcium 28mg; Fibre 1.5g; Sodium 141mg.

CORONATION CHICKEN

THIS DISH WAS ORIGINALLY DEVISED TO CELEBRATE THE CORONATION OF QUEEN ELIZABETH II IN 1953. THE SLIGHTLY SPICY, SWEET SAUCE IS FLAVOURED WITH A TOUCH OF APRICOT JAM AND LOOKS MOST ATTRACTIVE WHEN POURED OVER CHOPPED, COOKED CHICKEN. PERFECT FOR A SUMMER LUNCH.

SERVES 8

INGREDIENTS
  ½ lemon
  2.25kg/5lb chicken
  1 onion, quartered
  1 carrot, quartered
  1 large bouquet garni
  8 black peppercorns, crushed
  salt
  crisp lettuce leaves, to serve
For the sauce
  1 small onion, chopped
  15g/½oz/1 tbsp butter
  15ml/1 tbsp curry paste
  15ml/1 tbsp tomato purée (paste)
  125ml/4fl oz/½ cup red wine
  1 bay leaf
  juice of ½ lemon, or to taste
  10–15ml/2–3 tsp apricot jam
  300ml/½ pint/1¼ cups mayonnaise
  125ml/4fl oz/½ cup whipping cream
  salt and ground black pepper

1 Put the lemon half in the chicken cavity, then place it in a close-fitting pan. Add the vegetables, bouquet garni, peppercorns and a little salt.

2 Add water to come two-thirds of the way up the chicken, bring just to the boil, cover and cook gently for 1½ hours, until the juices run clear. When the chicken is cold, remove all the flesh from the bones and chop.

3 To make the sauce, cook the onion in the butter until soft. Add the curry paste, tomato purée, wine, bay leaf and lemon juice, then cook gently for 10 minutes. Add the jam, press through a sieve (strainer) and cool.

4 Beat the sauce into the mayonnaise. Whip the cream and fold it in; add seasoning and lemon juice, then stir in the chicken. Serve with crisp lettuce.

Energy 587kcal/2429kJ; Protein 10.1g; Carbohydrate 17.1g, of which sugars 4.7g; Fat 51.6g, of which saturates 8.8g; Cholesterol 228mg; Calcium 97mg; Fibre 1.1g; Sodium 401mg.

DEVILLED CHICKEN

MARINATING MEAT IN HOT, SPICY SEASONINGS BEFORE COOKING WAS VERY POPULAR IN THE 19TH CENTURY. THESE CHICKEN PIECES ABSORB ALL THE DELICIOUS TANGINESS OF SWEET CHUTNEY, HOT MUSTARD, SPICES AND PEPPER, AND ARE THEN OVEN-BAKED OR GRILLED TO SEAL IN THE FLAVOUR.

SERVES 4–6

INGREDIENTS

6 chicken drumsticks
6 chicken thighs
15ml/1 tbsp oil
45ml/3 tbsp chutney, finely
  chopped or mashed
15ml/1 tbsp Worcestershire sauce
10ml/2 tsp English (hot) mustard
1.5ml/¼ tsp cayenne pepper
1.5ml/¼ tsp ground ginger
salt and ground black pepper
watercress, to serve

1 With a sharp knife, make several deep slashes in the chicken pieces, cutting down to the bone.

2 In a large bowl, mix the oil, chutney, Worcestershire sauce, mustard, cayenne, ginger and seasoning. Add the chicken pieces and toss them in the mixture, until well coated. Cover and leave to stand for 1 hour.

3 Preheat the oven to 200°C/400°F/ Gas 6. Arrange the chicken pieces in a single layer on a non-stick baking sheet, brushing them with any extra sauce.

VARIATION
Instead of chutney, use the same quantity of tomato ketchup.

4 Put the chicken pieces into the hot oven and cook for about 35 minutes until crisp, deep golden brown and cooked through (test by inserting a small sharp knife or skewer – the juices should run clear). Turn them over once or twice during cooking. Serve hot or cold with watercress.

Energy 299kcal/1254kJ; Protein 47.4g; Carbohydrate 0.3g, of which sugars 0.3g; Fat 12g, of which saturates 2.6g; Cholesterol 236mg; Calcium 41mg; Fibre 0.6g; Sodium 207mg.

STUFFED ROAST TURKEY

ROAST TURKEY WITH ITS CRISP BUTTERY SKIN NOW TAKES PRIDE OF PLACE AS THE FIRST CHOICE FOR CHRISTMAS DINNER, BUT IS ALSO SOMETIMES EATEN AT EASTER. SERVED WITH A HERBY STUFFING AND CRANBERRY JELLY, THIS TRADITIONAL RECIPE IS A WINNER FOR A FAMILY GATHERING.

SERVES 6

INGREDIENTS
    1 turkey, about 4.5–5.5kg/10–12lb,
      washed and patted dry with
      kitchen paper
    25g/1oz/2 tbsp butter, melted
    salt and ground black pepper,
      to taste
    cranberry jelly, to serve
For the stuffing
    200g/7oz/3½ cups fresh white
      breadcrumbs
    175ml/6fl oz/¾ cup milk
    25g/1oz/2 tbsp butter
    1 egg, separated
    1 calf's liver, about 600g/1lb 6oz,
      finely chopped
    2 onions, finely chopped
    90ml/6 tbsp chopped fresh dill
    10ml/2 tsp clear honey
    salt and ground black pepper,
      to taste

1 To make the stuffing, put the breadcrumbs and milk in a large bowl and soak until swollen and soft. Melt the butter in a frying pan and mix 5ml/ 1 tsp with the egg yolk.

2 Heat the remaining butter in a frying pan and add the liver and onions. Fry gently for 5 minutes, until the onions are golden brown.

3 Remove from the heat and leave to cool. Preheat the oven to 180°C/ 350°F/Gas 4.

4 Add the cooled liver mixture to the soaked breadcrumbs and add the butter and egg yolk mixture, with the dill, honey and seasoning.

5 Whisk the egg white to soft peaks then fold into the stuffing.

6 Season the turkey inside and out. Stuff the cavity with the stuffing, then weigh to calculate the cooking time. Allow 20 minutes per 500g/1¼lb, plus an additional 20 minutes. Transfer the turkey to a roasting tin, brush the outside with melted butter and place in the oven.

7 Roast for the calculated time, basting regularly. Cover with foil for the final 30 minutes if the skin becomes too brown. To test whether the turkey is cooked, pierce the thickest part of the thigh with a knife; the juices should run clear. Rest for about 15 minutes when cooked. Carve into thin slices, then spoon over the juices and serve with the stuffing and cranberry jelly.

Energy 740kcal/3126kJ; Protein 112.3g; Carbohydrate 35.9g, of which sugars 7.3g; Fat 13.5g, of which saturates 6.6g; Cholesterol 507mg; Calcium 122mg; Fibre 1.7g; Sodium 517mg.

ROAST DUCK WITH APPLES

APPLE MAKES A DELICIOUS ACCOMPANIMENT TO DUCK, HELPING TO OFFSET THE RICH FLAVOUR. ROAST DUCK IS A DISH FOR ANY TIME OF YEAR BUT YOU CAN ALSO COOK GOOSE THIS WAY FOR SPECIAL OCCASIONS. SERVE THE ROAST BIRD WITH SOME MASHED POTATO AND GREENS.

2 Preheat the oven to 200C/400F/Gas 6. Remove any lumps of fat from inside the duck. With a fork, prick the skin all over then rub it all over with salt.

3 Spoon the stuffing into the neck end of the bird and, with a small skewer, secure the skin over the opening.

4 Sit the duck on a rack in a roasting pan and pour in 150ml/¼ pint/⅔ cup cold water. Cover the breast area of the duck with foil, and roast in the hot oven for 30 minutes.

5 Lift the duck and the rack out of the tin and drain off excess fat, leaving a little fat, all the sediment and juices.

6 Quarter and core the apples and cut them into thick wedges.

7 Add the wedges to the roasting pan, stirring until they are all evenly coated with fat and juices.

8 Replace the duck on the rack over the apples. Continue cooking for 30 minutes, turning the apples over once, until the duck is crisp, golden brown and cooked through. Check by inserting a skewer into the thickest part of the leg next to the breast – the juices should run clear.

9 Before carving, leave the duck in warm place to rest for 10–15 minutes.

SERVES 6

INGREDIENTS
   20g/¾oz/1½ tbsp butter
   1 onion, finely chopped
   5ml/1 tsp finely chopped fresh sage
      or 2.5ml/½ tsp dried sage
   75g/3oz/1¼ cups fresh breadcrumbs
   1 oven-ready duck, weighing about
      1.8–2.25kg/4–5lb
   3 crisp eating apples
   salt and ground black pepper

GRANDMOTHER'S TIP
Lots of fat will drain off the duck during cooking. Save it for roasting potatoes. It freezes well, packed in small plastic boxes or freezer bags.

1 To make the stuffing, melt the butter in a pan, add the onion and cook gently for about 5 minutes, stirring occasionally, until soft but not browned. Then remove from the heat and stir in the sage, breadcrumbs, salt and pepper.

Energy 270kcal/1138kJ; Protein 23.7g; Carbohydrate 23.3g, of which sugars 6g; Fat 9.9g, of which saturates 3.9g; Cholesterol 119mg; Calcium 51mg; Fibre 1.6g; Sodium 303mg.

DUCK WITH DAMSON AND GINGER SAUCE

IF YOU DON'T HAVE TIME TO COOK A WHOLE ROAST DUCK, THIS IS A SIMPLE AND EASY WAY OF SERVING THE TASTY AND TENDER BREAST PORTIONS. A TRADITIONAL WAY OF SERVING COLD DUCK WAS WITH A FRUIT AND GINGER CHUTNEY, AND THIS RECIPE REFLECTS THAT COMBINATION OF FLAVOURS.

SERVES 4

INGREDIENTS
    250g/9oz fresh damsons
    5ml/1 tsp ground ginger
    45ml/3 tbsp sugar
    10ml/2 tsp wine vinegar or sherry
      vinegar
    4 duck breast portions
    15ml/1 tbsp oil
    salt and ground black pepper

1 Put the damsons in a pan with the ginger and 45ml/3 tbsp water. Bring to the boil, cover and simmer gently for about 5 minutes, or until the fruit is soft. Stir frequently and add a little extra water if the fruit looks as if it is drying out or sticking to the bottom of the pan.

2 Stir in the sugar and vinegar. Press the mixture through a sieve (strainer), to remove stones (pits) and skin. Taste the sauce, add more sugar if necessary, and season to taste.

3 Meanwhile, with a sharp knife, score the fat on the duck breast portions in several places without cutting into the meat. Brush the oil over both sides of the duck. Sprinkle a little salt and pepper on the fat side only.

GRANDMOTHER'S TIP
Both the duck and the sauce are also good served cold. Serve with simple steamed vegetables or a crisp salad, such as a coleslaw made from thinly sliced white cabbage.

4 Preheat a griddle pan or heavy frying pan. When hot, add the duck breast portions, skin side down, and cook over medium heat for about 5 minutes or until the fat is evenly browned and crisp. Turn over and cook the meat side for 4–5 minutes. Lift out and leave to rest for 5–10 minutes.

5 Slice the duck on the diagonal. Serve with the sauce and green vegetables.

Energy 275kcal/1157kJ; Protein 29.9g; Carbohydrate 17.5g, of which sugars 17.5g; Fat 12.5g, of which saturates 2.4g, Cholesterol 165mg; Calcium 39mg; Fibre 1.1g; Sodium 167mg.

GAME PIE

THIS TRADITIONAL FARMHOUSE DISH IS VERY ADAPTABLE AND CAN BE MADE WITH WHATEVER GAME BIRDS ARE AVAILABLE. SERVE THE PIE WITH SEASONAL VEGETABLES: POTATOES BOILED IN THEIR SKINS, AND WINTER GREENS, SUCH AS PURPLE SPROUTING BROCCOLI OR BRUSSELS SPROUTS.

SERVES 8–10

INGREDIENTS

4 pheasant and/or pigeon skinless breast portions
225g/8oz lean stewing steak
115g/4oz streaky (fatty) bacon, trimmed
butter, for frying
2 medium onions, finely chopped
1 large garlic clove, crushed
15ml/1 tbsp plain (all-purpose) flour
about 300ml/½ pint/¼ cup pigeon or pheasant stock
15ml/1 tbsp tomato purée (paste) (optional)
15ml/1 tbsp chopped fresh parsley
a little grated lemon rind
15ml/1 tbsp rowan or redcurrant jelly
50–115g/2–4oz button (white) mushrooms, halved or quartered, if large
a small pinch of freshly grated nutmeg or ground cloves (optional)
milk or beaten egg, to glaze
sea salt and ground black pepper
For the rough-puff pastry
225g/8oz/2 cups plain (all-purpose) flour
2.5ml/½ tsp salt
5ml/1 tsp lemon juice
115g/4oz/½ cup butter, in walnut-sized pieces

1 To make the rough-puff pastry. Sift the flour and salt into a large mixing bowl. Add the lemon juice and the butter pieces, and just enough cold water to bind the ingredients together.

2 Turn the mixture on to a floured board and roll the pastry into a long strip. Fold it into three and press the edges together. Half-turn the pastry, rib it with the rolling pin to equalize the air in it and roll it into a strip once again. Repeat this folding and rolling process three more times.

3 Slice the pheasant or pigeon breasts from the bone and cut the meat into fairly thin strips. Trim away any fat from the stewing steak and slice it in the same manner.

4 Cut the bacon into thin strips, and then cook it very gently in a heavy frying pan until the fat runs. Add some butter and brown the sliced pheasant or pigeon, and the stewing steak in the fat, a little at a time.

5 Remove the meats from the pan and set aside. Cook the onions and garlic in the fat for 2–3 minutes over a medium heat. Remove and set aside with the meats, then stir the flour into the remaining fat.

6 Cook for 1–2 minutes, and then gradually stir in enough stock to make a fairly thin gravy. Add the tomato purée, if using, parsley, lemon rind and rowan or redcurrant jelly and the mushrooms. Season to taste and add the nutmeg or cloves, if you like.

7 Return the browned meats, chopped onion and garlic to the pan containing the gravy, and mix well before turning into a deep 1.75 litre/3 pint/7½ cup pie dish. Leave to cool. Meanwhile, preheat the oven to 220°C/425°F/Gas 7.

8 Roll the prepared pastry out to make a circle 2.5cm/1in larger all round than the pie dish, and cut out to make a lid for the pie. Wet the rim of the pie dish and line with the remaining pastry strip. Dampen the strip and cover with the lid, pressing down well to seal.

9 Trim away any excess pastry and knock up the edges with a knife. Make a hole in the centre for the steam to escape and use any pastry trimmings to decorate the top. Glaze the top of the pie with milk or beaten egg.

10 Bake in the oven for about 20 minutes, until the pastry is well-risen, then reduce the oven to 150°C/300°F/Gas 2 for another 1½ hours, until cooked. Protect the pastry from over-browning if necessary by covering it with a double layer of wet baking parchment. Serve piping hot, straight from the oven, with the vegetables of your choice.

GRANDMOTHER'S TIP
Ready-made puff pastry can be used instead of home-made, if you prefer.

BRAISED FARM PIGEON 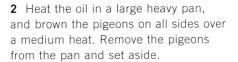 WITH ELDERBERRY

ELDERBERRY WINE IS AN OLD COUNTRYSIDE FAVOURITE, MADE WITH WILD ELDERBERRIES HARVESTED WHEN THEY ARE BLACK AND RIPE IN THE AUTUMN. THE RICH FLAVOUR OF THE WINE MAKES A CLASSIC PIGEON CASSEROLE WITH MUSHROOMS AND ONIONS, COOKED SLOWLY IN THE OVEN UNTIL TENDER.

SERVES 4

INGREDIENTS

4 pigeons
15ml/1 tbsp plain (all-purpose)
  flour
30ml/2 tbsp olive oil, plus extra
  if needed
1 onion, chopped
225g/8oz button (white) mushrooms,
  sliced
250ml/8fl oz/1 cup beef stock
100ml/3½fl oz/scant ½ cup elderberry
  wine
salt and ground black pepper
kale, to serve (optional)

1 Preheat the oven to 170°C/325°F/ Gas 3. Season the pigeons inside and out with salt and black pepper and roll liberally in the flour.

2 Heat the oil in a large heavy pan, and brown the pigeons on all sides over a medium heat. Remove the pigeons from the pan and set aside.

3 Brown the onion and then the mushrooms in the same pan, still over a medium heat, adding more oil if necessary. Add the vegetables to the casserole with the pigeon and mix together well.

4 Pour in the stock, elderberry wine and just enough water to cover. Bring to the boil, cover tightly with a lid and cook in the preheated oven for 2 hours, until the pigeons are tender.

5 Remove the birds from the casserole and keep warm. Boil the cooking liquor rapidly to thicken slightly. Return the pigeons to the pan and heat through. Serve with kale, if you like.

VARIATION
This recipe suits most small game birds, such as woodcock, quail or partridge.

Energy 296kcal/1237kJ; Protein 31g; Carbohydrate 6.8g, of which sugars 2.5g; Fat 14.3g, of which saturates 0.1g; Cholesterol 0mg; Calcium 35mg; Fibre 1g; Sodium 117mg.

QUAIL WITH APPLES

QUAILS ARE TINY BIRDS, SO THE COOKING TIME IS SHORT AND THEY CAN BE ROASTED IN A MERE 10 MINUTES. IN THIS RECIPE THEY ARE ACCOMPANIED BY SUCCULENT SLICED APPLES AND CRISPY FRIED BREAD. YOU CAN ASO SERVE THE QUAIL AS A STARTER, ALLOWING ONE BIRD PER PERSON.

SERVES 2 AS A MAIN COURSE

INGREDIENTS
4 oven-ready quail
120ml/4fl oz/½ cup olive oil
3 firm eating apples
115g/4oz/½ cup butter
4 slices white bread
salt and ground black pepper

1 Preheat the oven to 220°C/425°F/ Gas 7. Core the apples and slice them thickly (leave the peel on if it is pretty and not too tough).

2 Brush the quail with half the olive oil and roast them in a pan in the oven for 10 minutes, or until brown and tender.

3 Meanwhile, heat half the butter in a frying pan and sauté the apple slices for about 3 minutes until they are golden but not mushy. Season with pepper, cover and keep warm until required.

4 Remove the crusts from the bread. Heat the remaining olive oil and the butter in a frying pan and fry the bread on both sides until brown and crisp. Lay the fried bread on heated plates, place the quail on top, and serve immediately with the apple rings.

Energy 814Kcal/3389kJ; Protein 53.3g; Carbohydrate 33.3g, of which sugars 10.5g; Fat 43.6g, of which saturates 23.4g; Cholesterol 69mg; Calcium 169mg; Fibre 2.4g; Sodium 644mg.

RABBIT WITH RED WINE AND PRUNES

THIS IS A FAVOURITE FARMHOUSE DISH. THE PRUNES ADD A DELICIOUS SWEETNESS TO THE SAUCE, AND THE RED WINE AND BRANDY MAKE THIS CASSEROLE WARMING AND COMFORTING FOR AN AUTUMN OR WINTER SUPPER. SERVE WITH CRISP, GOLDEN SAUTEÉD POTATOES.

1 Season the rabbit portions liberally with salt and pepper. Heat the vegetable oil in a large, flameproof casserole and fry the rabbit portions in batches until they are golden brown on all sides.

2 Remove the browned rabbit portions from the casserole, add the chopped onion and garlic, and cook, stirring occasionally, until the onion is softened.

3 Return the rabbit pieces to the casserole, add the Armagnac or brandy and ignite it. When the flames have died down, pour in the wine. Stir in the sugar and prunes, cover and simmer for 30 minutes.

SERVES 4

INGREDIENTS
  8 rabbit portions
  30ml/2 tbsp vegetable oil
  2 onions, finely chopped
  2 garlic cloves, finely chopped
  60ml/4 tbsp Armagnac or brandy
  300ml/½ pint/1¼ cups dry red wine
  5ml/1 tsp soft light brown sugar
  16 ready-to-eat prunes
  150ml/¼ pint/⅔ cup double (heavy) cream
salt and ground black pepper

4 Remove the rabbit from the casserole, cover and keep warm. Add the cream to the sauce and simmer for 3–5 minutes, then season to taste and serve immediately.

VARIATION
The prunes can be replaced with ready-to-eat dried apricots if you prefer.

Energy 543Kcal/2259kJ; Protein 29.3g; Carbohydrate 19.4g, of which sugars 18.2g; Fat 29.9g, of which saturates 15.3g; Cholesterol 156mg; Calcium 99mg; Fibre 3g; Sodium 81mg.

SADDLE OF RABBIT WITH ASPARAGUS

THIS IS A PERFECT RECIPE FOR EARLY SUMMER, WHEN THE ASPARAGUS HARVEST HITS ITS PEAK. IT IS AN IMPRESSIVE AND TASTY DISH THAT IS EASILY AND QUICKLY MADE, WITH FEW INGREDIENTS. SERVE WITH PLAIN RICE OR NEW POTATOES FOR A REAL FLAVOUR OF THE SEASON.

SERVES 4

INGREDIENTS
  2 saddles of rabbit
  75g/3oz/6 tbsp butter
  sprig of fresh rosemary
  45ml/3 tbsp olive oil
  10 asparagus spears
  200ml/7fl oz/scant 1 cup chicken
    stock, plus extra for cooking the
    asparagus
  salt and ground black pepper

1 Preheat the oven to 200°C/400°F/ Gas 6. Trim the rabbit, removing the membrane and the belly flaps.

5 Add enough stock to just cover the asparagus and bring to a gentle boil. Allow the liquid to evaporate to a light glaze and the asparagus will be cooked.

6 Remove the rabbit from the oven and leave to rest for 5 minutes. Remove any fat from the pan then add the measured stock.

7 Bring to the boil, scraping up any residue from the base. Reduce the liquid by a half, then remove from the heat and whisk in the remaining butter. Strain the sauce and set aside.

8 Take the meat off the saddles in slices lengthways and place on a warmed serving dish. Serve with the asparagus on top and the sauce spooned over.

2 Heat an ovenproof pan, then add 50g/2oz/4 tbsp of the butter. Season the saddles and brown them lightly all over, by frying them gently in the butter for a few minutes on each side.

3 Tuck the rosemary underneath the saddles, with the fillets facing up, and put in the oven for 10 minutes.

4 Meanwhile, in a second pan, heat the olive oil then add the asparagus spears. Make sure they are coated in the oil and leave them to sweat gently for a few minutes.

GRANDMOTHER'S TIP
This is a good recipe if you are lucky enough to be given a number of rabbits for the pot. You can use the rest of the carcasses for making stock, and have the meat in a pie.

Energy 406kcal/1684kJ; Protein 33.7g; Carbohydrate 0.6g, of which sugars 0.6g; Fat 29.8g, of which saturates 13.4g; Cholesterol 146mg; Calcium 43mg; Fibre 0.4g; Sodium 215mg.

RAISED GAME PIE

This pie, made with hot-water pastry, was once an essential item for picnics or a buffet lunch. It contains all the richness of rabbit, partridge and pigeon, set in a delicious jelly flavoured with the quintessential herbs and spices of an English country kitchen.

SERVES 10-12

INGREDIENTS
For the pie filling
   1kg/2¼lb rabbit flesh, diced
   300g/11oz partridge flesh, diced
   300g/11oz pigeon flesh, diced
   300g/11oz fatty pork belly, minced
     (ground) or chopped in
     a food processor
   grated rind of 1 lemon
   15ml/1 tbsp chopped sage
   15ml/1 tbsp chopped thyme
   2.5ml/½ tsp freshly grated nutmeg
   15ml/1 tbsp English (hot)
     mustard powder
   60ml/4 tbsp ruby port
   sea salt and ground black pepper
For the jellied stock
   2 pig's trotters (feet), split
     lengthways, rabbit and game bones
   1 carrot, peeled
   1 small onion, peeled
   1 bay leaf
For the pastry
   150g/5oz/⅔ cup lard
   150g/5oz/⅔ cup butter
   350ml/12fl oz/1½ cups water
   850g/1lb 14oz/7½ cups plain
     (all-purpose) flour
   good pinch of sea salt
   1 egg, beaten, to glaze

1 The jellied stock must be made in advance. Place the ingredients in a pan, cover with plenty of water, bring to the boil and skim off any scum and fat. Reduce the heat to a simmer and cook for 6 hours, skimming and topping up with water as necessary.

2 At the end of the cooking time, strain the liquid and discard the meat. Return the stock to the pan and reduce to 600ml/1 pint/2½ cups.

3 Cool the stock, and when cold, store in the refrigerator: when completely chilled it should have formed a stiff jelly.

4 To make the pastry, place the fats and water in a pan and heat gently to melt – do not boil. Sift the flour and salt into a bowl, make a well in the centre, pour in the liquid and mix. Knead with your hands to form a soft dough.

5 Roll out three-quarters of the pastry to a circle 8mm/⅓in thick and line a 20cm/ 8in springform cake tin (pan). Cover the remaining pastry, do not chill.

6 To make the pie filling, combine all the ingredients in a bowl and mix thoroughly using your hands.

7 Spoon the pie filling into the pastry case, gently pushing the mixture into the corners and flattening the top. The meat should come to just below the top of the pastry case. Pre-heat the oven to 180°C/350°F/Gas 4.

8 Roll out the remaining pastry into a circle slightly smaller than the diameter of the tin and lower it on to the meat.

9 Dampen the edge with water, fold over the top of the pastry case and crimp the edges together with your fingertips. Cut a 1cm/½in hole in the centre of the lid and brush with the beaten egg.

10 Bake the pie in the preheated oven for 40 minutes to set the pastry, then reduce the heat to 140°C/275°F/Gas 1 and continue to cook for 2 hours. Remove from the oven and leave to cool to room temperature.

11 To finish the pie, warm the jellied stock gently until it is liquid, transfer it to a jug (pitcher) and, using a funnel, carefully pour it into the pie through the hole in the top, a little at a time, until the pie will accept no more.

12 The jelly now needs to set, so refrigerate the pie overnight.

13 Serve the pie cold, or at room temperature, cut into generous slices, accompanied by mustard, pickles, crisp lettuce and tomatoes.

Energy 728kcal/3045kJ; Protein 42.3g; Carbohydrate 55.7g, of which sugars 1.7g; Fat 38.2g, of which saturates 17.1g; Cholesterol 118mg; Calcium 135mg; Fibre 2.2g; Sodium 215mg.

VENISON PIE

DARK, STRONGLY FLAVOURED VENISON MAKES A TASTY ALTERNATIVE TO BEEF OR LAMB MINCE IN A RUSTIC SHEPHERD'S PIE. THE TOPPING IS MADE FROM MIXED ROOT VEGETABLES, MASHED TOGETHER WITH A TOUCH OF SPICY HORSERADISH SAUCE. SERVE WITH A PLAIN STEAMED GREEN VEGETABLE.

SERVES 6

INGREDIENTS
  30ml/2 tbsp olive oil
  2 leeks, washed, trimmed
    and chopped
  1kg/2¼lb minced (ground) venison
  30ml/2 tbsp chopped fresh parsley
  300ml/½ pint/1¼ cups game
    consommé
  salt and ground black pepper
For the topping
  1.4kg/3¼lb mixed root vegetables,
    such as sweet potatoes, parsnips
    and swede (rutabaga), coarsely
    chopped
  15ml/1 tbsp horseradish sauce
  25g/1oz/2 tbsp butter

GRANDMOTHER'S TIPS
• Use wild venison if possible as it has the best flavour and the lowest fat content. If you can't get it, then use farmed, organic venison, which will work well in this dish.
• If leeks aren't available, then use a large onion and chop it coarsely.

1 Heat the oil in a pan over a medium heat. Add the leeks and cook for about 8 minutes, or until they are softened and beginning to brown.

2 Add the minced venison to the pan and cook over a medium heat, stirring frequently, for about 10 minutes or until the venison is thoroughly browned all over.

3 Add the chopped parsley and stir it in, then add the consommé, salt and black pepper. Bring to the boil over a medium heat, then reduce the heat to low, cover and simmer gently for about 20 minutes, stirring occasionally.

4 Meanwhile, preheat the oven to 200°C/400°F/Gas 6 and prepare the pie topping. Cook the chopped root vegetables in enough boiling salted water to cover for 15–20 minutes.

5 Drain the vegetables and put them in a bowl. Mash them together with the horseradish sauce, butter and plenty of ground black pepper.

6 Spoon the venison mixture into a large ovenproof dish and cover the top evenly with the mashed vegetables. It is often easier to spoon it over in small quantities rather than pouring it on and then smoothing it out.

7 Bake in the preheated oven for 20 minutes, or until piping hot and beginning to brown. Serve immediately, with steamed green vegetables.

VARIATION
This pie can be made with other minced (ground) meats, such as beef, lamb or pork. You may need to adapt the cooking times for these, depending on the type and quantity that you use, although the basic recipe remains the same. You can also use other types of game meats for this pie, such as finely chopped or minced rabbit or hare.

VENISON SAUSAGES WITH RED WINE GRAVY

STRONGLY FLAVOURED, ROBUST VENISON SAUSAGES ARE AT THEIR BEST WHEN GENTLY SIMMERED IN A RED WINE GRAVY FLAVOURED WITH MUSHROOMS. SERVE THIS DISH WITH BUTTERY MASHED POTATOES OR PLENTY OF THICKLY SLICED CRUSTY BREAD TO MOP UP THE DELICIOUS SAUCE.

SERVES 4

INGREDIENTS

15ml/1 tbsp sunflower oil (optional)
12 venison or wild boar sausages
2 leeks, sliced
2 plump garlic cloves, sliced
225g/8oz/3 cups mushrooms,
  quartered
15ml/1 tbsp plain (all-purpose) flour
600ml/1 pint/2½ cups red wine
30ml/2 tbsp chopped mixed fresh
  herbs, such as flat leaf parsley
  and marjoram
salt and ground black pepper

1 Pour the sunflower oil, if using, into a large frying pan, add the venison or wild boar sausages and cook over a medium heat for 15–20 minutes, turning frequently.

2 Add the leeks, garlic and mushrooms and mix well. Cook the vegetables for 10–15 minutes, or until the leeks are soft and beginning to brown.

3 Sprinkle in the flour and gradually pour in the red wine, stirring with a wooden spoon and pushing the sausages around to mix the flour and the liquid smoothly with the leeks.

4 Bring slowly to the boil, reduce the heat and simmer for 10–15 minutes, stirring occasionally, or until the gravy is smooth and glossy.

5 Season the gravy with salt and pepper to taste and then sprinkle the mixed herbs over the sausages. Serve immediately with polenta or mashed potatoes.

Energy 246Kcal/1026kJ; Protein 7.8g; Carbohydrate 11.7g, of which sugars 2.9g; Fat 7.8g, of which saturates 3g; Cholesterol 15mg; Calcium 71mg; Fibre 3g; Sodium 447mg.

VENISON CASSEROLE

VENISON IS AN EXCELLENT CHOICE FOR CASSEROLES, AS IT IS FULL OF GOODNESS AND LOW IN FAT TOO. CRANBERRIES AND ORANGE BRING FESTIVE FRUITINESS AND A REMINDER OF CHRISTMAS TO THIS SPICY DISH. SERVE WITH PLAIN JACKET POTATOES AND BUTTER, AND A GREEN VEGETABLE.

SERVES 4

INGREDIENTS

   30ml/2 tbsp olive oil
   1 onion, chopped
   2 celery sticks, sliced
   10ml/2 tsp ground allspice
   15ml/1 tbsp plain (all-purpose) flour
   675g/1½lb stewing venison, cubed
   225g/8oz fresh or frozen cranberries
   grated rind and juice of 1 orange
   900ml/1½ pints/3¾ cups beef or
     venison stock
   salt and ground black pepper

1 Heat the oil in a flameproof casserole. Add the onion and celery and fry for about 5 minutes, until softened.

2 Meanwhile, mix the ground allspice with the flour and either spread the mixture out on a large plate or place in a large plastic bag. Toss a few pieces of venison at a time (to prevent them becoming soggy) in the flour mixture until they are all lightly coated.

3 When the onion and celery are softened, remove from the casserole using a slotted spoon and set aside. Add the venison pieces to the casserole in batches, and cook until browned and sealed on all sides.

VARIATION
Farmed venison is increasingly easy to find and makes a rich and flavourful stew, but lean pork or braising steak could be used in place of the venison.

4 Add the cranberries, orange rind and juice to the casserole along with the beef or venison stock, and stir well.

5 Return the vegetables and all the venison to the casserole and heat until simmering, then cover tightly and reduce the heat. Simmer for about 45 minutes, or until the venison is tender, stirring occasionally.

6 Season the venison casserole to taste with salt and pepper before serving.

GRANDMOTHER'S TIP
If you are baking potatoes at the same time, cook the casserole in the oven, to save on fuel costs.

Energy 242Kcal/1025kJ; Protein 38.3g; Carbohydrate 10.4g, of which sugars 7.1g; Fat 6.6g, of which saturates 1.8g; Cholesterol 84mg; Calcium 27mg; Fibre 1.4g; Sodium 105mg.

DAUBE OF VENISON WITH BAKED COURGETTES

THIS CLASSIC STEW BENEFITS FROM BEING ALLOWED TO SIT OVERNIGHT AFTER COOKING, AND IS EASILY REHEATED THE NEXT DAY. EVERYONE WILL ENJOY THE RICH AROMAS OF VENISON SIMMERING IN ITS SAUCE OF RED WINE AND HERBS, EVOCATIVE OF A COUNTRY HOUSE HUNTING PARTY.

SERVES 6

INGREDIENTS
30ml/2 tbsp olive oil
1kg/2¼lb stewing venison (shin or chuck), cut into 2.5cm/1in cubes
150g/5oz unsmoked streaky (fatty) bacon, cut into lardons
12 shallots, peeled
15ml/1 tbsp plain (all-purpose) flour
375ml/½ bottle rich red wine, such as Burgundy
200ml/7fl oz/scant 1 cup venison stock or two beef stock (bouillon) cubes dissolved in 200ml/7fl oz/ scant 1 cup hot water
2 garlic cloves, crushed
2 bay leaves
1 thyme sprig
4 cloves
5cm/2in cinnamon stick
3 strips orange rind and juice of 1 orange
1 large carrot, sliced
2 celery sticks, sliced
25g/1oz dried wild mushrooms reconstituted in 50ml/2fl oz warm water
sea salt and ground black pepper
crusty bread, to serve
For the courgette bake
25g/1oz butter
675g/1½lb courgettes (zucchini), diced
freshly grated nutmeg
250ml/8fl oz/1 cup double (heavy) cream
5ml/1 tsp thyme
1 garlic clove, crushed
75g/3oz Cheddar cheese
50g/2oz/1 cup fresh white breadcrumbs
10ml/2 tsp olive oil
sea salt and ground black pepper

1 Preheat the oven to 150°C/300°F/ Gas 2. Place a large casserole over high heat and heat the oil.

2 Season the meat and fry until browned all over before adding the bacon. Cook for 2–3 minutes, then add the shallots and brown them also.

3 Sprinkle the flour over the meat and onions and stir in well. Add the wine and stock gradually, stirring to combine with the flour.

4 Add all the remaining ingredients to the pan, bring to a simmer, cover and transfer to the oven for 1½–1¾ hours. Remove from the oven when the meat is tender, check the seasoning, cool and chill overnight.

5 About an hour before you want to serve, place the daube in a hot oven, preheated to 220°C/425°F/Gas 7.

GRANDMOTHER'S TIP
If you have a slow cooker this is a perfect recipe for it. Long gentle simmering will only improve the flavours. However, it is still a good idea to cook it the day before you plan to eat it.

6 To make the gratin, butter a 30cm/ 12in ovenproof dish and add the diced courgettes, nutmeg and seasoning.

7 Pour the cream over the courgettes and sprinkle over the thyme and garlic.

8 Mix the breadcrumbs, grated cheese and olive oil in a bowl, season, then spread over the gratin. Bake for 15–20 minutes, until the topping is crisp.

9 When the daube is piping hot and the gratin is cooked, serve on warmed plates with fresh bread.

Energy 976kcal/4066kJ; Protein 72.1g; Carbohydrate 22.2g, of which sugars 9.4g; Fat 64.9g, of which saturates 31.7g; Cholesterol 261mg; Calcium 256mg; Fibre 3.4g; Sodium 924mg.

MEAT DISHES

Once considered the most essential ingredient,
and the focus of every meal, meat is a staple of
the traditional kitchen, whether it's an expensive
joint for roasting, or an economical cut for
stews and casseroles. Many of these
old-fashioned dishes have been neglected, but
they are ready for revival as family suppers, are
easy to prepare, and make nourishing meals or
centrepieces for a special celebration.

RIB OF BEEF WITH YORKSHIRE PUDDINGS

MENTION TRADITIONAL ENGLISH FOOD, AND MANY PEOPLE THINK OF THIS QUINTESSENTIAL DISH, WHICH IS OFTEN THE MAIN COURSE FOR SUNDAY LUNCH WITH ROAST POTATOES AND OTHER VEGETABLES. THE YORKSHIRE PUDDINGS CAN BE SERVED FIRST, WITH PLENTY OF TASTY GRAVY.

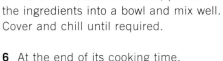

SERVES 6–8

INGREDIENTS
    rib of beef joint, weighing about
       3kg/6½lb
    oil, for brushing
    salt and ground black pepper
For the Yorkshire puddings
    115g/4oz/1 cup plain (all-purpose)
       flour
    1.5ml/¼ tsp salt
    1 egg
    200ml/7fl oz/scant 1 cup milk
    beef dripping, or oil, for greasing
For the horseradish cream
    60–75ml/4–5 tbsp finely grated fresh
       horseradish
    300ml/½ pint/1¼ cups soured cream
    30ml/2 tbsp cider vinegar or white
       wine vinegar
    10ml/2 tsp caster (superfine) sugar
For the gravy
    600ml/1 pint/2½ cups good beef stock

GRANDMOTHER'S TIP
To avoid the pungent smell (and tears) produced by grating horseradish, use a jar of preserved grated horseradish.

1 Preheat the oven to 220°C/425°F/Gas 7. Weigh the joint and calculate the cooking time required as follows: 10–15 minutes per 500g/1¼lb for rare beef, 15–20 minutes for medium and 20–25 minutes for well done.

2 Put the joint into a large roasting pan. Brush it all over with oil and season with salt and pepper. Put into the hot oven and cook for 30 minutes, until the beef is browned. Lower the oven temperature to 160°C/325°F/Gas 3 and cook for the calculated time, spooning the juices over the meat occasionally during cooking.

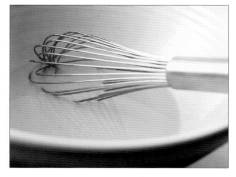

3 For the Yorkshire puddings, sift the flour and salt into a bowl and break the egg into it. Make the milk up to 300ml/½ pint/1¼ cups with water and gradually whisk into the flour to make a batter. Leave to stand while the beef cooks.

4 Generously grease eight Yorkshire pudding tins or muffin pans, measuring about 10cm/4in.

5 For the horseradish cream, put all the ingredients into a bowl and mix well. Cover and chill until required.

6 At the end of its cooking time, remove the beef from the oven, cover with foil and leave to stand for 30–40 minutes while you cook the Yorkshire puddings and make the gravy.

7 Increase the oven temperature to 220°C/425°F/Gas 7 and put the prepared tins on the top shelf for 5 minutes until very hot. Pour in the batter and cook for about 15 minutes until well risen, crisp and golden brown.

8 To make the gravy, transfer the beef to a warmed serving plate. Pour off the fat from the roasting pan, leaving the meat juices. Add the stock to the pan, bring to the boil and bubble until reduced by about half. Season to taste.

9 Carve the beef and serve with the gravy, Yorkshire puddings, roast potatoes and horseradish cream.

Energy 1037kcal/4338kJ; Protein 129g; Carbohydrate 15.1g, of which sugars 4.1g; Fat 51.5g, of which saturates 24.3g; Cholesterol 352mg; Calcium 123mg; Fibre 0.5g; Sodium 249mg.

STEAK WITH STOUT AND POTATOES

THIS RECIPE USES A VARIETY OF VEGETABLES AND HERBS TO FLAVOUR THE STOCK IN WHICH THE BEEF IS COOKED. HORSERADISH IS THE TRADITIONAL ACCOMPANIMENT TO BEEF, BUT ITS FIERCE FLAVOUR IS NOT TO EVERYONE'S LIKING, SO ADD IT SPARINGLY AND TASTE FREQUENTLY BEFORE SERVING.

SERVES 4

INGREDIENTS

675g/1½lb stewing beef
15ml/1 tbsp vegetable oil
25g/1oz/2 tbsp butter
225g/8oz baby (pearl) onions
175ml/6fl oz/¾ cup stout or dark beer
300ml/½ pint/1¼ cups beef stock
bouquet garni
675g/1½lb firm, waxy potatoes, cut into thick slices
225g/8oz/3 cups large mushrooms, sliced
15ml/1 tbsp plain (all-purpose) flour
2.5ml/½ tsp mild mustard
salt and ground black pepper
chopped thyme sprigs, to garnish

GRANDMOTHER'S TIP
To make onion peeling easier, first put the onions in a bowl and cover with boiling water. Allow them to soak for about 5 minutes and drain. The skins should now peel away easily.

1 Trim any excess fat from the steak and cut into four pieces. Season both sides of the meat. Heat the oil and 10g/¼oz/1½ tsp of the butter in a large heavy-based pan.

VARIATION
For a lighter dish, substitute four lamb leg steaks for the beef, dry cider for the stout, and chicken stock instead of beef.

2 Add the steak to the pan and brown on both sides, taking care not to burn the butter. Remove the steak from the pan and set aside.

3 Add the baby onions to the pan and cook for 3–4 minutes until lightly browned all over. Return the steak to the pan with the onions. Pour on the stout and stock, and season to taste.

4 Add the bouquet garni on top of the steak in the pan and top with the potato slices spreading them evenly over the surface of the pan.

5 Bring the ingredients in the pan to a boil then reduce the heat, cover with a tight-fitting lid and simmer gently for 1 hour.

6 Add the sliced mushrooms over the potatoes. Cover again and simmer for a further 30 minutes or so.

7 Remove the mushrooms, potatoes and steak from the pan using a slotted spoon and arrange on a platter. Keep warm.

7 Mix the remaining butter with the flour to make a roux. Whisk a little at a time into the cooking liquid in the pan. Stir in the mustard. Cook over a medium heat for 2–3 minutes, stirring all the while, until thickened.

8 Season the sauce, if necessary, and pour into the serving dish, over the steak and potatoes. Garnish with plenty of thyme sprigs and serve the dish at once.

Energy 538Kcal/2253kJ; Protein 43.4g; Carbohydrate 35.5g, of which sugars 6.2g; Fat 24.5g, of which saturates 10.2g; Cholesterol 111mg; Calcium 44mg; Fibre 3.2g; Sodium 172mg.

STEAK AND KIDNEY PIE

THIS IS A CLASSIC DISH, FULL OF GOODNESS, WITH CHUNKS OF BEEF AND KIDNEY IN A STRONG MEATY GRAVY AND A DELICIOUSLY LIGHT, PUFF PASTRY TOPPING. THE TRICK IS TO BAKE THE PASTRY SEPARATELY FROM THE MEAT, WHICH WILL ENSURE THAT IT REMAINS PERFECTLY CRISP.

SERVES 4

INGREDIENTS
    675g/1½lb stewing steak
    225g/8oz ox's or lamb's kidney
    45ml/3 tbsp oil
    15g/½oz/1 tbsp unsalted butter
    2 onions, chopped
    30ml/2 tbsp plain (all-purpose) flour
    300ml/½ pint/1¼ cups beef stock
    15ml/1 tbsp tomato purée (paste)
    10ml/2 tsp English (hot) mustard
    2 bay leaves
    375g/13oz ready-made, rolled,
      puff pastry
    beaten egg, to glaze
    15ml/1 tbsp chopped fresh parsley
    salt and ground black pepper
    creamed potatoes and green
      vegetables, to serve

1 Cut the steak into 2.5cm/1in cubes. Remove all fat and skin from the kidney and cut into cubes or thick slices.

2 Heat 30ml/2 tbsp of the oil in a frying pan and brown the beef. Remove from the pan with a slotted spoon and place in an ovenproof cooking pot.

3 Add the kidney to the frying pan and brown for 1–2 minutes before adding to the beef. Add the remaining oil and the butter to the pan, add the onions and cook for 5 minutes, until just beginning to colour. Sprinkle with the flour and stir in, then remove the pan from the heat.

4 Preheat the oven to 190°C/375°F/Gas 5. Gradually stir the stock into the pan, followed by the tomato purée and mustard. Return to the heat and bring to the boil, stirring constantly, until thickened. Pour the gravy over the meat, then add the bay leaves and season. Stir well and cover with the lid. Cook in the oven for 1½–2 hours.

5 While the beef is cooking, roll out the pastry and, using a dinner plate as a guide, cut out a 25cm/10in round. Transfer the pastry round to a baking sheet lined with baking parchment.

6 Using a sharp knife, mark the pastry into quarters, cutting almost but not quite through it. Decorate with pastry trimmings, then flute the edge. Cover with clear film (plastic wrap) and place in the refrigerator until ready to cook.

7 Half an hour before the beef is cooked, raise the oven temperature to 200°C/400°F/Gas 6. Brush the pastry all over with beaten egg to glaze, then bake for about 25 minutes, or until well risen, golden-brown and crisp.

8 To serve, stir the chopped parsley into the steak and kidney mixture and spoon on to warmed serving plates. Cut the baked pie crust into four, using the markings as a guide, and top each portion of meat with a wedge of pastry.

9 Serve immediately with rich, creamed potatoes and green vegetables.

Energy 637Kcal/2652kJ; Protein 18.7g; Carbohydrate 46.2g, of which sugars 5.2g; Fat 43.4g, of which saturates 13.1g; Cholesterol 259mg; Calcium 99mg; Fibre 2.7g; Sodium 578mg.

LIVER WITH FRIED ONIONS

DESPITE THE FACT THAT LIVER, KIDNEYS AND OTHER OFFAL CAN SEEM OFF-PUTTING, THESE WERE STAPLE INGREDIENTS IN THE PAST AND ARE EXTREMELY NUTRITIOUS. THIS RECIPE MAKES THE MOST OF DELICATE CALVES' LIVER, GARNISHED WITH CRISP FRIED ONION RINGS AND GLAZED APPLES.

SERVES 4

INGREDIENTS

  3 onions, finely sliced and separated
    into rings
  plain (all-purpose) flour, to dust
  45ml/3 tbsp sunflower oil
  800g/1¾lb calves' liver, sliced
    1cm/½in thick
  pinch of freshly grated nutmeg
  50g/2oz clarified butter
  3 small apples, peeled, cored and
    sliced 1cm/½in thick
  100ml/3½fl oz/scant ½ cup
    apple juice
  salt and ground white pepper
  chopped parsley, to garnish
  mashed potato, to serve

3 Season the liver with salt, pepper and ground nutmeg, and dust with flour. Heat the clarified butter in a frying pan over medium heat and fry the slices of liver for 2–3 minutes on each side. Remove from the pan and keep warm.

4 Add the apple rings to the same pan, and fry gently on one side until softening, then turn the rings over and cook on the other side. When golden, add the apple juice and boil to reduce so that the rings are glazed.

5 Arrange the liver on a serving dish with the apple slices on top, and garnish the dish with the crispy onion rings and chopped parsley. Serve with mashed potato.

VARIATION
You can use lamb's liver instead of calves' if you wish, but pig's liver is probably too tough for such a swiftly-cooked dish.

1 Dust the onion rings with flour. Heat the oil in a pan over high heat and fry the onion rings for 1–2 minutes.

2 When the onions are cooked, lift them out of the pan and drain on kitchen paper. Keep warm in a low oven, uncovered so they stay crisp.

Energy 584kcal/2438kJ; Protein 43.1g; Carbohydrate 29.6g, of which sugars 17.9g; Fat 33.6g, of which saturates 12.2g; Cholesterol 769mg; Calcium 71mg; Fibre 3.6g; Sodium 287mg.

FAGGOTS <u>WITH</u> ONION GRAVY

IN THE DAYS WHEN MOST HOUSEHOLDS REARED A PIG, FAGGOTS WERE MADE WITH THE FRESH LIVER ON SLAUGHTER DAY. THE MIXTURE WAS WRAPPED IN THE LACY NETTING OF THE PIG'S CAUL, WHICH HELD THE CONTENTS TOGETHER DURING COOKING. HERE, BEATEN EGG BINDS THE MIXTURE.

SERVES 4

INGREDIENTS
  450g/1lb pig's liver, trimmed and
    roughly chopped
  300g/11oz belly pork, chopped
  2 onions, roughly chopped
  100g/3½oz/1 cup fresh breadcrumbs
  1 egg, beaten
  2 sage leaves, chopped
  5ml/1 tsp salt
  2.5ml/½ tsp ground mace
  1.5ml/¼ tsp ground black pepper
  150ml/¼ pint/⅔ cup beef stock
  butter for greasing
For the onion gravy:
  50g/2oz/¼ cup butter
  4 onions, thinly sliced
  generous 10ml/2 tsp sugar
  15ml/1 tbsp plain (all-purpose) flour
  300ml/½ pint/1¼ cups beef stock
  300ml/½ pint/1¼ cups vegetable stock
  salt and black pepper

1 Preheat the oven to 180°C/350°F/ Gas 4. Put the liver, pork and onions in a food processor and process until finely chopped. Then turn the mixture out into a large mixing bowl and stir in the breadcrumbs, egg, sage, salt, mace and pepper until thoroughly combined.

2 With wet hands, shape the mixture into 10–12 patties and lay them in an ovenproof dish. Pour in the stock.

3 Use a buttered sheet of foil to cover the dish, butter side down. Crimp the edges around the dish to seal them.

4 Cook in the oven for 45–50 minutes (the juices should run clear when the faggots are pierced with a sharp knife).

5 For the onion gravy, melt the butter in a large pan and add the onions and sugar. Cover and cook gently for at least 30 minutes, until the onions are soft and evenly caramelized to a rich golden brown. Stir in the flour, remove from the heat and stir in both types of stock.

6 Return the pan to the heat and, stirring, bring just to the boil. Simmer gently for 20–30 minutes, stirring occasionally. Season to taste.

7 Once cooked, remove the foil and increase the oven temperature to 200°C/400°F/Gas 6. Cook for a further 10 minutes until lightly browned. Serve with the onion gravy.

Energy 664kcal/2768kJ; Protein 41.4g; Carbohydrate 31.2g, of which sugars 9.8g; Fat 42.5g, of which saturates 17.9g; Cholesterol 421mg; Calcium 84mg; Fibre 2.2g; Sodium 434mg.

SIMMERED BEEF TOPSIDE <u>WITH</u> HORSERADISH

THIS RECIPE USES A VARIETY OF VEGETABLES AND HERBS TO FLAVOUR THE STOCK IN WHICH THE BEEF IS GENTLY COOKED. THE HOT PUNGENCY OF THE HORSERADISH HELPS LIFT THE DISH AND COMPLEMENTS THE MILD FLAVOURS OF THE BEEF AND STOCK.

SERVES 4

INGREDIENTS
  1kg/2¼lb beef topside
  2 medium carrots, roughly chopped
  100g/3½oz celeriac, roughly chopped
  ½ leek, cleaned and roughly chopped
  2 onions, halved
  3 bay leaves
  4 allspice berries
  5 black peppercorns
  a few parsley stalks
  1 parsnip, sliced
  4 medium carrots, sliced
  2–3 sticks celery, sliced
  1 large potato, peeled and sliced
  200g/7oz swede (rutabaga), peeled
    and sliced
  beef stock cube (optional)
  30ml/2 tbsp butter
  30ml/2 tbsp plain (all-purpose) flour
  45ml/3 tbsp creamed horseradish
  juice of 1 lemon
  200ml/7fl oz/scant 1 cup single
    (light) cream
  30ml/2 tbsp chopped parsley
  salt

1 Put the beef in a pan with cold water to cover, bring to the boil and skim off any scum. Reduce the heat and leave the meat to simmer for 40–50 minutes.

2 Add the chopped vegetables, spices and parsley stalks to the pan. Continue to cook for about 90 minutes, until the beef is tender. Lift out the beef and keep it warm.

3 Season the stock with salt to taste and reserve. Put the sliced vegetables in a pan with 1 litre/1¾ pints/4 cups of the beef stock, bring to the boil, lower the heat and simmer until the vegetables are tender.

4 Season with salt; if the stock is not rich enough, add a beef stock cube. Add the chopped parsley.

5 Melt the butter in a pan and stir in the flour. Gradually add 500ml/17fl oz/ 2 cups of the beef stock, stirring. Bring it to the boil and add the creamed horseradish, lemon juice and cream.

6 Spoon on to serving plates. Slice the beef and arrange it on top. Serve the sauce separately.

Energy 653kcal/2747kJ; Protein 65g; Carbohydrate 44.3g, of which sugars 26g; Fat 25.3g, of which saturates 13g; Cholesterol 171mg; Calcium 281.5mg; Fibre 10.8g; Sodium 576mg

ESCALOPES OF VEAL WITH CREAM SAUCE

THIS IS A VERY QUICK, EASY DISH THAT IS IDEAL FOR SUPPER AFTER WORK. THE DELICATE FLAVOUR OF VEAL IS ENLIVENED BY A RUSTIC, CREAMY MUSHROOM SAUCE SPIKED WITH TARRAGON. THE BEST ACCOMPANIMENT IS A BOWL OF PASTA AND A GREEN VEGETABLE.

SERVES 4

INGREDIENTS

  15ml/1 tbsp plain (all-purpose) flour
  4 veal escalopes, each weighing
    about 75–115g/3–4oz
  30ml/2 tbsp sunflower oil
  1 shallot, chopped
  150g/5oz/2 cups chanterelle or oyster
    mushrooms, sliced
  30ml/2 tbsp Marsala or
    medium-dry sherry
  200ml/7fl oz/scant 1 cup
    crème fraîche
  30ml/2 tbsp chopped fresh tarragon
  salt and ground black pepper

1 Tip the flour into a bowl or on to a plate, mix in salt and pepper and then use to dust the veal escalopes. Set the escalopes aside.

2 Heat the oil in a large frying pan and cook the shallot for 5 minutes. Add the mushrooms, and cook for a further 5 minutes, then push the shallots and mushrooms to one side and add the escalopes. Cook over a high heat for about 1½ minutes on each side. Pour in the Marsala or sherry and cook until reduced by half.

3 Use a fish slice or spatula to remove the veal escalopes from the pan. Stir the crème fraîche and tarragon into the juices remaining in the pan and simmer gently for 2–3 minutes, or until the sauce is thick and creamy. Season to taste with salt and pepper.

4 Return the escalopes to the pan and heat through for 1 minute before serving.

GRANDMOTHER'S TIP
If the sauce seems to be too thick, add 30ml/2 tbsp water. Cooking the veal only takes a few minutes, so make sure you have the pasta and vegetables ready before you begin.

Energy 377Kcal/1567kJ; Protein 25.1g; Carbohydrate 5.9g, of which sugars 2.5g; Fat 27.5g, of which saturates 14.9g; Cholesterol 108mg; Calcium 45mg; Fibre 0.8g; Sodium 75mg.

SHEPHERD'S PIE

THIS DISH DEVELOPED IN VICTORIAN TIMES AS A THRIFTY AND WARMING WAY OF USING UP LEFTOVERS FROM THE SUNDAY ROAST. BY THE 1930S IT HAD BECOME PART OF A REGULAR WEEKLY PATTERN OF EATING, SERVED TO THE FAMILY EVERY MONDAY OR TUESDAY, TO THE CHILDREN'S GREAT DELIGHT.

SERVES 4

INGREDIENTS
- 1kg/2¼lb potatoes, peeled
- 60ml/4 tbsp milk
- about 25g/1oz/2 tbsp butter
- 15ml/1 tbsp oil
- 1 large onion, finely chopped
- 1 medium carrot, finely chopped
- 450g/1lb cold cooked lamb or beef, minced (ground) or finely chopped
- 150ml/¼ pint/⅔ cup lamb or beef stock
- 30ml/2 tbsp fresh parsley, finely chopped
- salt and ground black pepper

VARIATIONS
Add extra ingredients to the meat base, such as a clove or two of chopped garlic, a few mushrooms, a spoonful of tomato purée (paste) or ketchup, or a splash of Worcestershire sauce. You could also mix the potatoes with mashed parsnip, squash or swede (rutabaga), and add a dollop of wholegrain mustard.

1 Preheat the oven to 190°C/375°F/ Gas 5. Boil the potatoes in salted water for about 20 minutes or until soft. Drain, and mash with the milk, adding butter and seasoning to taste.

GRANDMOTHER'S TIP
Every home used to have a meat mincer (grinder), which could be used for cooked or raw meat. Nowadays you can easily buy minced beef or lamb to make this shepherd's pie, if you wish.

2 Heat the oil in a frying pan and add the onion and carrot. Cook over medium heat for 5–10 minutes, stirring occasionally, until soft. Stir in the minced meat, stock and parsley.

3 Spread the meat mixture in an ovenproof dish and spoon the mashed potato evenly over the top. Cook in the hot oven for about 30 minutes until the potatoes are crisped and browned.

Energy 487kcal/2045kJ; Protein 29.4g; Carbohydrate 50.1g, of which sugars 15.2g; Fat 20.2g, of which saturates 8.4g; Cholesterol 69mg; Calcium 54mg; Fibre 5.3g; Sodium 379mg.

ROAST LAMB

ROASTING LAMB WITH A SELECTION OF AROMATIC HERBS AND SPICES FOUND IN THE HERB GARDEN OR WHILE FORAGING IN THE FIELDS BRINGS OUT THE BEST IN THE MEAT. IN THIS DELICIOUS RECIPE THE HERBS AND GARLIC ARE INSERTED THROUGH THE SKIN OF THE JOINT FOR MAXIMUM FLAVOUR.

SERVES 6

INGREDIENTS
    2kg/4½lb leg of lamb
    fresh rosemary, separated into
      sprigs
    fresh thyme, separated into sprigs
    10 garlic cloves, cut into slivers
    5ml/1 tsp black peppercorns
    6 whole cloves
    6 allspice berries
    20g/¾oz butter, softened
    redcurrant jelly, to serve

1 Preheat the oven to 200°C/400°F/ Gas 6. Place the leg of lamb in a roasting pan.

2 Make about 20–30 small, deep slits all over the meat, then push a small sprig of rosemary and thyme and a sliver of garlic into each.

3 Using a mortar and pestle, grind the peppercorns, cloves and allspice to a coarse powder. Combine the powder with the softened butter and smear all over the lamb.

4 Place the roasting pan in the hot oven and cook for 15 minutes. Reduce the heat to 180°C/350°F/Gas 4 and roast the lamb for a further 1½ hours, or until cooked but still slightly pink.

5 Remove the joint from the oven, cover and allow to rest for 15 minutes.

6 Cut the meat into generous slices and serve immediately, with the redcurrant jelly.

Energy 562kcal/2340kJ; Protein 50.4g; Carbohydrate 0.4g, of which sugars 0.3g; Fat 39.9g, of which saturates 14.1g; Cholesterol 200mg; Calcium 36mg; Fibre 0.6g; Sodium 171mg.

LANCASHIRE HOTPOT

THIS DISH IS TRADITIONALLY MADE WITHOUT BROWNING THE LAMB OR VEGETABLES FIRST — ALL THE FLAVOUR DEVELOPS DURING THE LONG, SLOW COOKING. IT WORKS WELL IN AN ELECTRIC SLOW COOKER, BUT IT WOULD ORIGINALLY HAVE BEEN SIMMERED IN A LOW OVEN OR ON TOP OF THE STOVE.

SERVES 4

INGREDIENTS

    8 middle neck or loin lamb chops,
      about 900g/2lb in total weight
    900g/2lb potatoes, thinly sliced
    2 onions, peeled and sliced
    2 carrots, peeled and sliced
    1 stick celery, trimmed and sliced
    1 leek, peeled and sliced
    225g/8oz/generous 3 cups button
      (white) mushrooms, sliced
    5ml/1 tsp dried mixed herbs
    small sprig of rosemary
    475ml/16fl oz/2 cups lamb or beef
      stock
    15g/½oz/1 tbsp butter, melted
    salt and ground black pepper

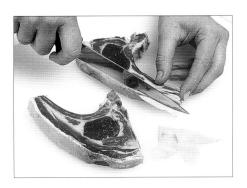

1 Trim the lamb chops of excess fat. Place a layer of sliced potatoes in the base of the ceramic cooking pot, and top with some sliced vegetables. Place four of the lamb chops on top.

2 Add a sprinkling of dried herbs, salt and black pepper. Repeat the layers of sliced potato, vegetables, dried herbs and meat, tucking the rosemary sprig down the side of the pot.

3 Continue layering up the remaining vegetables, finishing with a neat layer of potatoes on the top.

4 Pour the meat stock into the ceramic cooking pot, then cover with the lid and switch the slow cooker to high or auto. Cook for 1 hour, then reduce the temperature to low or leave on auto and cook for 6–8 hours or until tender.

5 Brush the top layer of potatoes with melted butter. Place under a preheated grill (broiler) and cook for 5 minutes, or until the potatoes are lightly browned. Serve immediately.

Energy 850Kcal/3544kJ; Protein 44.7g; Carbohydrate 45.3g, of which sugars 10.1g; Fat 55.8g, of which saturates 26.5g; Cholesterol 186mg; Calcium 72mg; Fibre 4.3g; Sodium 274mg.

PORK <u>WITH</u> CABBAGE <u>AND</u> BREAD DUMPLINGS

THIS RECIPE USES PORK KNUCKLE, AN ECONOMICAL CUT THAT BENEFITS FROM LONG, SLOW COOKING, GIVING THE MEAT TIME TO ABSORB ALL THE FLAVOURS OF THE BEER STOCK IN THIS HEARTY COUNTRY DISH. THE DUMPLINGS AND CABBAGE ARE COOKED SEPARATELY AND SERVED ALONGSIDE THE MEAT.

SERVES 4

INGREDIENTS

    4 pork knuckles with bones and skin,
      about 700g/1½lb each
    30ml/2 tbsp oil
    2 onions, roughly chopped
    2 garlic cloves, halved
    500ml/17fl oz/ 2 cups dark beer
    3 bay leaves
    5ml/1 tsp caraway seeds
    salt and ground white pepper
For the bread dumplings
    45ml/3 tbsp oil
    350g/12oz day-old white bread,
      broken into pieces
    1 small onion, finely chopped
    50g/2oz smoked bacon, finely diced
    250ml/8fl oz/1 cup milk
    pinch of freshly grated nutmeg
    10ml/2 tsp chopped parsley, plus
      extra to garnish
    5ml/1 tsp snipped chives
    2 egg yolks
For the cabbage
    15ml/1 tbsp oil
    100g/3½oz smoked bacon, diced
    1 small onion, finely chopped
    700ml/1¼ pints/3 cups chicken stock
    10ml/2 tsp white wine vinegar
    1 kg/2¼lb white cabbage, sliced
    5ml/1 tsp caraway seeds
    salt, ground white pepper and sugar

1 Preheat the oven to 180°C/350°F/ Gas 4. Heat the oil in a large casserole. Season the pork and brown on all sides. Add the onion and garlic and fry for 2 minutes, then add the beer.

2 Add 1 litre/1¾ pints/4 cups water, bay leaves and caraway seeds to the pan. Bring to the boil, cover and cook in the oven for 2½–3 hours, turning the knuckles occasionally.

3 Meanwhile, make the bread dumplings. Heat 30ml/2 tbsp oil in a frying pan over medium heat and fry the bread for 3–4 minutes, until crisp. Remove from the pan and put them in a large bowl.

4 Return the pan to the heat. Add the remaining oil to the pan and fry the onions and bacon for 2 minutes. Add the nutmeg, salt and pepper.

5 Pour the milk into the pan, and bring to the boil, then pour the mixture over the fried bread.

6 Add the chopped herbs and the egg yolks to the bread and milk and mix well. Set aside for 20 minutes for the bread to absorb the liquid.

7 To prepare the cabbage, heat the oil in a pan over high heat and fry the bacon and onion for 2–3 minutes. Add the stock, vinegar and cabbage.

8 Season with salt, pepper and sugar and add the caraway seeds. Reduce the heat, cover, and leave to cook for 30 minutes, stirring occasionally, until the cabbage is soft.

9 While the cabbage is cooking, form the bread mixture into eight dumplings.

10 Bring a pan of salted water to the boil, add the bread dumplings and simmer for 20–25 minutes. Remove with a slotted spoon and keep warm.

11 When the meat is ready, arrange some of the cabbage on each plate together with a pork knuckle and some of the juices from the pot. Put two bread dumplings on each plate and garnish with a little chopped parsley.

Energy 1377kcal/5743kJ; Protein 89.1g; Carbohydrate 70.1g, of which sugars 26.6g; Fat 81.2g, of which saturates 23.1g; Cholesterol 420mg; Calcium 392mg; Fibre 8.4g; Sodium 1365mg.

PORK FILLETS WITH PRUNE STUFFING

THE SWEET FLAVOUR OF DRIED FRUIT SUCH AS PRUNES OR APRICOTS GOES PARTICULARLY WELL WITH PORK. HERE THE PRUNES ARE BLENDED WITH LEFTOVER BREADCRUMBS AND MADE INTO A FRUITY STUFFING WITH CHOPPED SHALLOTS AND CELERY, PLUS A TOUCH OF ORANGE RIND.

SERVES 4

INGREDIENTS

15g/½oz/1 tbsp butter
1 shallot, very finely chopped
1 stick celery, very finely chopped
finely grated rind of ½ orange
115g/4oz/½ cup (about 12) stoned
  (pitted), ready-to-eat prunes,
  chopped
25g/1oz/½ cup fresh white
  breadcrumbs
30ml/2 tbsp chopped
  fresh parsley
pinch of grated nutmeg
two 225g/8oz pork fillets,
  trimmed
6 slices Parma ham or prosciutto
15ml/1 tbsp olive oil
150ml/¼ pint/⅔ cup dry white wine
salt and ground black pepper
mashed root vegetables and
  steamed greens, to serve

1 Melt the butter in a frying pan, add the shallot and celery, and fry gently until soft. Transfer to a bowl and stir in the orange rind, prunes, breadcrumbs, parsley and nutmeg. Season and leave to cool.

2 Slice down the length of each fillet, cutting three-quarters of the way through. Open out each pork fillet and lay it out on a board.

3 Cover the meat with a piece of oiled clear film (plastic wrap), then gently flatten with a rolling pin until the meat is about 5mm/¼in thick.

4 Arrange 3 slices of the ham on a board and place one pork fillet on top. Repeat with the remaining ham and fillet. Divide the prune and breadcrumb stuffing between the two fillets, then fold over to enclose the filling.

5 Wrap the ham around each stuffed fillets, and secure with one or two wooden cocktail sticks (toothpicks). Preheat the oven to 180°C/350°F/Gas 4.

6 Heat the oil in the clean frying pan and quickly brown the wrapped pork fillets all over, taking care not to dislodge the cocktail sticks, before transferring them to an ovenproof casserole dish.

7 Pour the white wine into the frying pan and bring almost to the boil, then pour over the pork. Cover the casserole dish with a lid and cook in the oven for 30 minutes.

8 When the meat is cooked, remove the meat from the dish and remove the cocktail sticks. Cut the pork into slices.

9 Arrange on warmed plates and spoon over some of the cooking juices. Serve with mashed root vegetables and steamed greens.

Energy 245Kcal/1027kJ; Protein 17.3g; Carbohydrate 14.6g, of which sugars 11.3g; Fat 10.8g, of which saturates 4g; Cholesterol 59mg; Calcium 34mg; Fibre 2g; Sodium 378mg.

TOAD IN THE HOLE

THIS CLASSIC NURSERY DISH IS EVERY CHILD'S FAVOURITE SUPPER. ORIGINALLY IT WAS MADE WITH SMALL CHUNKS OF MEAT, BUT TODAY IT IS SAUSAGES THAT NESTLE IN THE LIGHT, CRUNCHY BATTER. THIS DISH MUST BE SERVED AS SOON AS IT COMES OUT OF THE OVEN FOR THE BEST RESULTS.

SERVES 6

INGREDIENTS
175g/6oz/1½ cups plain (all-purpose) flour
2.5ml/½ tsp salt
2 eggs
300ml/½ pint/1¼ cups milk
30ml/2 tbsp oil
500g/1¼lb meaty butcher's sausages

1 Preheat the oven to 220°C/425°F/ Gas 7. To make the batter, sift the flour and salt into a bowl, make a well in the centre and break the eggs into it.

2 Mix the milk with 300ml/½ pint/ 1¼ cups cold water. Using a whisk, gradually stir the milk mixture into the bowl with the eggs, incorporating the flour and beating well to make a smooth batter. Leave to stand.

GRANDMOTHER'S TIP
To help the batter rise and become crispy use a roasting pan rather than a ceramic dish.

3 Pour the oil into a roasting pan and add the sausages (cut in half crosswise if large). Put into the hot oven and cook for about 10 minutes until the oil is very hot and the sausages begin to brown.

4 Stir the batter and quickly pour it around the sausages, then return to the oven. Cook for about 45 minutes or until the batter is puffed up, set and golden brown. Serve immediately.

Energy 497kcal/2070kJ; Protein 14.5g; Carbohydrate 32.1g, of which sugars 3.8g; Fat 35.4g, of which saturates 13.6g; Cholesterol 109mg; Calcium 141mg; Fibre 1.3g; Sodium 616mg

POTATO AND SAUSAGE CASSEROLE

THERE ARE MANY VARIATIONS OF THIS TRADITIONAL SUPPER DISH, BUT THE BASIC INGREDIENTS ARE THE SAME WHEREVER YOU GO — POTATOES, SAUSAGES AND BACON. THIS VERSION REALLY BENEFITS FROM A LITTLE CHOPPED SAGE, WITH ITS FRESH, WOODY TASTE, BLENDED WITH THE STOCK.

SERVES 6

INGREDIENTS
    15ml/1 tbsp vegetable oil
    8 large pork sausages
    4 bacon rashers (strips), cut into
      2.5cm/1in pieces
    1 large onion, chopped
    2 garlic cloves, crushed
    4 large baking potatoes, peeled
      and thinly sliced
    1.5ml/¼ tsp fresh sage
    300ml/½ pint/1¼ cups vegetable
      stock
    salt and ground black pepper

GRANDMOTHER'S TIPS
Choose good-quality sausages with a high meat percentage, because it will make all the difference to the final result. Many local butchers make their own, and it is always worth trying them rather than the vacuum-packed ones from the supermarket.

1 Heat the oil in a frying pan and fry the sausages for about 10 minutes, turning until they are golden brown. Remove from the pan and tip away all but about 10ml/2 tsp of fat. Preheat the oven to 200°C/400°F/Gas 6.

2 Add the bacon to the pan and fry for 2 minutes. Add the onion and fry for about 8 minutes, stirring frequently until golden. Add the garlic and fry for a further 1 minute, then turn off the heat.

3 Arrange half the potato slices in the base of a casserole. Spoon the bacon and onion mixture on top. Season well with salt and ground black pepper, and sprinkle with the fresh sage. Cover with the remaining potato slices.

4 Pour the stock over the potatoes and top with the sausages. Cover with the lid and cook for 45 minutes to 1 hour, or until the potatoes are tender and the sausages cooked through. Serve hot.

Energy 717Kcal/2984kJ; Protein 20.5g; Carbohydrate 49.9g, of which sugars 6.1g; Fat 49.8g, of which saturates 18.1g; Cholesterol 78.1mg; Calcium 73mg; Fibre 4g; Sodium 1322mg.

BLACK PUDDING, POTATO AND APPLE MASH

*BLACK PUDDING IS A SUCCULENT, NUTRITIOUS SAUSAGE WITH A STRONG FLAVOUR. IT USED TO BE
PARTICULARLY POPULAR IN THE NORTH OF ENGLAND. IN THIS DISH, FRIED SLICES OF BLACK PUDDING
SIT ON TOP OF A PILE OF MASHED POTATOES WITH ONIONS AND APPLES.*

SERVES 4

INGREDIENTS
    45ml/3 tbsp oil
    2 onions, chopped
    500g/1¼lb apples, peeled and diced
    juice of 1 lemon
    5ml/1 tsp sugar
    100g/3½oz/7 tbsp butter
    500g/1¼lb floury potatoes, boiled
      and kept hot
    pinch of freshly grated nutmeg
    100g/3½oz bacon
    500g/1¼lb black pudding (blood
      sausage)
    salt and ground white pepper
    fresh parsley, to garnish

VARIATION
If you don't like black pudding, replace
it with mini burgers made from minced
(ground) pork, or some thinly sliced
spicy sausages.

1 Heat 15ml/1 tbsp of the oil in a pan
over medium heat and cook the onions
for 2–3 minutes. Add the apples, lemon
juice, sugar and 15ml/1 tbsp water.
Simmer gently until the apple is soft,
and add the butter.

2 Add the apple mixture to the hot
boiled potatoes and mash together.
Season with salt, pepper and nutmeg.
Keep warm.

3 Heat the remaining oil in two frying
pans over high heat. Fry the bacon
cubes in one for 4–5 minutes until crisp
and browned. Slice the black pudding
and fry the slices in the other pan until
browned on both sides.

4 Spoon the mash on to four plates,
then put the fried black pudding on top
and sprinkle some bacon cubes over it.
Garnish with chopped parsley.

Energy 855kcal/3559kJ; Protein 20.8g; Carbohydrate 61g, of which sugars 19.7g; Fat 60.4g, of which saturates 26.7g; Cholesterol 156mg; Calcium 193mg; Fibre 4.9g; Sodium 1767mg

PORK AND POTATO HOTPOT

LONG, SLOW COOKING MAKES THE PORK CHOPS MELTINGLY TENDER AND ALLOWS THE POTATO SLICES TO SOAK UP ALL THE DELICIOUS JUICES FROM THE MEAT. THIS DISH IS PERFECT FOR A FAMILY MEAL, AND ONLY NEEDS SOME STEAMED GREEN VEGETABLES TO GO WITH IT.

SERVES 4

INGREDIENTS
    25g/1oz/2 tbsp butter
    15ml/1 tbsp oil
    1 large onion, very thinly sliced
    1 garlic clove, crushed
    225g/8oz/generous 3 cups button
      (white) mushrooms, sliced
    1.5ml/¼ tsp dried mixed herbs
    900g/2lb potatoes, thinly sliced
    4 thick pork chops
    750ml/1¼ pints/3 cups vegetable
      or chicken stock
    salt and ground black pepper

1   Use 15g/½oz/1 tbsp of the butter to grease the base and halfway up the sides of the ceramic cooking pot.

2   Preheat the oven to 180°C/350°F/ Gas 4.Heat the oil in a frying pan, add the sliced onion and cook gently for about 5 minutes, until softened.

3   Add the garlic and mushrooms to the pan and cook for a further 5 minutes until softened. Remove the pan from the heat and stir in the mixed herbs.

4   Spoon half the mushroom mixture into the base of a casserole, then arrange half the potato slices on top and season with salt and black pepper.

5   Using a sharp knife, trim as much fat as possible from the pork chops, then place them on top of the potatoes in a single layer. Pour about half the stock over the top to cover the potatoes and prevent them discolouring.

6   Repeat the layers of the mushroom mixture and potatoes, finishing with a layer of neatly overlapping potatoes. Pour over the remaining stock; it should just cover the potatoes, so use a little more or less if necessary. Dot the remaining butter on top of the potatoes.

7   Cook in the oven for 1½–2 hours, or until the potatoes are tender and golden brown. If you like, place the hotpot under a medium grill (broiler) for 5–10 minutes to brown before serving.

Energy 511Kcal/2132kJ; Protein 17.9g; Carbohydrate 41.5g, of which sugars 6.5g; Fat 31.5g, of which saturates 12.1g; Cholesterol 67mg; Calcium 40mg; Fibre 3.7g; Sodium 529mg.

ROAST BELLY OF PORK

OF ALL THE PORK CUTS, NOTHING QUITE COMPARES WITH THE FLAVOUR OF BELLY OF PORK,
PARTICULARLY WHEN IT IS TOPPED WITH A LAYER OF CRISP CRACKLING. THIS RECIPE INCLUDES
WINTER VEGETABLES TUCKED UNDER THE MEAT, WHICH COOK TO PERFECTION IN THE JUICES.

SERVES 4–6

INGREDIENTS
   1 small swede (rutabaga), weighing
     about 500g/1lb 2oz
   1 onion
   1 parsnip
   2 carrots
   15ml/1 tbsp olive oil
   1.5kg/3lb 6oz belly of pork, well
     scored
   15ml/1 tbsp fresh thyme leaves or
     5ml/1 tsp dried thyme
   sea salt flakes and ground black
     pepper

GRANDMOTHER'S TIP
Ask your butcher to score (slash) the
pork rind well, or use a strong sharp
blade and do it yourself.

1 Preheat the oven to 220°C/425°F/
Gas 7. Cut the vegetables into small
cubes (about 2cm/¾in) and stir them
with the oil in a roasting pan, tossing
them until evenly coated. Pour in
300ml/½ pint/1¼ cups water.

2 Sprinkle the pork rind with thyme,
salt and pepper, rubbing them well into
the scored slashes in the pork belly.
Place the pork on top of the vegetables,
with the skin side uppermost.

3 Put the pork and vegetables into the
hot oven and cook for 30 minutes, by
which time the liquid will have almost
evaporated to leave a golden crust in
the bottom of the pan.

4 Add 600ml/1 pint/2½ cups cold water
to the vegetables in the pan. Reduce
the oven temperature to 180°C/350°F/
Gas 4, and cook for 1½ hours, until the
pork is tender and the juices run clear
when the centre of the meat is pierced.

5 Check the oven during the last half
hour to make sure the liquid does not
dry up completely, adding a little extra
water if necessary. If the crackling is not
yet crisp enough, increase the oven
temperature to 220°C/425°F/Gas 7 and
continue cooking for another 10–20
minutes, adding extra water if necessary
– just enough to prevent the vegetables
from burning on the bottom of the tin.

6 With a sharp knife, slice off the
crackling, and break into pieces. Slice
the pork thickly, and serve on warmed
plates with the vegetables, pieces of
crackling, and the golden juices
spooned over.

Energy 1014kcal/4194kJ; Protein 39.5g; Carbohydrate 9.4g, of which sugars 7.3g; Fat 91.2g, of which saturates 33.1g; Cholesterol 180mg; Calcium 81mg; Fibre 3.3g; Sodium 202mg.

SOMERSET CIDER-GLAZED HAM

THIS WONDERFUL OLD WEST COUNTRY RECIPE FOR HAM GLAZED WITH CIDER AND DOTTED WITH CLOVES IS TRADITIONALLY SERVED WITH CRANBERRY SAUCE. IT IS AN IDEAL DISH TO SERVE ON CHRISTMAS DAY, ALONGSIDE ROAST TURKEY, OR THE DAY AFTER WITH THE COLD SLICED LEFTOVERS.

SERVES 8-10

INGREDIENTS
  2kg/4½lb middle gammon (cured
    ham) joint
  1 large or 2 small onions
  about 30 whole cloves
  3 bay leaves
  10 black peppercorns
  1.3 litres/2¼ pints/5⅔ cups medium-
    dry cider
  45ml/3 tbsp soft light brown sugar
For the cranberry sauce
  350g/12oz/3 cups cranberries
  175g/6oz/¾ cup light brown sugar
  grated rind and juice of 2
    clementines
  30ml/2 tbsp port

1 Weigh the joint and calculate the cooking time at 20 minutes per 450g/1lb, then place it in a large casserole or pan. Stud the onion or onions with 5–10 of the cloves and add to the casserole or pan with the bay leaves and peppercorns.

2 Add 1.2 litres/2 pints/5 cups of the cider and enough water to cover the ham. Heat until simmering and skim off any scum that rises to the surface. Start timing the cooking from the moment the stock begins to simmer.

3 Cover with a lid or foil and simmer gently for the calculated time. Towards the end of the cooking time, preheat the oven to 220°C/425°F/Gas 7.

4 Heat the sugar and remaining cider in a pan; stir until the sugar has completely dissolved.

5 Simmer for 5 minutes to make a dark, sticky glaze. Remove the pan from the heat and leave to cool for 5 minutes.

6 Lift the ham out of the casserole or pan using a slotted spoon and a large fork. Carefully and evenly, cut the rind from the ham, then score the fat into a neat diamond pattern. Place the ham in a roasting pan or ovenproof dish.

7 Press a clove into the centre of each diamond, then carefully spoon over the glaze. Bake for 20–25 minutes, or until the fat is brown, glistening and crisp.

8 Simmer all the cranberry sauce ingredients in a heavy-based saucepan for 15–20 minutes, stirring frequently. Transfer the sauce to a jug (pitcher). Serve the ham accompanied by the cranberry sauce.

Energy 368Kcal/1541kJ; Protein 39.6g; Carbohydrate 15.2g, of which sugars 15.2g; Fat 16.9g, of which saturates 5.6g; Cholesterol 52g; Calcium 25mg; Fibre 0.6g; Sodium 1982mg.

BACON WITH PARSLEY SAUCE

THIS IS A BASIC RECIPE FOR COOKING A LARGE JOINT OF BACON TO TENDER PERFECTION. IN PAST CENTURIES, A BACON JOINT WOULD NEED TO BE SOAKED IN WATER AND RINSED TO EXTRACT THE PRESERVING SALT, BUT THESE DAYS IT CAN BE COOKED AS IT IS IN FLAVOURED STOCK.

SERVES 6-8

INGREDIENTS
  joint of bacon such as corner or
    collar, weighing about 1.35kg/3lb
  1 large onion, thickly sliced
  1 large carrot, thickly sliced
  2 celery sticks, roughly chopped
  6 black peppercorns
  4 whole cloves
  2 bay leaves
  600ml/1 pint/2½ cups milk
  25g/1oz/2 tbsp butter
  25g/1oz/¼ cup plain (all-purpose)
    flour
  fresh parsley, finely chopped
  salt and ground black pepper
  herby mash, to serve

GRANDMOTHER'S TIP
Use the stock from the bacon to make a delicious soup. Simply boil the stock with whatever vegetables you have to hand, potatoes, carrots and peas for example, or a bag of frozen peas for a quick and easy lunch. Add seasoning with care, as the stock is likely to already be salty enough.

1 Put the bacon in a large pan and cover it with cold water. Bring the water to the boil, then drain off and discard it. Replace the bacon in the pan.

2 Add the onion, carrot, celery, peppercorns, cloves and bay leaves to the pan. Pour in enough cold water to cover the bacon by about 2.5cm (1in) or slightly more.

3 Bring slowly to the boil and, if necessary, skim any scum off the surface. Cover and simmer very gently for 1 hour 20 minutes.

4 To make the parsley sauce, put the milk, butter and flour into a pan. Stirring continuously with a whisk, cook over medium heat until the sauce thickens and comes to the boil.

5 Stir the parsley into the sauce and allow it to bubble gently for 1–2 minutes before seasoning to taste with salt and pepper.

6 Lift the bacon joint on to a warmed serving plate, cover with foil and leave to rest for at least 15 minutes before slicing thinly, and serving with the parsley sauce and herby mash.

Energy 467kcal/1937kJ; Protein 32.7g; Carbohydrate 5.7g, of which sugars 3.7g; Fat 34.8g, of which saturates 14.4g; Cholesterol 87mg; Calcium 118mg; Fibre 0.4g; Sodium 2045mg.

SIDE DISHES
AND SALADS

This chapter gives a whole variety of recipes for traditional accompaniments to the main course, from warming dishes of sliced root vegetables to crisp salads fresh from the garden. They will inspire you to try something new to accompany a Sunday roast or a weekday meal.

CELERIAC PURÉE

AN UNUSUAL VEGETABLE, CELERIAC HAS A STRONG FLAVOUR THAT COMBINES WONDERFULLY WELL IN THIS PUREE WITH THE BLANDER TASTE OF POTATOES. THE PUREE IS SHARPENED WITH A LITTLE LEMON JUICE AND BLENDED WITH HOT CREAM FOR A COMFORTING ACCOMPANIMENT TO ROAST MEATS.

SERVES 4

INGREDIENTS

 1 celeriac bulb, peeled
 1 lemon, cut in half
  and squeezed
 2 potatoes, peeled and cut into
  chunks
 300ml/½ pint/1¼ cups double
  (heavy) cream
 salt and ground black pepper
 chopped chives, to garnish

1 Chop the celeriac into chunks, and place in a pan.

2 Add the lemon juice to the pan, dropping the two halves in also.

3 Add the potatoes to the pan and just cover with cold water. Place a disc of baking parchment over the vegetables. Bring to the boil, reduce the heat and simmer for about 20 minutes.

4 Remove the lemon halves and drain through a colander. Return to the pan and allow to steam dry for a few minutes over a low heat.

5 Remove from the heat and purée in a food processor. This mixture can be set aside until you need it.

6 When ready to serve, pour the cream into a pan and bring to the boil. Add the celeriac mixture and stir until heat through. Season, garnish with the chopped chives and serve.

Energy 403kcal/1661kJ; Protein 2.2g; Carbohydrate 7.9g, of which sugars 2.3g; Fat 40.5g, of which saturates 25.1g; Cholesterol 103mg; Calcium 65mg; Fibre 1.1g; Sodium 58mg

FENNEL, POTATO AND GARLIC MASH

THIS DELICIOUS MASH OF POTATO, FENNEL AND GARLIC GOES PARTICULARLY WELL WITH DELICATE FISH SUCH AS TROUT OR SALMON, OR SUCCULENT ROAST CHICKEN. THE WHOLE HEAD OF GARLIC BECOMES LESS STRONG WHEN COOKED, AND COMPLEMENTS THE ANISEED FLAVOUR OF THE FENNEL.

SERVES 4

INGREDIENTS

1 head of garlic, separated into cloves
800g/1¾lb boiling potatoes, cut into chunks
2 large fennel bulbs
65g/2½oz/5 tbsp butter or 90ml/ 6 tbsp extra virgin olive oil
120–150ml/4–5fl oz/½–⅔ cup milk or single (light) cream
freshly grated nutmeg
salt and ground black pepper

VARIATIONS

• To give a stronger fennel flavour, cook 2.5–5ml/½–1 tsp ground fennel seeds with the fennel.

• For a slightly less rich mash, substitute hot stock for some or all of the milk or cream. Mash made with fish stock is particularly good with grilled fish or as a topping for fish pie.

1 If using a food mill to mash the potato, leave the garlic unpeeled, otherwise peel it. Boil the garlic with the potatoes in salted water for 20 minutes.

2 Meanwhile, trim and roughly chop the fennel, reserving any feathery tops. Chop the tops and set them aside.

3 Heat 25g/1oz/2 tbsp of the butter or 30ml/2 tbsp of the oil in a heavy-based saucepan. Add the fennel, cover and cook over a low heat for 20–30 minutes, until soft but not browned.

4 Drain and mash the potatoes and garlic. Purée the fennel in a food mill or blender and beat it into the potato with the remaining butter or olive oil.

5 Warm the milk or cream and beat sufficient into the potato and fennel to make a creamy, light mixture. Season to taste and add a little grated nutmeg.

6 Reheat gently, then beat in any chopped fennel tops. Transfer to a warmed dish and serve immediately.

GRANDMOTHER'S TIP
A food mill is good for mashing potatoes as it ensures a smooth texture. Never mash potatoes in a food processor or blender as this releases the starch, giving an overprocessed result that resembles wallpaper paste.

Energy 144Kcal/608kJ; Protein 4g; Carbohydrate 24.4g, of which sugars 4.6g; Fat 4.1g, of which saturates 2.3g; Cholesterol 10mg; Calcium 60mg; Fibre 4g; Sodium 61mg.

POTATO AND ONION GRATIN

THIS IS A SIMPLE WAY OF COOKING TWO MAINSTAYS OF THE KITCHEN GARDEN, POTATOES AND ONIONS, TOGETHER IN A DELICIOUS GRATIN. CHOOSE STOCK TO COMPLEMENT THE MAIN DISH THAT IT IS ACCOMPANYING. THE GARLIC CAN BE OMITTED FOR A MILDER FLAVOUR, IF YOU WISH.

SERVES 4–6

INGREDIENTS
  40g/1½oz/3 tbsp butter or bacon fat,
    or 45ml/3 tbsp olive oil
  2–4 garlic cloves, finely chopped
  900g/2lb waxy potatoes, thinly sliced
  450g/1lb onions, thinly sliced
  450ml/3⁄4 pint/scant 2 cups fish,
    chicken, beef or lamb stock
  salt and ground black pepper

VARIATIONS
• For a main course, layer thinly sliced cheese and rashers of bacon with the potatoes. About 15–20 minutes before the end of cooking time, sprinkle the gratin with another 50g/2oz/½ cup grated cheese, dot with more butter and finish baking. Serve with a green salad.
• For a simple topping, crumble 165g/5½oz soft goat's cheese on the gratin 15 minutes before the end of cooking.

1 Use half the butter, bacon fat or oil to grease a 1.5 litre/2½ pint/6¼ cup gratin dish. Preheat the oven to 180°C/350°F/Gas 4.

2 Sprinkle a little of the chopped garlic over the base of the dish and then layer the potatoes and onions in the dish, seasoning each layer with a little salt and pepper and adding the remaining garlic. Finish with a layer of overlapping potato slices on top.

3 Bring the stock to the boil in a saucepan and pour it over the gratin. Dot the top with the remaining butter or bacon fat, cut into pieces, or drizzle the remaining olive oil over the top. Cover the gratin tightly with foil and bake for 1½ hours.

4 Increase the oven temperature to 200°C/400°F/Gas 6. Uncover the gratin and then cook for a further 35–50 minutes, until the potatoes are completely cooked and the top layer is browned and crusty. Serve immediately.

Energy 181Kcal/762kJ; Protein 3.5g; Carbohydrate 30.1g, of which sugars 6.2g; Fat 6.1g, of which saturates 3.8g; Cholesterol 15mg; Calcium 29mg; Fibre 2.6g; Sodium 69mg.

JERUSALEM ARTICHOKES ᴬᵁ GRATIN

THESE STRANGE-LOOKING, KNOBBLY ROOT VEGETABLES ARE NOT RELATED TO GLOBE ARTICHOKES, BUT TO THE SUNFLOWER, AND WERE MUCH MORE POPULAR IN THE PAST. THEY ABSORB THE RICHNESS OF THE CREAM AND SOUR CREAM TO MAKE THIS DISH A REAL WINTER WARMER.

SERVES 4

INGREDIENTS

    250ml/8fl oz/1 cup sour cream
    50ml/2fl oz/¼ cup single (light) cream
    675g/1½ lb Jerusalem artichokes, coarsely chopped
    40g/1½ oz/½ cup mature Cheddar cheese, grated
    60ml/4 tbsp fresh breadcrumbs
    salt

1 Preheat the oven to 190°C/375°F/Gas 5. Lightly grease an ovenproof dish. Stir together the sour cream and single cream in a mixing bowl and season with salt.

2 Add the chopped Jerusalem artichokes to the cream and toss to coat evenly with the mixture. Spread the artichokes over the bottom of the prepared dish.

3 Sprinkle evenly with the cheese, then the breadcrumbs. Bake for about 30 minutes, until the cheese melts and the top is brown and bubbling.

GRANDMOTHER'S TIP
This is a very good way of using up any leftover cheese, as you can mix varieties depending on what you have. Try Parmesan mixed with Cheshire or Red Leicester, or add a sharper tang with some Wensleydale. You can also use blue cheese such as Stilton inside the gratin, but use a grated hard cheese on top.

Energy 296kcal/1230kJ; Protein 6.9g; Carbohydrate 27.6g, of which sugars 15.5g; Fat 18.1g, of which saturates 11.1g; Cholesterol 52mg; Calcium 186mg; Fibre 4.4g; Sodium 240mg.

ONION CAKE

THIS SIMPLE BUT DELICIOUS RECIPE WAS ONCE A FAMILY FAVOURITE, WHICH CAN BE SERVED AS A MAIN DISH IN ITS OWN RIGHT. IT ALSO GOES WONDERFULLY WELL WITH SAUSAGES, CHOPS OR ROAST MEAT. THE COOKING TIME DEPENDS ON THE SIZE AND VARIETY OF THE POTATOES.

SERVES 6

INGREDIENTS

900g/2lb new potatoes, peeled and
  thinly sliced
2 medium onions, very finely
  chopped
salt and ground black pepper
about 115g/4oz/½ cup butter

1 Preheat the oven to 190°C/375°F/ Gas 5. Butter a 20cm/8in round cake tin (pan) and line the base with a circle of baking parchment.

2 Arrange a single layer of potato slices to fill the bottom of the tin and then sprinkle some of the chopped onions over them. Season.

3 Reserve 25g/1oz/2 tbsp of the butter and dot the onion layer with half of the remaining butter, cut into cubes.

4 Repeat these layers, using up all the ingredients, and finishing with an overlapping layer of potatoes.

5 Melt the reserved butter and brush it over the top. Cover with foil and cook for 1–1½ hours, until tender and golden. Remove from the oven and leave to stand, covered, for 10–15 minutes, then turn out the onion cake on to a warmed plate and serve.

Energy 272kcal/1133kJ; Protein 3.5g; Carbohydrate 29.5g, of which sugars 5.8g; Fat 16.3g, of which saturates 10.1g; Cholesterol 41mg; Calcium 29mg; Fibre 2.4g; Sodium 135mg.

CAULIFLOWER CHEESE

THIS RECIPE IS A TRUE STAPLE OF TRADITIONAL COOKERY. IT IS ANOTHER DISH THAT CAN BE SERVED AS A MAIN COURSE OR AS A SIDE VEGETABLE WITH A SPLENDID SUNDAY ROAST. IT NEEDS A GOOD OLD-FASHIONED CHEESE SUCH AS MATURE CHEDDAR TO MAKE IT REALLY MOUTHWATERING.

SERVES 4

INGREDIENTS
  1 medium cauliflower
  25g/1oz/2 tbsp butter
  25g/1oz/4 tbsp plain (all-purpose)
    flour
  300ml/½ pint/1¼ cups milk
  115g/4oz mature Cheddar or
    Cheshire cheese, grated
  salt and ground black pepper

1 Trim the cauliflower and cut it into florets. Bring a large pan of lightly salted water to the boil.

2 Drop the cauliflower florets into the pan and cook for 5–8 minutes or until just tender. When cooked, drain the florets, tip into an ovenproof dish, and keep warm.

3 To make the sauce, melt the butter in a pan, stir in the flour and cook gently, stirring constantly, for about 1 minute.

4 Remove from the heat and gradually stir in the milk. Return the pan to the heat and cook, stirring, until the mixture thickens and comes to the boil. Simmer gently for 1–2 minutes.

5 Stir in three-quarters of the cheese and season to taste. Spoon the sauce over the cauliflower and scatter the remaining cheese on top. Put under a hot grill (broiler) until golden brown.

GRANDMOTHER'S TIP
Boost the flavour by adding a little English (hot) mustard to the sauce.

Energy 318kcal/1318kJ; Protein 17.4g; Carbohydrate 4.4g, of which sugars 3.9g; Fat 25.8g, of which saturates 16.3g; Cholesterol 71mg; Calcium 371mg; Fibre 1.8g; Sodium 453mg.

CREAMED LEEKS

THIS DISH IS A COMFORTING AND YET SIMPLE WINTER TREAT, BLENDING THE ONION FLAVOUR OF THE LEEKS WITH A CREAMY SAUCE. LOOK FOR LEEKS THAT ARE FAIRLY YOUNG AND FRESH, AS THEY WILL BE FIRM AND MELLOW-FLAVOURED, WITH NO TOUGH CORE.

2 Melt the butter in a large pan and when melted add the leeks, stirring to coat them in the butter, and heat through. They will wilt but should not exude water. You need to create a balance between steaming the water out of the vegetable, so they stay bright green, but not burning the leeks.

3 Keeping the heat high, pour the cream in to the leeks, mix in thoroughly, making sure they are all coated with cream, and allow to bubble and reduce slightly.

4 Season to taste with salt and ground black pepper.

5 When the texture is smooth and creamy the leeks are ready to serve.

SERVES 4

INGREDIENTS
  2 large leeks, tops trimmed and roots
    removed
  50g/2oz/½ stick butter
  200ml/7fl oz/scant 1 cup double
    (heavy) cream
  salt and ground black pepper

VARIATION
Although these leeks have a wonderful taste themselves, you may like to add extra flavourings, such as a little chopped garlic or some chopped fresh tarragon or thyme.

1 Split the leeks down the middle then cut across so you make pieces approximately 2cm/¾in square. Wash thoroughly and drain in a colander.

GRANDMOTHER'S TIP
You can make this with whole baby leeks, but make sure you clean them well. Cut the leeks down through the middle, hold upside down under cold running water, and fan out the layers.

Energy 363kcal/1496kJ; Protein 2.5g; Carbohydrate 3.8g, of which sugars 3.1g; Fat 37.6g, of which saturates 23.3g; Cholesterol 95mg; Calcium 51mg; Fibre 2.2g; Sodium 89mg.

BRAISED LEEKS WITH CARROTS

SWEET, NEW SEASON CARROTS AND LEEKS GO WELL TOGETHER AND TASTE EVEN BETTER SPRINKLED WITH SOME CHOPPED HERBS FROM THE GARDEN. THIS RECIPE WORKS WELL AS A SIDE DISH WITH ROAST BEEF, AND TRANSFORMS TWO EVERYDAY VEGETABLES INTO SOMETHING SPECIAL.

SERVES 6

INGREDIENTS
    65g/2½oz/5 tbsp butter
    675g/1½lb carrots, thickly sliced
    2 fresh bay leaves
    caster (superfine) sugar
    75ml/5 tbsp water
    675g/1½lb leeks, cut into 5cm/
        2in lengths
    120ml/4fl oz/½ cup white wine
    30ml/2 tbsp chopped fresh mint,
        chervil or parsley
    salt and ground black pepper

1 Melt 25g/1oz/2 tbsp of the butter in a pan and cook the carrots gently, without allowing them to brown, for 4–5 minutes.

2 Add the bay leaves, seasoning, a good pinch of sugar and water. Bring to the boil, cover and cook for 10–15 minutes, until tender. Uncover, then boil until the juices have evaporated, leaving the carrots moist and glazed.

3 Meanwhile, melt another 25g/1oz/ 2 tbsp of the remaining butter in a frying pan large enough to take the leeks in a single layer. Fry the leeks in the butter over a low heat for 4–5 minutes, without browning them.

4 Add seasoning, a good pinch of sugar, the wine and half the chopped herbs. Heat until simmering, then cover and cook gently for 5–8 minutes, until the leeks are tender, but not collapsed.

5 Uncover the leeks and turn them in the buttery juices. Increase the heat, then boil the liquid rapidly until reduced to a few tablespoons. Add the carrots to the leeks and reheat them gently, then swirl in the remaining butter.

6 Adjust the seasoning, if necessary. Transfer to a warmed serving dish and serve, sprinkled with the remaining chopped herbs.

VARIATION
Braised leeks in tarragon cream
Cook 900g/2lb leeks in 40g/1½oz/3 tbsp butter as above. Season, add a pinch of sugar, 45ml/3 tbsp tarragon vinegar, 6 fresh tarragon sprigs or 5ml/1 tsp dried tarragon, and 60ml/4 tbsp white wine. Cover and cook as above. Add 150ml/ ¼ pint/⅔ cup double cream and allow to bubble and thicken. Adjust the seasoning and serve, sprinkled with chopped fresh tarragon. A spoonful of tarragon-flavoured mustard is good stirred into these leeks.

Energy 163Kcal/677kJ; Protein 3.8g; Carbohydrate 18.5g, of which sugars 16.4g; Fat 6.5g, of which saturates 3.6g; Cholesterol 13g; Calcium 87mg; Fibre 7.8g; Sodium 85mg.

POTATO SALAD

THIS RECIPE IS BEST MADE WITH FRESH NEW POTATOES IN SUMMER SO THAT THEY HOLD THEIR SHAPE.
ANY WAXY SALAD VARIETY WILL DO, SO LONG AS THEY DO NOT BECOME FLOURY AFTER COOKING.
THE SOUR CREAM DRESSING IS FAR SUPERIOR TO SHOP-BOUGHT MAYONNAISE.

SERVES 6–8

INGREDIENTS
1.8kg/4lb potatoes
45ml/3 tbsp finely chopped onion
2 celery sticks, finely chopped
250ml/8fl oz/1 cup sour cream
250ml/8fl oz/1 cup mayonnaise
5ml/1 tsp mustard powder
4ml/¾ tsp celery seed
75ml/5 tbsp chopped fresh dill
salt and ground white pepper

1 Boil the potatoes in lightly salted water for 20–25 minutes, until tender, then drain and allow to cool.

2 Peel and coarsely chop the potatoes and place them in a large mixing bowl. Add the onion and celery.

3 In a separate bowl, stir together the sour cream, mayonnaise, mustard, celery seed, dill, salt and pepper.

4 Add the dressing to the potatoes and toss gently to coat evenly with the dressing. Adjust the seasoning, cover the bowl and chill until ready to serve.

GRANDMOTHER'S TIP
Add chopped cucumber, crumbled bacon rashers (strips), or chopped hard-boiled eggs to the potato salad.

Energy 440kcal/1834kJ; Protein 5.2g; Carbohydrate 38.5g, of which sugars 4.9g; Fat 30.5g, of which saturates 7.7g; Cholesterol 42mg; Calcium 50mg; Fibre 2.4g; Sodium 183mg.

CUCUMBER SALAD

THIS IS A PERFECT RECIPE FOR USING UP A GLUT OF CUCUMBERS FROM THE COLD FRAME. UNLIKE MANY SALADS, IT CAN BE PREPARED AND DRESSED WELL IN ADVANCE, CHILLED AND SERVED WITH ANY DELICATE MAIN COURSE. IT GOES PARTICULARLY WELL WITH SALMON.

SERVES 4–6

INGREDIENTS
    2 medium cucumbers
    2.5ml/½ tsp salt
    120ml/4fl oz/½ cup sour cream
    juice from ½ lemon
    2.5ml/½ tsp sugar (optional)
    1.5ml/¼ tsp ground black pepper
    15ml/1 tbsp chopped chives, to
      garnish

GRANDMOTHER'S TIP
This fresh summer salad makes a lovely accompaniment to poached salmon, and can be garnished with chopped dill instead of chives.

1 Peel the cucumbers, slice them thinly and place in a sieve (strainer). Sprinkle over the salt, leave for a few minutes, then rinse to remove the salt and pat dry with kitchen paper.

2 To make the dressing, mix together the sour cream, lemon juice, sugar and pepper. Add to the cucumber, then chill in the refrigerator for 1 hour. Garnish with chives before serving.

Energy 48kcal/196kJ; Protein 1.1g; Carbohydrate 1.8g, of which sugars 1.7g; Fat 4.1g, of which saturates 2.5g; Cholesterol 12mg; Calcium 31mg; Fibre 0.4g; Sodium 10mg.

FRESH SPRING SALAD

THIS CLASSIC ENGLISH SALAD CAN BE SERVED AS AN ACCOMPANIMENT TO MOST COLD MEAT AND FISH DISHES. SLICED HARD-BOILED EGGS NESTLE INTO CRISP LETTUCE ALONGSIDE CUCUMBER, RADISHES, SPRING ONIONS AND HERBS FROM THE GARDEN, WITH A SHARP LEMONY DRESSING.

SERVES 4

INGREDIENTS
  2 eggs
  1 large cos or romaine lettuce
  1 cucumber
  10 radishes
  1 bunch spring onions (scallions)
  45ml/3 tbsp roughly chopped fresh
    dill, to garnish
For the dressing
  200ml/7fl oz/scant 1 cup crème
    fraîche
  juice of 1 lemon
  15ml/1 tbsp caster (superfine)
    sugar
  pinch of salt

GRANDMOTHER'S TIP
Prepare this salad no more than 1 hour before serving and add the dressing just before it is served.

1 First make the dressing. Put the crème fraîche and lemon juice in a bowl and whisk together. Add the sugar and salt to the bowl, and stir until the sugar is dissolved. Set aside.

2 Put the eggs in a pan, cover with water and bring to the boil. Reduce the heat to low, and simmer for 10 minutes. Drain and put under cold running water. Remove the shells and slice the eggs.

3 Using a sharp knife, cut the lettuce into 5–6cm/2–2½in pieces and put in a serving dish. Peel and finely slice the cucumber, slice the radishes and finely slice the spring onions.

4 Place the cucumber on top of the shredded lettuce, then the radishes, then the egg and finally the spring onions. Spoon the dressing over, garnish with dill and serve immediately.

Energy 268kcal/1107kJ; Protein 6g; Carbohydrate 8.7g, of which sugars 8.5g; Fat 23.5g, of which saturates 14.5g; Cholesterol 152mg; Calcium 96mg; Fibre 1.8g; Sodium 55mg.

BEETROOT SALAD

THIS SIMPLE RECIPE IS MUCH EASIER THAN PICKLING, AND CREATES A LIGHTER, FRESHER TASTING ACCOMPANIMENT, WHICH CAN BE SERVED WITH SIMPLY COOKED, OR SMOKED, FIRM-TEXTURED OILY FISH SUCH AS MACKEREL OR TROUT. IT WILL ALSO KEEP FOR A FEW DAYS IN THE REFRIGERATOR.

SERVES 4

INGREDIENTS

    450g/1lb evenly-sized raw
      beetroot (beets)
    grated rind and juice of ½ lemon
    about 150ml/¼ pint/⅔ cup extra
      virgin olive oil (or a mixture of
      olive and sunflower oil, blended
      to taste)
    sea salt and ground black pepper

GRANDMOTHER'S TIP
To avoid the beetroots 'bleeding' during cooking, twist off the tops rather than cutting them with a knife. Peeling them after they are cooked also helps to stop the red juices draining out.

1 Twist off the tops from the beetroot (see Grandmother's tip), and cook in a large pan of salted boiling water for about 30 minutes, or until the beetroot is tender. Pinch the skin between two fingers: when cooked, the skin will come away easily. Drain the beetroot and allow it to cool.

2 Peel when cool and slice into wedges into a bowl. Add the lemon rind and juice, and the oil; season to taste. Mix gently in the dressing and serve.

VARIATION
Serve as a side dish or a first course, with a crème fraîche and chive dressing.

Energy 265Kcal/1097kJ; Protein 1.9g; Carbohydrate 8.6g, of which sugars 7.9g; Fat 25.1g, of which saturates 3.6g; Cholesterol 0mg; Calcium 23mg; Fibre 2.2g; Sodium 74mg.

DESSERTS

*Nothing quite beats a proper pudding at the end
of a meal, and it brings a smile to everyone's
face, from the youngest to the oldest. This
chapter holds a whole treasure trove of
favourite desserts and puddings from past
times to be explored — hot pies, crumbles,
sponges and suet puddings, as well as chilled
fruit fools and sorbets — something for
every occasion and every season.*

DEEP-DISH APPLE PIE

PERHAPS THE DESSERT WE MOST ASSOCIATE WITH HOME, NO-ONE CAN RESIST A REALLY GOOD APPLE PIE, TOPPED WITH CRUMBLY HOME-MADE SHORTCRUST PASTRY. IN THIS RECIPE THE APPLES ARE TOSSED IN CARAMEL BUTTER BEFORE BAKING TO MAKE THEM EVEN MORE IRRESISTIBLE.

2 Peel, core and thickly slice the apples. Melt the butter in a frying pan, add the sugar and cook for 3–4 minutes, until melted and caramelized.

3 Add the apples to the pan and stir around to coat. Cook over a brisk heat until the apples take on a little colour, add the spice mixture and tip out into a bowl to cool slightly.

4 Divide the pastry in two and, on a lightly floured surface, roll into two rounds to fit a deep 23cm/9in pie plate. Line the plate with one round of pastry. Spoon in the apples and mound up in the centre.

SERVES 6

INGREDIENTS
  900g/2lb eating apples
  75g/3oz/6 tbsp unsalted butter
  45–60ml/3–4 tbsp demerara
    (raw) sugar
  2.5ml/½ tsp mixed (apple pie)
    spice
For the pastry
  250g/9oz/2¼ cups plain
    (all-purpose) flour
  pinch of salt
  50g/2oz/¼ cup white cooking fat,
    chilled and diced
  75g/3oz/6 tbsp unsalted butter,
    chilled and diced
  30–45ml/2–3 tbsp chilled water
  a little milk, for brushing
  caster (superfine) sugar,
    for dredging

1 Preheat the oven to 200°C/400°F/ Gas 6. Make the pastry first. Sift the flour and salt into a bowl. Rub in the fat and butter until the mixture resembles fine breadcrumbs. Stir in enough chilled water to bring the pastry together. Knead lightly then wrap in cling film (plastic wrap) and chill for 30 minutes.

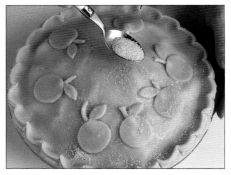

5 Cover with the remaining pastry, sealing and crimping the edges. Make a slit on the top of the pastry to allow steam to escape. Brush the pie with milk and dredge with caster sugar.

6 Bake in the oven for 25–35 minutes until golden and firm. Serve with clotted cream or ice cream.

Energy 591Kcal/2488kJ; Protein 7.4g; Carbohydrate 89.9g, of which sugars 39.8g; Fat 25g, of which saturates 15.3g; Cholesterol 62mg; Calcium 117mg; Fibre 4.4g; Sodium 193mg.

BAKEWELL TART

THIS TRADITIONAL TART COMES ORIGINALLY FROM THE DERBYSHIRE VILLAGE OF BAKEWELL, WHERE IT IS KNOWN AS BAKEWELL PUDDING. A CRISP PASTRY SHELL IS TOPPED WITH JAM AND THEN A LIGHT ALMOND SPONGE. IT CAN BE SERVED AT TEA TIME OR AS A SPECIAL DESSERT WITH CREAM.

SERVES 4

INGREDIENTS
   225g/8oz puff pastry
   30ml/2 tbsp raspberry or apricot
    jam
   2 eggs, plus 2 egg yolks
   115g/4oz/½ cup caster (superfine)
    sugar
   115g/4oz/½ cup butter, melted
   50g/2oz/⅔ cup ground almonds
   a few drops of almond extract
   icing (confectioners') sugar,
    for dusting

1 Preheat the oven to 200°C/400°F Gas 6. Roll out the pastry on a lightly floured surface and use to line an 18cm/7in pie plate. Trim the edge.

2 Prick the pastry case all over, then spread the jam over the base. Collect up the pastry trimmings.

3 Re-roll the trimmings and cut out wide strips of pastry. Use these to decorate the edge of the pastry case by gently twisting them around the rim, joining the strips together as necessary. Brushing the edge with a little milk first will help the pastry hold.

GRANDMOTHER'S TIP
Since this pastry case is not baked blind before being filled, place a baking sheet in the oven while it preheats, then place the tart on the hot sheet. This will ensure that the base of the pastry case cooks right through.

4 Whisk the eggs, egg yolks and sugar together in a bowl until the mixture is thick and pale. Gently stir the melted butter, ground almonds and almond essence into the whisked egg mixture.

5 Pour the mixture into the pastry case and bake for 30 minutes, or until the filling is just set and is lightly browned. Dust with icing sugar before serving hot, warm or cold.

Energy 700Kcal/2919kJ; Protein 10.8g; Carbohydrate 57.1g, of which sugars 36.7g; Fat 49.9g, of which saturates 17.1g; Cholesterol 257g; Calcium 110mg; Fibre 0.9g; Sodium 394mg.

FRESH PLUM TART

THIS SPECIAL DESSERT WOULD WORK SPLENDIDLY AS THE FINAL FLOURISH AFTER A FAMILY SUNDAY DINNER. THE CIRCLES OF SLICED PLUMS ARE SET IN A TASTY SWEET YEAST DOUGH, WHICH IS A LITTLE MORE COMPLICATED TO MAKE THAN A PASTRY CASE, BUT IS WELL WORTH THE EXTRA EFFORT.

SERVES 6–8

INGREDIENTS
  250g/9oz/2¼ cups plain (all-purpose) flour, plus extra for dusting
  50g/2oz/¼ cup caster (superfine) sugar
  15ml/1 tbsp easy-blend (rapid-rise) dried yeast
  2.5ml/½ tsp salt
  1 egg, beaten
  100ml/3½fl oz/scant ½ cup milk
  50–75g/2–3oz/4–6 tbsp unsalted butter, softened
For the filling
  675g/1½lb fresh ripe plums, quartered
  60ml/4 tbsp soft light brown sugar
  15ml/1 tbsp ground cinnamon
  15ml/1 tbsp rum or dessert wine
  5ml/1 tsp cornflour (cornstarch)

1 Sift the flour into a large mixing bowl. Stir in the sugar, dried yeast and salt. Make a well in the centre and pour in the beaten egg and half the milk.

2 Stir, gradually incorporating the dry ingredients until the mixture starts to hold together. Add the extra milk, if needed. Finally add the softened butter and mix with your fingertips to a soft dough.

3 On a lightly floured surface, knead the dough lightly, form it into a ball and place in a large, lightly oiled bowl. Cover with clear film (plastic wrap) and leave to rise in a warm, draught-free place for about 30 minutes or until doubled in bulk.

4 Preheat the oven to 220°C/425°F/ Gas 7. Grease a 23cm/9in loose-bottomed tart or flan tin (pan) and dust it lightly with flour.

5 Meanwhile, prepare the filling. Put the plums in a bowl. Sprinkle with 45ml/3 tbsp of the brown sugar and two-thirds of the cinnamon. Add the rum or dessert wine, and leave to stand while the dough is rising.

6 Knock back (punch down) the dough. Roll it out on a lightly floured surface and line the tart or flan tin (pan) without stretching the dough. Trim and crimp the edges and prick the base of the pastry case (pie shell) with a fork. Sprinkle the base with the remaining brown sugar and cinnamon, then leave to stand for 15 minutes.

7 Sift the cornflour over the plums, then layer them in the pastry case. Place the tin on a hot baking sheet in the oven. Bake for 30–45 minutes or until the pie is cooked and the pastry is golden brown.

8 Leave to cool on a wire rack for about 15 minutes before removing from the tin. Serve immediately, in slices.

VARIATION
Instead of plums, try other fruits for this tart, such as apricots, cherries, berries, apples or pears.

Energy 304kcal/1285kJ; Protein 5.9g; Carbohydrate 57.5g, of which sugars 23.6g; Fat 6.7g, of which saturates 3.7g; Cholesterol 38mg; Calcium 100mg; Fibre 2.7g; Sodium 56mg.

SWEET APPLE CAKE WITH HOMEMADE CUSTARD

SWEET EATING APPLES ARE BEST FOR MAKING THIS SPECIAL CAKE. THE SPICED APPLE LAYER IS BAKED UNDER A VERY LIGHT ALMOND SPONGE AND IT IS SERVED WITH A DELECTABLE FRESH CUSTARD. THIS IS AN OLD-FASHIONED RECIPE DESIGNED TO MAKE BEST USE OF AN APPLE GLUT IN THE AUTUMN.

SERVES 6-8

INGREDIENTS
   115g/4½oz/½ cup plus 1 tbsp
      unsalted (sweet) butter
   7 eating apples
   200g/7oz/1 cup caster (superfine)
      sugar, plus 30ml/2 tbsp extra
   10ml/2 tsp ground cinnamon
   2 egg yolks and 3 egg whites
   100g/4oz/1 cup ground almonds
   grated rind and juice of ½ lemon
For the vanilla cream
   250ml/8fl oz/1 cup milk
   250ml/8fl oz/1 cup double (heavy)
      cream
   15ml/1 tbsp sugar
   1 vanilla pod (bean), split
   4 egg yolks, beaten

1 Preheat the oven to 180°C/350°F/Gas 4. Butter a 20cm/8in flan tin (pan) using 15g/½oz/1 tbsp of the butter. Peel, core and thinly slice the apples and put the slices in a bowl.

2 Add 30ml/2 tbsp caster sugar and cinnamon to the apples, mix together, then transfer the spiced apples to the prepared tin and spread evenly.

3 Put the remaining butter and sugar in a bowl and whisk them together until they are light and fluffy.

4 Beat the egg yolks, one at a time, into the sugar and butter mixture, then stir in the ground almonds and lemon rind and juice.

5 Whisk the egg whites until stiff then fold into the mixture. Pour the mixture over the apples in the flan tin. Bake in the oven for about 40 minutes until golden brown.

6 Meanwhile, make the custard. Put the milk, cream, sugar and vanilla pod in a pan and heat gently. Add a little of the warm milk mixture to the eggs then slowly add the egg mixture to the pan and continue to heat gently, stirring all the time, until the mixture thickens. Do not allow the mixture to boil or it will curdle.

7 Remove the vanilla pod and serve the custard with the apple cake.

Energy 541kcal/2254kJ; Protein 7.6g; Carbohydrate 39.7g, of which sugars 39.3g; Fat 40.3g, of which saturates 20g; Cholesterol 227mg; Calcium 122mg; Fibre 2.1g; Sodium 135mg.

LEMON MERINGUE PIE

THIS IS SURELY ONE OF THE MOST POPULAR ITEMS ON THE DESSERT MENU. THE FRESH LEMONY FLAVOUR WAS ESPECIALLY RELISHED AFTER WARTIME RATIONING, WHEN AT LAST LEMONS, SUGAR AND EGGS BECAME PLENTIFUL ONCE MORE AND THIS DELIGHTFUL PIE WAS REDISCOVERED.

SERVES 6

INGREDIENTS
For the pastry
  115g/4oz/1 cup plain (all-purpose)
    flour
  pinch of salt
  25g/1oz/2 tbsp lard, diced
  25g/1oz/2 tbsp butter, diced
For the filling
  50g/2oz/¼ cup cornflour (cornstarch)
  175g/6oz/¾ cup caster (superfine)
    sugar
  finely grated rind and juice of
    2 lemons
  2 egg yolks
  15g/½oz/1 tbsp butter, diced
For the meringue topping
  2 egg whites
  75g/3oz/½ cup caster
    (superfine) sugar

1 To make the pastry, sift the flour and salt into a bowl and add the lard and butter. With the fingertips, lightly rub the fats into the flour until the mixture resembles fine crumbs.

2 Stir in about 20ml/2 tbsp cold water until the mixture can be gathered together into a smooth ball of dough. (Alternatively, make the pastry using a food processor.)

3 Wrap the pastry and refrigerate for at least 30 minutes. Meanwhile, preheat the oven to 200°C/400°F/Gas 6.

4 Roll out the pastry on a lightly floured surface and use to line a 20cm/8in flan tin (pan). Prick the base with a fork, line with baking parchment or foil and bake in the oven for 15 minutes.

5 Remove the parchment or foil, return the pastry to the oven and cook for a further 5 minutes. Reduce the temperature to 150°C/300°F/Gas 2.

6 To make the lemon filling, put the cornflour into a pan and add the sugar, lemon rind and 300ml/½ pint/1¼ cups water. Heat the mixture, stirring, until it comes to the boil and thickens. Reduce the heat and simmer very gently for 1 minute. Remove the pan from the heat and stir in the lemon juice.

7 Add the the egg yolks to the lemon mixture, one at a time and beating after each addition, and then stir in the butter. Pour the mixture into the pastry case (pie shell and level the surface.

8 To make the meringue topping, whisk the egg whites until stiff peaks form, then whisk in half the sugar. Fold in the rest of the sugar using a metal spoon. Spread the meringue over the lemon filling, covering it completely. Cook for about 20 minutes until lightly browned.

Energy 357Kcal/1497kJ; Protein 6.8g; Carbohydrate 42.8g, of which sugars 25.1g; Fat 18.9g, of which saturates 9g; Cholesterol 129mg; Calcium 108mg; Fibre 0.7g; Sodium 137mg.

TREACLE TART

TRADITIONAL HOME-MADE SHORTCRUST PASTRY IS PERFECT FOR THIS OLD-FASHIONED FAVOURITE. THE STICKY LEMON-FLAVOURED SYRUP FILLING IS TOPPED WITH TWISTED LATTICES OF LEFTOVER PASTRY FOR A REALLY AUTHENTIC LOOK. IT CAN BE SERVED WARM OR COLD WITH CUSTARD OR CREAM.

SERVES 4-6

INGREDIENTS

    260g/9½oz/generous ¾ cup golden
      (light corn) syrup
    75g/3oz/1½ cups fresh
      white breadcrumbs
    grated rind of 1 lemon
    30ml/2 tbsp lemon juice
For the pastry
    150g/5oz/1¼ cups plain (all-purpose)
      flour
    2.5ml/½ tsp salt
    130g/4½oz/9 tbsp chilled butter,
      diced
    45–60/3–4 tbsp chilled water

1 To make the pastry, combine the flour and salt in a bowl. Rub or cut in the butter until the mixture resembles coarse breadcrumbs.

2 With a fork, stir in just enough water to bind the dough. Gather into a smooth ball, knead lightly for a few seconds until smooth, then wrap in clear film (plastic wrap) and chill for 20 minutes.

3 On a lightly floured surface, roll out the pastry to a thickness of 3mm/⅛in. Transfer to a 20cm/8in fluted flan tin (quiche pan) and trim off the overhang. Chill the pastry case (pie shell), for 20 minutes. Reserve the pastry trimmings.

4 Put a baking sheet in the oven and preheat to 200°C/400°F/Gas 6. To make the filling, begin by warming the syrup in a pan until it melts.

5 Remove the syrup from the heat and stir in the breadcrumbs and lemon rind. Leave to stand for 10 minutes, then add more breadcrumbs if the mixture is too thin and moist. Stir in the lemon juice, then spread the mixture evenly in the pastry case.

6 Roll out the pastry trimmings and cut into 10–12 thin strips.

7 Twist the strips into spirals, then lay half of them on the filling. Arrange the remaining strips at right angles to form a lattice. Press the ends on to the rim.

8 Place the tart on the hot baking sheet and bake for 10 minutes. Lower the oven temperature to 190°C/375°F/Gas 5. Bake for 15 minutes more, until golden. Serve warm or cold.

Energy 420Kcal/1764kJ; Protein 4.1g; Carbohydrate 63.5g, of which sugars 35.1g; Fat 18.4g, of which saturates 11.3g; Cholesterol 46g; Calcium 62mg; Fibre 1.1g; Sodium 344mg.

ONE-CRUST RHUBARB PIE

THIS IS SUCH AN EASY PIE TO MAKE, AND IT CAN BE FILLED WITH ALL KINDS OF FRUIT. IT DOESN'T MATTER HOW ROUGH THE PIE LOOKS WHEN IT GOES INTO THE OVEN — THE UNEVENNESS OF THE PASTRY IS PART OF ITS CHARM. TOPPED WITH A SPRINKLING OF SUGAR, IT IS THE PERFECT RUSTIC PUDDING.

SERVES 6

INGREDIENTS
- 350g/12oz ready-made shortcrust pastry, thawed if frozen
- 1 egg yolk, beaten
- 25g/1oz/3 tbsp semolina
- 25g/1oz/¼ cup hazelnuts, coarsely chopped
- 30ml/2 tbsp golden granulated sugar

For the filling
- 450g/1lb rhubarb, cut into 2.5cm/1in pieces
- 75g/3oz/⅓ cup caster (superfine) sugar
- 1–2 pieces stem ginger in syrup, drained and finely chopped

GRANDMOTHER'S TIP
Egg yolk glaze brushed on to pastry gives it a nice golden sheen. However, be careful not to drip the glaze on the baking sheet, or it will burn.

1 Preheat the oven to 200°C/400°F/ Gas 6. Roll out the pastry to a circle 35cm/14in across. Lay it over the rolling pin and transfer it to a large baking sheet. Brush a little egg yolk over the pastry. Scatter the semolina over the centre, leaving a wide rim all round.

2 Make the filling. Place the rhubarb pieces, caster sugar and chopped ginger in a large bowl and mix well.

3 Pile the rhubarb mixture into the middle of the pastry. Fold the rim roughly over the filling so that it almost covers it. Some of the fruit will remain visible in the centre.

4 Glaze the pastry rim with any remaining egg yolk and scatter the hazelnuts and golden sugar over. Bake for 30–35 minutes or until the pastry is golden brown. Serve warm.

Energy 389Kcal/1633kJ; Protein 5.6g; Carbohydrate 49.7g, of which sugars 19.6g; Fat 20.1g, of which saturates 5.6g; Cholesterol 42g; Calcium 139mg; Fibre 2.5g; Sodium 239mg.

APPLE AND BLACKBERRY CRUMBLE

AUTUMN HERALDS THE HARVEST OF APPLES AND OTHER SUCCULENT FRUITS. THE PERFECT COMPANION TO THE SWEET APPLES IS A BASKET OF TART LITTLE BLACKBERRIES FROM THE FIELD EDGES. FINELY TEXTURED OATMEAL IS ADDED TO THE CRUMBLE TOPPING FOR AN EXTRA NUTRITIOUS CRUNCH.

SERVES 6–8

INGREDIENTS
900g/2lb cooking apples
450g/1lb/4 cups blackberries
squeeze of lemon juice (optional)
175g/6oz/scant 1 cup granulated
   (white) sugar
For the topping
115g/4oz/½ cup butter
115g/4oz/1 cup wholemeal
   (whole-wheat) flour
50g/2oz/½ cup fine or medium
   pinhead oatmeal
50g/2oz/¼ cup soft light brown sugar
a little grated lemon rind (optional)

1 Preheat the oven to 200°C/400°F/ Gas 6. To make the crumble topping, rub the butter into the flour until the mixture resembles rough breadcrumbs.

GRANDMOTHER'S TIP
This delicious topping can be used with most fruits; try plums or raspberries.

2 Add the oatmeal and brown sugar to the bowl and continue to rub in until the mixture begins to stick together, forming larger crumbs. Using a fork, mix in the grated lemon rind, if using.

3 Peel, core and slice the cooking apples into wedges.

4 Put the apples, blackberries, lemon juice (if using), 30ml/2 tbsp water and the sugar into a shallow ovenproof dish, about 2 litres/3½ pints/9 cups capacity.

5 Cover the fruit with the topping. Sprinkle with a little cold water. Bake in the oven for 15 minutes, then reduce the heat to 190°C/375°F/Gas 5 and cook for another 15–20 minutes until crunchy and brown on top. Serve hot.

Energy 470Kcal/1974kJ; Protein 5.1g; Carbohydrate 78.2g, of which sugars 60.3g; Fat 17.2g, of which saturates 10g; Cholesterol 41mg; Calcium 71mg; Fibre 7g; Sodium 128mg.

STICKY COFFEE AND GINGER PUDDING

GINGER HAS BEEN USED IN BOTH SWEET AND SAVOURY COOKING FOR CENTURIES. HERE IT IS BLENDED WITH COFFEE TO FLAVOUR THE FEATHER-LIGHT SPONGE. WHEN THE PUDDING IS TURNED OUT, THE COFFEE AND GINGER SAUCE WILL TRICKLE DOWN THE SIDES. SERVE WITH CREAM OR ICE CREAM.

2 Put the ground coffee in a small bowl. Heat the ginger syrup until almost boiling; pour into the coffee. Stir well and leave for 4 minutes. Pour through a sieve (strainer) into the heatproof bowl.

3 In a clean bowl, beat half the caster sugar and egg yolks until light and fluffy. Fold in the sifted flour and ginger, breadcrumbs and ground almonds.

4 In a third bowl, whisk the egg whites until stiff, then gradually whisk in the remaining caster sugar. Fold this into the cake mixture. Transfer the mixture into the heatproof bowl.

5 Cover the basin with a piece of pleated greased greaseproof paper and secure with string. Bake for 40 minutes, or until the sponge is firm to the touch. Turn out and serve immediately.

GRANDMOTHER'S TIP
This pudding can also be baked in a 900ml/1½ pint/3¾ cup loaf tin and served thickly sliced.

SERVES 4

INGREDIENTS
  30ml/2 tbsp soft light brown sugar
  25g/1oz/2 tbsp stem ginger, chopped
  30ml/2 tbsp ground coffee
  75ml/5 tbsp stem ginger syrup (from a jar of preserved stem ginger)
  115g/4oz/generous ½ cup caster (superfine) sugar
  3 eggs, separated
  25g/1oz/¼ cup plain (all-purpose) flour, sifted with 5ml/1 tsp ground ginger
  65g/2½oz/generous 1 cup fresh white breadcrumbs
  25g/1oz/¼ cup ground almonds

1 Preheat the oven to 180°C/350°F/ Gas 4. Grease and line the base of a 750ml/1¼ pint/3 cup heatproof bowl, then sprinkle in the soft light brown sugar and chopped stem ginger.

Energy 382Kcal/1617kJ; Protein 9.7g; Carbohydrate 70.6g, of which sugars 53.5g; Fat 8.9g, of which saturates 1.7g; Cholesterol 171g; Calcium 93mg; Fibre 1g; Sodium 240mg.

QUEEN OF PUDDINGS

THIS DELICATE DESSERT MAKES THE MOST OF EGGS IN THRIFTY STYLE, WITH THE YOLKS STIRRED WITH BREADCRUMBS, SUGAR AND LEMON TO FORM THE BASE AND THE WHITES BEATEN UP INTO A LIGHT MERINGUE TOPPING. THE FAMOUS MRS BEETON CALLED THIS RECIPE 'QUEEN OF BREAD PUDDING'.

SERVES 4

INGREDIENTS
  80g/3oz/1½ cups fresh breadcrumbs
  60ml/4 tbsp caster (superfine) sugar,
    plus 5ml/1 tsp
  grated rind of 1 lemon
  600ml/1 pint/2½ cups milk
  4 eggs
  45ml/3 tbsp raspberry jam, warmed

1 Stir the breadcrumbs, 30ml/2 tbsp of the sugar and the lemon rind together in a bowl. Bring the milk to the boil in a pan, then stir it into the breadcrumb and sugar mixture.

2 Separate three of the eggs and beat the yolks with the remaining whole egg.

3 Stir the eggs into the breadcrumb mixture, then pour into a buttered ovenproof dish and leave to stand for 30 minutes.

4 Meanwhile, preheat the oven to 160°C/325°F/Gas 3. Cook the pudding for 50–60 minutes, until set.

5 Whisk the egg whites in a large, clean bowl until stiff, then gradually whisk in the remaining 30ml/2 tbsp caster sugar until the mixture is thick and glossy. Be careful not to overwhip.

GRANDMOTHER'S TIP
The traditional recipe stipulates that raspberry jam should be used, but you could ring the changes by replacing it with a different jam, such as strawberry or plum, you could also use lemon curd, marmalade or fruit purée.

6 Spread the jam over the set custard, then spoon on the egg whites. Sprinkle the remaining sugar over the top, then bake for a further 15 minutes, until the meringue is light golden. Serve warm.

Energy 297kcal/1259kJ; Protein 13.7g; Carbohydrate 45g, of which sugars 31g; Fat 8.5g, of which saturates 3.2g; Cholesterol 199mg; Calcium 242mg; Fibre 0.4g; Sodium 281mg.

Bread AND Butter Pudding

PLATES OF BREAD AND BUTTER WERE A STANDARD FEATURE OF AN ENGLISH TEA OR NURSERY SUPPER IN VICTORIAN AND EDWARDIAN TIMES. FRUGAL COOKS NEEDED TO COME UP WITH WAYS TO USE UP THE LEFTOVERS, AND THIS BREAD AND BUTTER PUDDING WAS THE VERY TASTY RESULT.

SERVES 4–6

INGREDIENTS
  50g/2oz/4 tbsp soft butter
  about 6 large slices of day-old
    white bread
  50g/2oz dried fruit, such as raisins,
    sultanas (golden raisins) or chopped
    dried apricots
  40g/1½oz/3 tbsp caster (superfine)
    sugar
  2 large eggs
  600ml/1 pint/2½ cups full cream
    (whole) milk

1 Preheat the oven to 160°C/325°F/ Gas 5. Lightly butter a 1.2 litre/2 pint/ 5 cup ovenproof dish.

2 Butter the slices of bread and cut them into small triangles or squares.

3 Arrange half the bread pieces, buttered side up, in the dish. Sprinkle the dried fruit and half the sugar on top.

4 Lay the remaining bread slices, again buttered side up, evenly on top of the fruit. Sprinkle the remaining sugar evenly over the bread.

5 Beat the eggs lightly together, just to break up the yolks and whites, and stir in the milk.

6 Strain the egg mixture and pour it over the bread in the dish. Push the top slices down into the liquid if necessary so that it is evenly absorbed.

7 Leave the pudding to stand for 30 minutes to allow the bread to soak up all the liquid (this is an important step so don't be tempted to skip it).

8 Put the dish into the hot oven and cook for about 45 minutes, or until the custard is set and the top is crisp and golden brown. Serve the pudding immediately.

VARIATION
To make a special occasion chocolate bread and butter pudding, complete steps 1–4, omitting the dried fruit if you wish. Break 150g/5oz dark (bittersweet) chocolate into 500ml/17fl oz/generous 2 cups milk, and heat gently (on the stove or on low power in the microwave) until the milk is warm and the chocolate has melted. Stir frequently during heating and do not allow the milk to boil. Stir the warm chocolate milk into the beaten eggs in step 5, and then continue with the remaining steps.

Energy 622kcal/2597kJ; Protein 10.5g; Carbohydrate 55.6g, of which sugars 37.8g; Fat 39g, of which saturates 23g; Cholesterol 186mg; Calcium 203mg; Fibre 1.6g; Sodium 350mg.

RICE PUDDING <u>WITH</u> RHUBARB COMPOTE

THIS DESSERT COMBINES TWO TRADITIONAL FAVOURITES: RICE PUDDING, A YEAR-ROUND SWEET TREAT FROM THE STORE CUPBOARD, AND GENTLY COOKED ORANGE-FLAVOURED RHUBARB, AT ITS BEST IN THE SUMMER WHEN THE RHUBARB IS GROWING STRONGLY IN THE KITCHEN GARDEN.

SERVES 4

INGREDIENTS
    175g/6oz/scant 1 cup short-grain
      rice
    1 litre/1¾ pints/4 cups milk
    50g/2oz/¼ cup caster (superfine)
      sugar, plus extra for sprinkling
    5g/⅒oz vanilla sugar (about) or
      ½ tsp vanilla extract
    50g/2oz/4 tbsp butter
    pinch of salt
    pinch of ground cinnamon
For the compote
    500g/1¼lb rhubarb
    75g/3oz/⅔ cup caster (superfine)
      sugar
    juice of 1 orange
    2 pieces of star anise
    cornflour (cornstarch)

1 Wash the rice thoroughly and drain. Put the milk in a pan with the sugar, vanilla sugar, butter and salt. Bring to the boil, then reduce the heat and add the rice.

2 Cook gently for about 15 minutes, stirring constantly, until the rice is cooked. Turn into a serving dish and sprinkle with sugar, mixed with ground cinnamon. Keep warm.

GRANDMOTHER'S TIP
This rice pudding is also delicious if served cold. Simply make both the rice pudding and the fruit compote in advance, and chill both in the refrigerator before serving.

3 While the rice cooks, cut the rhubarb stems into pieces 2cm/¾in thick.

4 Heat a heavy pan over a medium heat and pour in the sugar. Heat the sugar until it starts to dissolve, and slightly caramelizes, then remove from the heat, stir in the orange juice and add the star anise.

5 Return the pan to the heat, add the rhubarb, bring to the boil, then reduce the heat and simmer for 8–10 minutes.

6 If there is too much juice, add a little cornflour slaked in a spoonful of cold water and cook until the sauce has thickened. Serve the rice with the rhubarb.

Energy 557Kcal/2348kJ; Protein 12g; Carbohydrate 80g, of which sugars 45g; Fat 21g, of which saturates 12g; Cholesterol 61mg; Calcium 394mg; Fibre 2g; Sodium 244mg.

JAM ROLY POLY

THIS WARMING WINTER PUDDING, MADE WITH JAM SPREAD INSIDE A SUET PASTRY ROLL, FIRST APPEARED IN THE 19TH CENTURY. IT CAN BE MADE WITH A SWEET OR SAVOURY FILLING, BUT THIS SWEET VERSION WILL UNDOUBTEDLY BE THE CHILDREN'S FAVOURITE. SERVE IT WITH CREAMY CUSTARD.

SERVES 4–6

INGREDIENTS
175g/6oz/1½ cups self-raising
   (self-rising) flour
pinch of salt
75g/3oz shredded suet (or vegetarian
   equivalent)
finely grated rind of 1 small lemon
90ml/6 tbsp strawberry jam

1 Preheat the oven to 180°C/350°F/ Gas 4 and line a baking sheet with baking parchment.

2 Sift the flour and salt into a bowl and stir in the suet and lemon rind. Stir in just enough cold water to enable you to gather the mixture into a ball of soft dough, finishing off with your fingers.

3 Remove the ball of dough from the bowl, and on a lightly floured work surface or board, knead it very lightly until smooth.

4 Gently roll out the pastry into a rectangle that measures approximately 30 x 20cm/12 x 8in.

5 Using a palette knife or metal spatula, spread the jam evenly over the pastry, leaving the side edges and ends clear.

6 Brush the edges of the pastry with a little water and, starting at one of the short ends, carefully roll up the pastry. Try to keep the roll fairly loose so that the jam is not squeezed out.

7 Place the roll, seam side down, on the prepared baking sheet. Put into the hot oven and cook for 30–40 minutes until risen, golden brown and cooked through. Leave the pudding to cool for a few minutes before cutting into thick slices to serve.

GRANDMOTHER'S TIP
For the lightest suet pastry, use as little cold water as possible to mix the dough, and handle it as gently and lightly as you can.

VARIATION
To make a steamed pudding, try the traditional nursery favourite, Spotted Dick, replace half the flour with 115g/4oz/2 cups fresh white breadcrumbs; add 50g/2oz/½ cup caster (superfine) sugar and 175g/6oz/¾ cup currants to the flour in step 2.

Instead of water to mix, use about 75ml/5 tbsp milk. Leave out the jam and just form into a sausage shape without rolling.

Shape the mixture into a roll and wrap loosely (to allow room for the pudding to rise and expand) first in baking parchment and then in a large sheet of foil. Twist the ends of the paper and foil to seal them securely and tie a string handle from one end to the other.

Lower the package into a wide pan of boiling water on the stove, cover and boil for about 1½ hours. Check the water level occasionally and top up with boiling water if necessary. Serve the pudding hot with custard.

Energy 240kcal/1008kJ; Protein 2.8g; Carbohydrate 33.7g, of which sugars 10.7g; Fat 11.3g, of which saturates 5.7g; Cholesterol 0mg; Calcium 104mg; Fibre 0.9g; Sodium 111mg

LEMON SURPRISE PUDDING

The surprise in this pudding is the pool of tangy lemon sauce that forms during cooking beneath a light sponge topping. A few simple ingredients work their magic to make a special dessert that children will love, with a delicious taste and texture.

2 Beat the butter and sugar together in a large bowl until pale and fluffy. Beat in one egg yolk at a time and gradually add in the lemon rind and juice until well mixed; do not worry if the mixture curdles a little.

3 Sift the flour and stir it into the lemon mixture until well mixed, then gradually stir in the milk.

4 Whisk the egg whites in a separate bowl until stiff, but not dry, then lightly, but thoroughly, fold into the lemon mixture in three batches. Carefully pour the mixture into the soufflé dish, then pour boiling water into the roasting pan.

5 Bake the pudding in the middle of the oven for 45 minutes, or until golden on top. Dust with icing (confectioners') sugar and serve immediately.

SERVES 4

INGREDIENTS
   75g/3oz/6 tbsp butter
   175g/6oz/¾ cup soft light
     brown sugar
   4 eggs, separated
   grated rind and juice of 4 lemons
   50g/2oz/½ cup self-raising
     (self-rising) flour
   120ml/4fl oz/½ cup milk

1 Preheat the oven to 180°C/350°F/ Gas 4. Butter an 18cm/7in soufflé dish and stand it in a roasting pan.

VARIATION
This pudding is also delicious made with oranges instead of lemons.

GRANDMOTHER'S TIP
When whisking egg whites, use a grease-free bowl and make sure that there are no traces of yolk.

Energy 446Kcal/1872kJ; Protein 10g; Carbohydrate 51g, of which sugars 43g; Fat 23g, of which saturates 21g; Cholesterol 283mg; Calcium 114mg; Fibre 0.4g; Sodium 270mg.

APPLE PUDDING

THIS IS ONE OF THE SIMPLEST AND YET MOST TASTY DESSERT RECIPES, MADE WITH APPLES FROM THE GARDEN AND ALL OTHER INGREDIENTS FROM THE STORE CUPBOARD. SLICED APPLES ARE SPREAD OUT IN A CAKE TIN AND TOPPED WITH A LIGHT SOUFFLÉ-LIKE SPONGE BEFORE BAKING.

SERVES 4

INGREDIENTS

4 crisp eating apples
a little lemon juice
300ml/½ pint/1¼ cups milk
40g/1½oz/3 tbsp butter
40g/1½oz/⅓ cup plain (all-purpose)
  flour
25g/1oz/2 tbsp caster (superfine) sugar
2.5ml/½ tsp vanilla extract
2 eggs, separated

1 Preheat the oven to 200°C/400°F/ Gas 6. Butter a dish measuring 20–23cm/8–9in diameter and 5cm/2in deep. Peel, core and slice the apples, into the dish, and add the lemon juice.

2 Put the milk, butter and flour in a pan. Whisking continuously, cook over medium heat until the sauce thickens and comes to the boil. Let it bubble gently for 1–2 minutes, stirring to make sure it does not stick on the bottom. Pour into a bowl, add the sugar and vanilla, and then stir in the egg yolks.

3 In a separate bowl, whisk the egg whites until stiff peaks form. With a large metal spoon fold the egg whites into the custard. Pour the custard mixture over the apples in the dish.

4 Put into the hot oven and cook for about 40 minutes until firm to the touch. Serve straight out of the oven, before the topping begins to fall.

VARIATION
Stewed fruit, such as cooking apples, plums or rhubarb sweetened with honey or sugar, would also make a good base for this pudding, as would fresh summer berries (blackberries, raspberries, redcurrants and blackcurrants).
You could also use a layer of tinned pineapple if you don't have any fresh fruit to hand.

Energy 240kcal/1006kJ; Protein 7g; Carbohydrate 26.8g, of which sugars 19.2g; Fat 12.5g, of which saturates 6.8g; Cholesterol 121mg; Calcium 127mg; Fibre 1.9g; Sodium 131mg

EVE'S PUDDING

THIS RECIPE WAS ORIGINALLY KNOWN AS 'MOTHER EVE'S PUDDING'. IT WOULD HAVE BEEN MADE WITH SUET PASTRY AND BOILED IN A BASIN COVERED WITH A CLOTH. THIS VERSION IS BAKED IN THE OVEN, AND IS MADE FROM A LIGHTER LEMON AND ALMOND-FLAVOURED SPONGE.

SERVES 4-6

INGREDIENTS

115g/4oz/½ cup butter
115g/4oz/½ cup caster (superfine)
  sugar
2 eggs, beaten
grated rind and juice of 1 lemon
90g/3¼oz/scant 1 cup self-raising
  (self-rising) flour
40g/1½oz/⅓ cup ground almonds
115g/4oz/scant ½ cup soft light
  brown sugar
550–675g/1¼–1½lb cooking apples,
  cored and thinly sliced
25g/1oz/¼ cup flaked (sliced)
  almonds

1 Preheat the oven to 180°C/350°F/
Gas 4. Butter an ovenproof dish.

2 Beat together the butter and caster sugar in a large mixing bowl until the mixture is very light and fluffy.

3 Gradually beat the eggs into the butter mixture, beating well after each addition, then fold in the lemon rind, flour and ground almonds.

4 Mix the brown sugar, apples and lemon juice and tip the mixture into the ovenproof dish, spreading it out evenly.

5 Spoon the sponge mixture over the top and spread evenly. Sprinkle the almonds over. Bake for 40–45 minutes until risen and golden brown.

Energy 507kcal/2128kJ; Protein 6.9g; Carbohydrate 65.5g, of which sugars 52.7g; Fat 26.1g, of which saturates 12g; Cholesterol 114mg; Calcium 91mg; Fibre 2.8g; Sodium 159mg.

SUMMER PUDDING

NOTHING COULD BE MORE REDOLENT OF LATE SUMMER THAN THIS TRADITIONAL PUDDING. IT IS WONDERFULLY EASY TO MAKE, AND FRUGAL TOO, USING UP SLICES OF LEFTOVER BREAD AND WHATEVER SUMMER BERRIES AND OTHER FRUITS ARE AVAILABLE IN THE HEDGEROWS OR THE KITCHEN GARDEN.

SERVES 4-6

INGREDIENTS

8 x 1cm/½in thick slices of day-old white bread, crusts removed
800g/1¾lb/6–7 cups mixed berries, such as strawberries, raspberries, blackcurrants and redcurrants
50g/2oz/¼ cup golden caster (superfine) sugar
double (heavy) cream, to serve

1 Trim a slice of bread to fit in the base of a 1.2 litre/2 pint/5 cup bowl, then trim another 5–6 slices to line the sides of the bowl, making sure the bread comes up above the rim.

2 Place all the fruit in a pan with the sugar. Do not add any water. Cook gently for 4–5 minutes until the juices begin to run.

3 Allow the mixture to cool then spoon the berries, and enough of their juices to moisten, into the bread-lined bowl. Reserve any remaining juice to serve with the pudding.

4 Fold over the excess bread from the side of the bowl. Cover the fruit with the remaining bread, trimming to fit.

5 Place a small plate that fits inside the bowl on top of the pudding. Weight it down with a 900g/2lb weight, if you have one, or use a couple of full cans.

6 Chill the pudding in the refrigerator for at least 8 hours. To serve, run a knife between the pudding and the bowl and turn out on to a serving plate. Spoon any reserved juices over the top.

Energy 230kcal/977kJ; Protein 6.2g; Carbohydrate 51.7g, of which sugars 26.5g; Fat 1.2g, of which saturates 0g; Cholesterol 0mg; Calcium 98mg; Fibre 3g; Sodium 294mg.

BAKED CHEESECAKE

THIS IS THE TRADITIONAL BAKED CHEESECAKE, MADE WITH COTTAGE OR RICOTTA CHEESE STUDDED WITH DRIED FRUITS. IT IS SET ON A LOVELY BUTTER AND BREADCRUMB BASE, AND MAKES A LIGHT AND DELICIOUS DESSERT, IDEAL FOR A SUMMER PICNIC, OR SUNDAY LUNCH IN THE GARDEN.

SERVES 6–8

INGREDIENTS
15g/½oz/1 tbsp butter
45ml/3 tbsp fresh white breadcrumbs
4 eggs
100g/3¾oz mixed (candied) peel
500g/1¼lb/2 cups cottage or
  ricotta cheese
90g/3½oz/½ cup caster (superfine)
  sugar
50g/2oz/scant ½ cup raisins
grated rind of 1 lemon
45ml/3 tbsp semolina
icing (confectioners') sugar, for dusting
crème fraîche or whipped cream, and
  fresh berries, to serve

1 Use the butter to grease the bottom and sides of a 20cm/8in loose-bottomed cake tin (pan). Pour in the breadcrumbs and tip and shake until the insides of the tin are well coated with the breadcrumbs.

2 Preheat the oven to 180°C/350°F/ Gas 4. Separate the egg yolks from the egg whites into two separate large bowls. Finely chop the candied peel and add to the egg yolks. Add the cottage or ricotta cheese, sugar, raisins, lemon rind and semolina and mix well.

3 Whisk the egg whites until they are stiff and hold their shape, then carefully fold into the cheese mixture. Spoon the mixture into the prepared tin.

4 Bake the cake in the oven for 30–40 minutes, until a skewer, inserted in the centre, comes out dry. Leave the cake to cool in the tin.

5 Slide a knife around the edge of the cake and carefully remove it from the tin. Place on a serving plate and dust with sifted icing sugar.

6 Serve with crème fraîche or whipped cream and fresh berries.

Energy 297kcal/1239kJ; Protein 7.6g; Carbohydrate 27.2g, of which sugars 19g; Fat 18g, of which saturates 9g; Cholesterol 83mg; Calcium 56mg; Fibre 1.1g; Sodium 139mg.

BAKED APPLES WITH MARZIPAN

THIS IS A TRADITIONAL RECIPE FOR THE WINTER, WHEN APPLES WERE ONCE THE ONLY FRESH FRUITS AVAILABLE AND COOKS NEEDED TO BE VERY CREATIVE TO FIND DIFFERENT WAYS TO SERVE THEM. THE BRANDY, RAISINS, NUTS AND MARZIPAN IN THE FILLING GIVE IT A REAL FLAVOUR OF CHRISTMAS.

SERVES 4

INGREDIENTS

5ml/1 tsp raisins
10ml/2 tsp brandy
4 large, crisp eating apples, such
  as Braeburn
75g/3oz marzipan, chopped
juice of ½ lemon
20g/¾oz/¼ cup chopped nuts
single (light) cream, to serve

VARIATION
You can vary the nuts in the recipe – walnuts, hazelnuts and almonds, or even pistachios, can be used.

1 Preheat the oven to 160°C/325°F/ Gas 3. Soak the raisins in the brandy for 20 minutes.

2 Meanwhile, core the apples with a corer or cut them out with a sharp knife. Cut a small slice off the bottom of each apple, if necessary, so that they will stand up while they are cooking. Score the skin around the apple in three places to prevent it rolling up during baking.

3 Mix the marzipan with the lemon juice, chopped nuts, raisins and brandy, and push the filling into the centre of the apples. Put the apples on a baking tray lined with baking parchment, and bake them for 20–25 minutes. Serve the apples warm with single cream.

Energy 150kcal/631kJ; Protein 2.2g; Carbohydrate 22.9g, of which sugars 22.7g; Fat 5.3g, of which saturates 0.6g; Cholesterol 0mg; Calcium 23mg; Fibre 2.3g; Sodium 33mg.

POACHED PEARS WITH CHOCOLATE

PEARS AND CHOCOLATE ARE ONE OF THE GREAT COMBINATIONS THAT COOKS HAVE KNOWN ABOUT FOR CENTURIES. THIS IS A VERY SIMPLE RECIPE FOR HALVED PEARS, SIMMERED WITH SUGAR AND TOPPED WITH HOME-MADE CHOCOLATE SAUCE, THEN SERVED WARM WITH ICE CREAM.

SERVES 4

INGREDIENTS

    4 firm dessert pears, peeled
    250g/9oz/1¼ cups caster (superfine)
      sugar
    600ml/1 pint/2½ cups water
    500ml/17fl oz/2¼ cups vanilla
      ice cream, to serve
For the chocolate sauce
    250g/9oz good quality dark
      (bittersweet) chocolate (minimum
      70 per cent cocoa solids)
    40g/1½oz unsalted butter
    5ml/1 tsp vanilla extract
    75ml/5 tbsp double (heavy) cream

1 Cut the pears in half lengthways and remove the core. Place the sugar and water in a large pan and gently heat until the sugar has dissolved.

2 Add the pear halves to the pan, then simmer for about 20 minutes, or until the pears are tender but not falling apart. Lift out of the sugar syrup with a slotted spoon and leave to cool.

3 To make the chocolate sauce, break the chocolate into small pieces and put into a pan. Add the butter and 30ml/ 2 tbsp water to the pan. Heat gently over a low heat, without stirring, until the chocolate has melted. Remove the pan from the heat.

4 Add the vanilla extract and cream to the melted chocolate, and mix gently.

5 When you are ready to serve, place a scoop of ice cream into each of four glasses. Add two cooled pear halves to each and pour over the hot chocolate sauce. Serve immediately.

Energy 1014kcal/4255kJ; Protein 8.8g; Carbohydrate 145.1g, of which sugars 143.2g; Fat 46.7g, of which saturates 29.6g; Cholesterol 81mg; Calcium 206mg; Fibre 4.9g; Sodium 152mg.

FRUIT AND WINE JELLY

IN 17TH-CENTURY ENGLAND, MAKING JELLY WAS A LENGTHY PROCESS THAT INVOLVED THE BOILING OF CALF'S HOOF, HARTSHORN OR ISINGLASS. NOW, THOUGH, GELATINE IS USED TO MAKE A LIGHT AND ELEGANT DESSERT. ALLOW PLENTY OF TIME FOR SIEVING THE FRUIT AND COOLING THE JELLY.

SERVES 6

INGREDIENTS
   600g/1lb 6oz fresh raspberries
   140g/5oz/¾ cup white sugar
   300ml/½ pint/1¼ cups medium-dry
      white wine
   5 leaves of gelatine (6 if the jelly
      is to be set in a mould and
      turned out)

GRANDMOTHER'S TIP
Instead of making your own fruit juice, use a carton of juice, such as mango, cranberry or orange, sweetened to taste.

1 Put the raspberries and sugar in a pan with 100ml/3½fl oz/scant ½ cup water and heat gently until the fruit releases its juices and becomes very soft, and the sugar has dissolved.

2 Remove the pan from the heat, pour the mixture into a fine nylon sieve (strainer) or jelly bag over a large bowl, and leave to strain – this will take some time, but do not squeeze the fruit or the resulting juice may be cloudy.

3 When the juice has drained into the bowl, make it up to 600ml/1 pint/2½ cups with water if necessary. Soften the gelatine in cold water for 5 minutes.

4 Heat half the juice until very hot but not quite boiling. Remove from the heat. Squeeze the softened gelatine to remove excess water, then stir it into the hot juice until dissolved. Add the remaining raspberry juice and the wine.

5 Pour into stemmed glasses and chill until set. Alternatively, set the jelly in a wetted mould and turn out onto a pretty plate for serving.

Energy 178kcal/758kJ; Protein 8.6g; Carbohydrate 29.3g, of which sugars 29.3g; Fat 0.3g, of which saturates 0.1g; Cholesterol 0mg; Calcium 42mg; Fibre 2.5g; Sodium 6mg.

SYLLABUB

THE ORIGINS OF THIS DISH CAN BE TRACED BACK AT LEAST AS FAR AS THE 17TH CENTURY. IT IS SAID TO HAVE BEEN MADE BY POURING MILK FRESH FROM THE COW ON TO SWEETENED, SPICED CIDER OR ALE. THIS MORE ADULT VERSION USES SHERRY AND CREAM FOR A GREAT CLASSIC DESSERT.

1 Finely grate 2.5ml/½ tsp rind from the orange, then squeeze out its juice.

2 Put the orange rind and juice, sugar and sherry into a large bowl and stir until the sugar is completely dissolved. Stir in the cream. Whip the mixture until it is thick and soft peaks form.

3 Carefully spoon the syllabub into wine glasses.

4 Chill the glasses of syllabub until ready to serve, then decorate with strips of crystallized orange.

SERVES 6

INGREDIENTS
  1 orange
  65g/2½oz/⅓ cup caster (superfine) sugar
  60ml/4 tbsp medium dry sherry
  300ml/½ pint/1¼ cups double (heavy) cream
  crystallized orange, to decorate

GRANDMOTHER'S TIPS
• Syllabub is lovely spooned over a bowl of fresh soft fruit such as strawberries, apricots, raspberries or blackberries. You can also serve it with traditional sponge fingers, or thin crisp biscuits (cookies).
• Add a pinch of ground cinnamon to the mixture in step 2 if you are making this at Christmas time.

Energy 310kcal/1282kJ; Protein 1.1g; Carbohydrate 14.5g, of which sugars 14.5g; Fat 26.9g, of which saturates 16.7g; Cholesterol 69mg; Calcium 41mg; Fibre 0.3g; Sodium 15mg.

GOOSEBERRY FOOL

*THIS QUICKLY MADE, SIMPLE DESSERT NEVER FAILS TO IMPRESS. THE BASIC RECIPE WORKS WELL WITH
ANY GARDEN FRUIT, SUCH AS RASPBERRIES, RHUBARB OR BLACKCURRANTS. ADJUST THE SWEETNESS TO
SUIT THE FRUIT — FOR INSTANCE, GOOSEBERRIES WILL NEED MORE SUGAR THAN RASPBERRIES.*

SERVES 4

INGREDIENTS
    450g/1lb gooseberries, cut into half
        or chopped
    125g/4½oz/¼ cup caster (superfine)
        sugar, or to taste
    300ml/½ pint/1¼ cups double
        (heavy) cream
    sweet biscuits, to serve

1 Put the gooseberries into a pan with
30ml/2 tbsp water. Cover and cook
gently for about 10 minutes until the
fruit is soft. Stir in the sugar to taste.

2 Pour the fruit into a sieve (strainer)
and press through. Leave to cool.

3 Whip the cream until stiff enough to
hold soft peaks. Stir in the gooseberry
purée without over-mixing (it looks
pretty with some streaks).

4 Spoon the mixture into serving
glasses and refrigerate until required.

Energy 517kcal/2147kJ; Protein 2.6g; Carbohydrate 37.3g, of which sugars 37.3g; Fat 40.7g, of which saturates 25.1g; Cholesterol 103mg; Calcium 85mg; Fibre 2.7g; Sodium 21mg.

Raspberry Trifle

This is the recipe that best sums up childhood. It is ideal for using up cake that is past its best, mixed with jam from the larder and seasonal soft fruit from the garden. There is also the addition of a little sherry to tempt the grown-ups.

SERVES 6 OR MORE

INGREDIENTS
6oz (170g) trifle sponges, or
  1in (2.5cm) cubes of plain Victoria
  sponge, or coarsely crumbled
  sponge fingers
4 tablespoons medium sherry
4oz (115g) raspberry jam
10oz (300g) raspberries
¾ pint (450ml) custard, flavoured
  with 2 tablespoons medium or sweet
  sherry (optional)
½ pint (300ml) double (heavy)
  cream, whipped
toasted flaked almonds and mint
  leaves, to decorate

VARIATIONS
Try other fruit in the trifle, with a jam and liqueur flavour to suit: apricots, peaches, nectarines, strawberries, etc. Another traditional cake to use in a trifle is Swiss roll (jelly roll). If you are serving the trifle to children, use fruit juice instead of sherry to moisten the cake.

1 Spread half of the sponges, cake cubes or sponge fingers over the bottom of a large serving bowl. (A glass bowl is best for presentation.)

2 Sprinkle half of the sherry over the cake to moisten it. Spoon over half of the jam, dotting it evenly over the cake.

3 Reserve a few raspberries for decoration. Make a layer of half of the remaining raspberries on top.

4 Pour over half of the custard, covering the fruit and cake. Repeat the layers. Cover and chill in the refrigerator for at least 2 hours.

5 Before serving, spoon the whipped cream evenly over the top. To decorate, sprinkle the trifle with toasted flaked almonds and arrange the reserved raspberries and the mint leaves on the top.

Energy 330Kcal/1382kJ; Protein 5.1g; Carbohydrate 35.9g, of which sugars 29.1g; Fat 17.7g, of which saturates 9.9g; Cholesterol 90mg; Calcium 102mg; Fibre 1.1g; Sodium 59mg.

STRAWBERRY SNOW

STRAWBERRIES HAVE A DELICATE, FRAGRANT TASTE AND TEXTURE, AND MOST DESSERTS MADE FROM CHOPPED OR CRUSHED STRAWBERRIES ARE BEST EATEN AS SOON AS POSSIBLE AFTER THEY ARE MADE. THIS IS AN IDEAL FAMILY PUDDING, OR AN AFTERNOON TREAT, TO EAT IN SUMMER.

SERVES 4

INGREDIENTS
    120ml/4fl oz/½ cup water
    15ml/1 tbsp powdered gelatine
    300g/11oz/2¾ cups strawberries,
       lightly crushed
    250ml/8fl oz/1 cup double
       (heavy) cream
    4 egg whites
    90g/3½oz/½ cup caster (superfine)
       sugar
    halved strawberries, to decorate

1 Put the water in a heatproof bowl and sprinkle in the gelatine. Stand the bowl over a pan of hot water and heat gently until dissolved. Remove the bowl from the pan and leave to cool slightly.

2 Put half the crushed strawberries in a pan and bring to the boil.

3 Remove from the heat, then stir in the dissolved gelatine. Chill the mixture in the refrigerator for about 2 hours until it has a syrupy consistency.

4 Pour the cream into a bowl and whisk until it holds its shape. Set it aside while you prepare the egg whites.

5 In a large, clean bowl, whisk the egg whites until stiff, gradually adding the sugar as they rise. Fold the egg whites into the cream and strawberry mixture, then fold in the remaining crushed strawberries, followed by the whipped cream.

6 Turn the mixture into individual serving dishes and serve immediately, or chill until required. Serve, decorated with halved strawberries.

GRANDMOTHER'S TIP
Strawberry Snow freezes well and can then be served in slices. All you have to do is spoon the mixture into a loaf tin (pan) lined with clear film (plastic wrap) and freeze for a couple of hours, until it is firm, slice and serve.

Energy 443kcal/1841kJ; Protein 7.8g; Carbohydrate 29.1g, of which sugars 29.1g; Fat 33.7g, of which saturates 20.9g; Cholesterol 86mg; Calcium 56mg; Fibre 0.8g; Sodium 81mg.

CHOCOLATE AND COFFEE MOUSSE

A LIGHT CHOCOLATE MOUSSE IS ALWAYS A POPULAR WAY TO END A MEAL. THIS INDULGENT VERSION IS MADE WITH A GOOD STRONG CHOCOLATE FLAVOURED WITH COFFEE AND RUM. BRANDY OR VODKA COULD ALSO BE USED. YOU CAN OMIT THE COFFEE OR ALCOHOL, DEPENDING ON YOUR PREFERENCE.

SERVES 4–6

INGREDIENTS
　250g/9oz dark (bittersweet)
　　chocolate (minimum 70 per cent
　　cocoa solids)
　60ml/4 tbsp cooled strong black
　　coffee
　8 eggs, separated
　200g/7oz/1 cup caster (superfine)
　　sugar
　60ml/4 tbsp rum, brandy or
　　vodka (optional)

1 Break the chocolate into small pieces and melt in a heatproof bowl over a pan of gently simmering water. Ensure the water does not touch the base of the bowl, or the chocolate may seize and crystallize.

2 Once the chocolate has completely melted, stir in the cold coffee. Leave to cool slightly.

3 Beat the egg yolks with half the sugar until it is pale, thick and creamy. Add the rum, Polish spirit or vodka and stir in the melted chocolate mixture.

4 Whisk the egg whites in a separate bowl until stiff peaks form.

5 Stir in the remaining sugar, then fold into the chocolate mixture. Spoon into chilled glasses or ramekins. Chill the mousse for at least an hour before serving.

Energy 464kcal/1951kJ; Protein 10.6g; Carbohydrate 61.3g, of which sugars 60.9g; Fat 19.1g, of which saturates 9.1g; Cholesterol 256mg; Calcium 70mg; Fibre 1.1g; Sodium 98mg.

APPLE SNOW

THIS COMFORTING NURSERY DISH IS AS SIMPLE AS IT IS DELICIOUS — AND IS BEST MADE WITH LATE-CROPPING COOKING APPLES, HARVESTED IN THE AUTUMN. THEY 'FALL' (DON'T HOLD THEIR SHAPE) WHEN COOKED, AND MAKE A FLUFFY PURÉE. SERVE WITH CRISP COOKIES, OR SPONGE FINGERS.

SERVES 6

INGREDIENTS
   675g/1½lb cooking apples
   a little thinly peeled lemon rind
   about 115g/4oz/generous ½ cup
     caster (superfine) sugar
   3 egg whites

1 Peel, core and slice the apples. Turn into a pan with 45ml/3 tbsp water and the lemon rind.

2 Cover and simmer gently for 15 minutes, until the apples break down.

3 Remove the pan from the heat, take out the lemon rind, and sweeten to taste with caster sugar.

4 Beat the apples well with a wooden spoon to make a purée, or rub through a sieve if a smoother texture is preferred. Leave to cool.

5 When the purée is cold, whisk the egg whites until stiff.

6 Fold the egg whites into the apple using a metal spoon. Whisk together until the mixture is thick and light.

7 Turn into a serving bowl, or divide between six individual dishes, and chill until required.

Energy 121Kcal/516kJ; Protein 1.8g; Carbohydrate 30.1g, of which sugars 30.1g; Fat 0.1g, of which saturates 0g; Cholesterol 0mg; Calcium 7mg; Fibre 1.8g; Sodium 34mg.

CAKES AND BREADS

There are hundreds of classic recipes for cakes and breads that have been passed down to us by previous generations of cooks. From the lightest, airiest sponge cake, suitable for serving for afternoon tea, to a rustic tea bread, packed with fruit, that will keep you going for a hard afternoon's gardening or walking the dog, there is something in this chapter for everyone.

VANILLA SPONGE WITH STRAWBERRIES

This sponge cake is fat-free and ideal to make for a summer tea, filled with fresh soft fruit. The classic name for the cake is 'Genoese', and it became popular in the 1800s. It helps to have all the ingredients ready at room temperature.

SERVES 8–10

INGREDIENTS
    white vegetable fat (shortening),
       for greasing
    115g/4oz/generous ½ cup caster
       (superfine) sugar, plus extra for
       dusting
    90g/3½oz/¾ cup plain (all-purpose)
       flour, sifted, plus extra for dusting
    4 eggs
    icing (confectioners') sugar, for
       dusting
For the filling
    300ml/½ pint/1¼ cups double (heavy)
       cream
    about 5ml/1 tsp icing (confectioners')
       sugar, sieved
    450g/1lb/4 cups strawberries,
       washed and hulled
    a little Cointreau, or other fruit
       liqueur (optional)

GRANDMOTHER'S TIPS
• Like all fatless sponges, this cake is best eaten on the day of baking.
• One trick for a lighter cake is to whisk the sponge mixture over hot water to help make it rise.

1 Preheat the oven to 190°C/375°F/ Gas 5. Grease a loose-based 20cm/ 8in deep cake tin (pan) with white vegetable fat, and dust it with 5ml/1 tsp caster sugar mixed with 5ml/1 tsp flour. Shake off any excess sugar and flour mixture and discard.

2 Put the eggs and sugar into the bowl of an electric mixer and whisk at high speed until it is light and thick, and the mixture leaves a trail as it drops from the whisk. Alternatively, whisk by hand, or with a hand-held electric whisk; set the bowl over a pan one quarter filled with hot water and whisk until thick and creamy, then remove from the heat.

3 Sift the flour evenly over the whisked eggs and carefully fold it in with a metal spoon, mixing thoroughly but losing as little volume as possible.

4 Pour the mixture into the prepared cake tin. Shake gently to level off the top and bake in the preheated oven for 25–30 minutes, or until the sponge feels springy to the touch.

5 Leave in the tin for 1–2 minutes to allow the cake to cool a little and shrink slightly from the sides, then loosen the sides gently with a knife and turn out on to a rack to cool.

6 When the sponge is cold, make the filling. Whip the double cream with a little icing sugar until it is stiff enough to hold its shape. Slice the sponge across the middle with a sharp knife and divide half of the cream between the two inner sides of the cake.

7 Select some well-shaped even-sized strawberries for the top of the cake, and then slice the rest.

8 Lay the bottom half of the sponge on a serving plate and arrange the sliced strawberries on the cream. Sprinkle with liqueur, if using. Cover with the second half of the cake and press down gently so that it holds together.

9 Spread the remaining cream on top of the cake, and arrange the reserved strawberries, whole or halved according to size, on top.

10 Set aside for an hour or so for the flavours to develop, then dust lightly with icing sugar and serve as a dessert.

VARIATION
For raspberry sponge, halve the amount of cream in the recipe, omit the strawberries and replace with raspberry jam. After halving the cake, whip the cream to form soft peaks. Spread the bottom half of the cake with jam. Cover with cream, put the second half of the cake on top and dust with icing sugar. Leave in the refrigerator, or in a cool place, for 1 hour before serving.

Energy 333Kcal/1387kJ; Protein 5.3g; Carbohydrate 27.8g, of which sugars 19.2g; Fat 23.1g, of which saturates 13.3g; Cholesterol 147mg; Calcium 65mg; Fibre 1g; Sodium 48mg.

CHERRY CAKE

BOTH DRIED AND GLACÉ CHERRIES ARE USED IN THIS CAKE, PARTNERED WITH THE DELICATE FLAVOUR OF ALMONDS AND DECORATED WITH A DRIZZLE OF ICING. IT IS A COMBINATION THAT IS PERFECT FOR A SUMMER TEA PARTY ON THE LAWN WHEN FRIENDS OR FAMILY COME TO CALL.

SERVES 10

INGREDIENTS
175g/6oz/¾ cup unsalted butter, softened, plus extra for greasing
175g/6oz/scant 1 cup caster (superfine) sugar
3 eggs, beaten
150g/5oz/1¼ cups self-raising (self-rising) flour
50g/2oz/½ cup plain (all-purpose) flour
75g/3oz/¾ cup ground almonds
75g/3oz/scant ½ cup glacé (candied) cherries, washed, dried and halved
25g/1oz dried cherries
a few drops of almond extract
For the decoration
115g/4oz/1 cup icing (confectioners') sugar, sifted
5ml/1 tsp lemon juice
50g/2oz/½ cup flaked (sliced) almonds, toasted
10 natural glacé (candied) cherries

1 Preheat the oven to 160°C/325°F/Gas 3. Grease and line a 20cm/8in round deep cake tin (pan).

2 In a bowl, beat the butter with the sugar until light and fluffy, using an electric whisk, if possible. Add the eggs a little at a time, including 5ml/1 tsp of flour with each addition.

3 Sift the flour into the bowl, together with the ground almonds and both types of cherries and fold into the butter and sugar mixture until smooth.

4 Stir the almond extract into the mixture, then spoon into the cake tin and smooth level.

5 Bake for 45–50 minutes, or until a skewer inserted into the centre comes out clean. Cool slightly, then turn on to a wire rack to go cold. Remove the lining paper.

6 In a bowl, mix the icing sugar with the lemon juice, and 10–15ml/2–3 tsp water, to make a soft icing.

7 Drizzle half the icing over the cake. Sprinkle the almonds in the centre. Place the cherries around the edge and drizzle over the remaining icing.

Energy 367kcal/1535kJ; Protein 5g; Carbohydrate 43.7g, of which sugars 26.6g; Fat 20.4g, of which saturates 12g; Cholesterol 118mg; Calcium 75mg; Fibre 0.9g; Sodium 309mg.

LEMON DRIZZLE CAKE

THIS CLASSIC RECIPE IS A FAVOURITE AT COFFEE MORNINGS, FOR A TEATIME SNACK OR A SUPPERTIME TREAT. THE WONDERFULLY MOIST CAKE IS TRANSFORMED INTO SOMETHING SPECIAL BY POURING LEMON AND SUGAR SYRUP OVER THE COOKED SPONGE WHILE IT IS STILL WARM FROM THE OVEN.

SERVES 6

INGREDIENTS
 225g/8oz/1 cup unsalted butter,
   softened, plus extra for greasing
 finely grated rind of 2 lemons
 175g/6oz/scant 1 cup caster
   (superfine) sugar, plus 5ml/1 tsp
 4 eggs
 225g/8oz/2 cups self-raising
   (self-rising) flour, sifted with 5ml/
   1 tsp baking powder
 grated rind of 1 lemon,
   to decorate
For the syrup
 juice of 1 lemon
 150g/5oz/¾ cup caster
   (superfine) sugar

1 Preheat the oven to 160°C/325°F/ Gas 3. Grease and line an 18–20cm/ 7–8in round deep cake tin (pan) with baking parchment so the paper is higher than the sides of the tin.

2 Mix the lemon rind and sugar together in a bowl.

3 In a large bowl, beat the butter with the lemon and sugar mixture until light and fluffy, then beat in the eggs one at a time. Sift the flour and baking powder into the mixture in three batches and beat well.

GRANDMOTHER'S TIPS
Leaving the cake in the tin to cool means that all of the delicious lemon syrup soaks into the cake.

4 Turn the batter into the prepared tin and smooth the top level. Bake for 1½ hours, or until golden brown and springy to the touch.

5 To make the syrup, slowly heat the juice with the sugar until dissolved.

6 Prick the cake top with a skewer and pour over the syrup, then leave to cool. When completely cool, take the cake out of the tin. Remove the lining paper, then sprinkle over the grated lemon rind together with 5ml/1 tsp sugar, and slice to serve.

Energy 659kcal/2765kJ; Protein 8g; Carbohydrate 84.1g, of which sugars 56.2g; Fat 34.8g, of which saturates 21.4g; Cholesterol 213mg; Calcium 184mg; Fibre 1.2g; Sodium 466mg.

ICED WALNUT LAYER CAKE

MANY A VILLAGE TEA ROOM FEATURES THIS TRADITIONAL CAKE ON A PRETTY STAND. THE CHOPPED WALNUTS IN THE SPONGE MIXTURE BLEND WELL WITH THE BUTTERCREAM FILLING, AND HALVED NUTS MAKE A LOVELY DECORATION ON TOP OF THE SWIRLED FROSTING. IT KEEPS WELL IN AN AIRTIGHT TIN.

SERVES 12

INGREDIENTS
 225g/8oz/1 cup butter, softened, plus
  extra for greasing
 225g/8oz/2 cups self-raising (self-
  rising) flour
 5ml/1 tsp baking powder
 225g/8oz/1 cup soft light brown sugar
 75g/3oz/¾ cup walnuts, finely
  chopped
 4 eggs
 15ml/1 tbsp treacle (molasses)
For the buttercream
 75g/3oz/6 tbsp unsalted butter
 5ml/1 tsp vanilla extract
 175g/6oz/1½ cups icing
  (confectioners') sugar
For the meringue frosting
 2 large (US extra large) egg whites
 350g/12oz/1¾ cups golden caster
  (superfine) sugar
 pinch of salt
 pinch of cream of tartar
 15ml/1 tbsp warm water
 whole walnut halves, to decorate

1 Preheat the oven to 160°C/325°F/
Gas 3. Grease and line two 20cm/8in
round shallow cake tins (pans) with
baking parchment.

2 Sift the flour and baking powder into
a large bowl, then add all the remaining
ingredients. Beat vigorously for 2
minutes until smooth, then divide the
mixture between the tins and spread
level. Bake for 25 minutes until golden
and springy to the touch in the centre.

3 Allow the tins to stand for 5 minutes,
then turn the cakes out on to a wire
rack to cool. Remove the lining papers.
Cut each cake in half horizontally using
a long-bladed sharp knife.

4 Meanwhile make the buttercream.
Beat the butter, vanilla extract and icing
sugar together until light and fluffy.
Spread a third thinly over one sponge
half and place a sponge layer on top.

5 Continue layering the other 3 halves
of sponge cakes with the buttercream.
Then transfer the cake on to a plate.

6 To make the frosting, put the
egg whites in a large heatproof bowl
and add the caster sugar, salt, cream of
tartar and water. Put the bowl over a
pan of hot water and whisk with an
electric mixer for 7 minutes, or until the
mixture is thick and stands in peaks.

7 Immediately, use a metal spatula to
swirl the frosting over the top and sides
of the cake.

8 Arrange the walnut halves on top of
the cake and leave it to set for at least
10 minutes before serving.

Energy 563kcal/2349kJ; Protein 8.5g; Carbohydrate 50.6g, of which sugars 39.2g; Fat 35.3g, of which saturates 10.1g; Cholesterol 108mg; Calcium 114mg; Fibre 1.5g; Sodium 177mg.

CHOCOLATE CAKE WITH COFFEE ICING

THIS IS AN EASY ALL-IN-ONE VERSION OF A TRADITIONAL FAMILY FAVOURITE. IT CAN BE DECORATED WITH SWIRLS OF ICING AND WHOLE NUTS TO MAKE A BIRTHDAY CAKE OR FOR ANY SPECIAL OCCASION. THE COFFEE ICING BEAUTIFULLY COMPLEMENTS THE RICH CHOCOLATE FLAVOUR OF THE CAKE.

MAKES AN 18CM/7IN CAKE

INGREDIENTS
175g/6oz/1½ cups self-raising (self-rising) flour
25ml/1½ tbsp unsweetened cocoa powder
pinch of salt
175g/6oz/¾ cup butter, softened, or soft margarine
175g/6oz/¾ cup soft dark brown sugar
50g/2oz/½ cup ground almonds
3 large (US extra large) eggs, lightly beaten
For the coffee butter icing
175g/6oz/¾ cup unsalted butter, at warm room temperature
350g/12oz/3 cups sifted icing (confectioners') sugar
30ml/2 tbsp coffee essence (extract)
whole hazelnuts or pecan nuts, to decorate (optional)

VARIATION
For a deliciously rich touch, 15–30ml/ 1–2 tbsp of coffee liqueur can be included in the icing – beat in with the coffee essence at the end of step 4.

1 Preheat the oven to 180°C/350°F/ Gas 4 and butter two 18cm/7in diameter sandwich tins (pans).

2 Sift the flour, cocoa and salt into a mixing bowl. Cut in the butter or margarine and add the sugar, ground almonds and eggs.

3 Mix with a wooden spoon for 2–3 minutes, until thoroughly mixed; the mixture should be smooth, with no traces of butter remaining.

4 Divide the mixture between the prepared tins and bake in the centre of the preheated oven for 25–30 minutes, or until springy to the touch. Turn the cakes out and cool on a wire rack.

5 Meanwhile, make the icing: cream the butter well in a large bowl, then gradually beat in the sifted icing sugar and the coffee essence.

6 When the cakes are cold, sandwich them together with some of the icing and cover the top and sides with most of the remainder. Pipe the remaining icing around the top in rosettes, if you like, and decorate with whole hazelnuts or pecan nuts.

Per cake: Energy 5899Kcal/24,684kJ; Protein 56.2g; Carbohydrate 691.1g, of which sugars 556.9g; Fat 343.1g, of which saturates 193.7g; Cholesterol 1.43g; Calcium 1.06g; Fibre 12.2g; Sodium 3.28g

BOILED FRUIT CAKE

THE TEXTURE OF THIS FRUIT CAKE IS REALLY SPECIAL, WITH PLUMP DRIED FRUIT MADE EVEN MORE SUCCULENT BY HEATING IT GENTLY WITH THE BUTTER, SUGAR AND MILK BEFORE BAKING. THE IDEA ORIGINALLY COMES FROM WALES, WHICH HAS A LONG TRADITION OF DELICIOUS FRUIT CAKE RECIPES.

2 Put the dried fruit in a large pan and add the butter and sugar. Bring slowly to boil, stirring occasionally.

3 When the butter has melted and the sugar has dissolved, bubble the mixture gently for about 2 minutes. Remove from the heat and cool slightly.

4 Sift the flour with the bicarbonate of soda and mixed spice. Add this, this milk and the eggs to the fruit mixture and mix together well.

5 Pour the mixture into the prepared tin and smooth the surface.

6 Bake for about 1½ hours or until firm to the touch and the cake is cooked through – a skewer inserted in the centre should come out free of sticky mixture.

MAKES A 20cm/8in CAKE

INGREDIENTS
    350g/12oz/2 cups mixed dried fruit
    225g/8oz/1 cup butter
    225g/8oz/1 cup soft dark brown
        sugar
    400ml/14fl oz/1⅔ cup milk
    450g/1lb/4 cups self-raising (self-
        rising) flour
    5ml/1 tsp bicarbonate of soda
        (baking soda)
    5ml/1 tsp mixed (apple pie) spice
    2 eggs, beaten

1 Preheat the oven to 160°C/325°F/ Gas 3. Butter a 20cm/8in cake tin (pan) and line it with baking parchment.

7 Leave in the tin to cool for 20–30 minutes, then turn out and cool completely on a wire rack.

Per cake: Energy 5150kcal/21689kJ; Protein 72.2g; Carbohydrate 796g, of which sugars 498.8g; Fat 209.1g, of which saturates 125.4g; Cholesterol 884mg; Calcium 2352mg; Fibre 20.1g; Sodium 3297mg.

OLD-FASHIONED TREACLE CAKE

THIS IS A GOOD HEARTY CAKE WHICH IS RELATIVELY QUICK TO MAKE. THE TREACLE ADDS EXTRA COLOUR AND FLAVOUR. IT WOULD BE AN IDEAL TREAT FOR HUNGRY CHILDREN AFTER SCHOOL, OR FOR SUSTAINING EVERYONE IN THE FAMILY ON A WALK THROUGH THE COUNTRYSIDE.

MAKES A 20cm/8in CAKE

INGREDIENTS
- 250g/9oz/2 cups self-raising (self-rising) flour
- 2.5ml/½ tsp mixed (apple pie) spice
- 75g/3oz/6 tbsp butter, cut into small dice
- 35g/1oz/2 tbsp caster (superfine) sugar
- 150g/5oz/1 cup mixed dried fruit
- 1 egg
- 15ml/1 tbsp treacle (molasses)
- 100ml/3½fl oz/scant ½ cup milk

3 Beat the egg and, with a small whisk or a fork, stir in the treacle and then the milk; add a little extra milk if necessary.

4 Transfer the cake mixture to the prepared dish or tin with a spoon and level out the surface.

5 Bake the cake in the hot oven and cook for about 1 hour until it has risen, is firm to the touch and fully cooked through. To check if the cake is cooked, insert a small skewer in the centre – it should come out free of sticky mixture.

6 Leave the cooked treacle cake to cool completely. Serve, cut into wedges, straight from the dish.

1 Preheat the oven to 180°C/350°F/ Gas 5. Butter a shallow 20–23cm/ 8–9in ovenproof flan dish (pan) or baking tin (pan).

2 Sift the flour and spice into a large mixing bowl. Add the butter and, with your fingertips, rub it into the flour until the mixture resembles fine crumbs. Alternatively, you could make this in a food processor. Stir in the sugar and mixed dried fruit.

GRANDMOTHER'S TIP
You can vary the fruit for this cake, depending on what you have in the storecupboard. Try using chopped ready-to-eat dried apricots and preserved stem ginger, or a packet of luxury dried fruit.

Per cake: Energy 2089kcal/8805kJ; Protein 37.4g; Carbohydrate 343g, of which sugars 152.4g; Fat 72.8g, of which saturates 42.2g; Cholesterol 356mg; Calcium 720mg; Fibre 11.1g; Sodium 676mg.

CHOCOLATE GINGER CRUNCH CAKE

THIS IS ONE OF THE EASIEST CAKES TO MAKE. IT IS A PERFECT RECIPE FOR CHILDREN TO COOK THEMSELVES WITH A LITTLE SUPERVISION — THEY WILL ENJOY BREAKING UP THE BISCUITS WITH A ROLLING PIN AND STIRRING THE MELTING CHOCOLATE. THE CHOPPED GINGER ADDS A SPICY TOUCH.

3 Chop the stem ginger fairly finely and mix with the crushed biscuits.

4 Stir the biscuit mixture, ginger syrup and coconut into the melted chocolate and butter, mixing well until combined.

5 Tip the mixture into the prepared flan ring and press down firmly and evenly.

6 Chill in the fridge until set. Remove the flan ring and slide the cake on to a plate. Melt the milk chocolate, drizzle it over the top and decorate with the pieces of crystallized ginger.

SERVES 6

INGREDIENTS
150g/5oz plain (unsweetened) chocolate, broken into squares
50g/2oz/4 tbsp unsalted butter
115g/4oz ginger nut biscuits (gingersnaps)
4 pieces preserved stem ginger
30ml/2 tbsp stem ginger syrup
45ml/3 tbsp desiccated (dry unsweetened) coconut
To decorate
25g/1oz milk chocolate
pieces of crystallized ginger

1 Crush the biscuits into small pieces and tip into a bowl.

2 Grease a 15cm/6in loose-bottomed flan ring (tart pan); and place it on a sheet of non-stick baking paper. Melt the plain chocolate with the butter in a heatproof bowl over simmering water. When melted, remove from the heat.

GRANDMOTHER'S TIP
Do not process the biscuits, as you need some crunchy pieces for texture. Put them in a stout plastic bag and crush them with a rolling pin.

Energy 340Kcal/1420kJ; Protein 3.1g; Carbohydrate 33.9g, of which sugars 25.4g; Fat 22.3g, of which saturates 14.5g; Cholesterol 20mg; Calcium 46mg; Fibre 2g; Sodium 121mg.

IRISH WHISKEY CAKE

THIS IS A GROWN-UP CAKE FOR THOSE WHO LOVE THE EARTHY, STRONG FLAVOUR OF IRISH WHISKEY. IT HAS ALL THE FLAVOUR OF LEMON AND SPICY CLOVES, WITH PLENTY OF SUCCULENT SULTANAS SOAKED OVERNIGHT. A DRIZZLE OF LEMON-FLAVOURED ICING ON TOP ADDS THE FINISHING TOUCH.

MAKES AN 18cm/7in CAKE

INGREDIENTS
225g/8oz/1⅓ cups sultanas (golden raisins)
grated rind of 1 lemon
150ml/¼ pint/⅔ cup Irish whiskey
175g/6oz/¾ cup butter, softened
175g/6oz/¾ cup soft light brown sugar
175g/6oz/1½ cups plain (all-purpose) flour
pinch of salt
1.5ml/¼ tsp ground cloves
5ml/1 tsp baking powder
3 large (US extra large) eggs, separated
For the icing
juice of 1 lemon
225g/8oz/2 cups icing (confectioners') sugar
crystallized lemon slices, to decorate (optional)

1 Put the sultanas and grated lemon rind into a bowl with the whiskey and leave overnight to soak.

2 Preheat the oven to 180°C/350°F/Gas 4. Grease a loose-bottomed 18cm/7in deep cake tin (pan), and line the base with baking parchment..

3 Cream the butter and sugar until light and fluffy. Sift the flour, salt, cloves and baking powder together into a bowl.

4 Beat the yolks into the butter and sugar one at a time, adding a little of the flour with each egg and beating well after each addition.

5 Gradually blend in the sultana and whiskey mixture, alternating with the remaining flour. Do not overbeat.

GRANDMOTHER'S TIP
For an additional whiskey flavour you could add a shot to the icing before you mix in the water.

6 Whisk the egg whites until stiff and fold them into the mixture with a metal spoon. Turn the mixture into the prepared tin and bake in the preheated oven for 1½ hours, or until well risen and springy to the touch. Turn the cake out of the tin, and leave to cool completely on a rack.

7 To make the icing, mix the lemon juice with the sieved icing sugar and enough warm water to make a pouring consistency. Lay a plate under the cake rack and slowly pour the icing over the cake. Scoop up and reuse any icing dripping on to the plate. When the icing has set, decorate with lemon slices.

Per cake: Energy 4691Kcal/19,730kJ; Protein 48.1g; Carbohydrate 711.2g, of which sugars 577.8g; Fat 167g, of which saturates 97.1g; Cholesterol 1.06g; Calcium 735mg; Fibre 9.9g; Sodium 1.38g.

COUNTRY-STYLE APPLE TART

This classic apple tart is packed with fruit and flavoured with cinnamon. The crust resembles a cake mixture, rather than pastry, which gives a wonderfully light result. Eating apples rather than cooking apples are used for added sweetness.

SERVES 6

INGREDIENTS

215g/7½oz/scant 2 cups plain (all-purpose) flour, plus extra for rolling
5ml/1 tsp baking powder
pinch of salt
115g/4oz/½ cup cold unsalted butter, cubed
finely grated rind of ½ lemon
75g/3oz/scant ½ cup caster (superfine) sugar, plus extra for sprinkling
2 small (US medium) eggs
3 eating apples, peeled and cubed
ground cinnamon
whipped cream, to serve

1 Sift the flour, baking powder and salt into a food processor. Add the butter and grated lemon rind and process briefly to combine, then add the sugar, 1 whole egg and the yolk of the second egg to the flour mixture, and process to make a soft dough.

2 Divide the dough into two pieces, one portion nearly double the size of the other. Wrap in clear film (plastic wrap) and chill for at least 2 hours until firm.

3 Preheat the oven to 180°C/350°F/ Gas 4. Place a baking sheet in the oven and grease a 20cm/8in loose-bottomed flan tin (tart pan).

4 Place the larger piece of dough on a lightly floured piece of clear film (plastic wrap) and cover with another piece of film. Roll out to a 25cm/10in round. Remove the film and place the dough in the tin. Press into the tin so that it stands just clear of the top.

5 Pack the tin with the apples and sprinkle with cinnamon. Roll out the second piece of dough in the same way, to exactly the same size as the tin. Lay the dough on top of the apples and fold the overlapping edges of the bottom piece of dough inward. Gently press the edges together with a fork, to seal.

6 Prick the dough a few times, brush with egg white and sprinkle with sugar. Place on the hot baking sheet and bake for 20 minutes, then reduce the temperature to 160°C/325°F/Gas 3 for a further 25–30 minutes until golden.

7 Leave the tart to cool in the tin for 30 minutes, then unmould and cool on a wire rack. Serve with whipped cream.

Energy 232Kcal/984kJ; Protein 5.7g; Carbohydrate 45.4g, of which sugars 18.1g; Fat 4.4g, of which saturates 1.9g; Cholesterol 69mg; Calcium 69mg; Fibre 1.9g; Sodium 41mg.

SWISS ROLL

ROLLED SPONGE CAKE IS A NURSERY TREAT THAT IS NOT DIFFICULT TO MAKE IF YOU FOLLOW THE INSTRUCTIONS BELOW. THIS ONE IS FILLED WITH CHOCOLATE BUTTERCREAM, BUT A FRUITY JAM AND SOME FRESHLY CHOPPED BERRIES SUCH AS STRAWBERRIES OR RASPBERRIES WOULD TASTE DELICIOUS.

SERVES 12

INGREDIENTS
  50g/2oz/½ cup self-raising (self-rising) flour
  25g/1oz/¼ cup cornflour
  5ml/1 tsp baking powder
  3 eggs
  250g/9oz/1¼ cups caster (superfine) sugar
  30ml/2 tbsp water
For the chocolate buttercream filling
  50g/2oz/¼ cup unsalted butter
  90g/3oz/⅔ cup icing (confectioner's) sugar, sifted
  1 egg yolk
  30ml/2tbsp unsweetened cocoa powder, sifted, plus extra for dusting

1 Preheat the oven to 190°C/375°F /Gas 5. Lightly grease a 27 x 38cm/ 10½ x 15in Swiss roll tin (jelly roll pan). Line with baking parchment and lightly grease it.

2 Sift together the cornflour, flour and baking powder in a mixing bowl. Whisk the eggs and 150g/5oz/¾ cup of the sugar together in a separate bowl until light and foamy.

3 Gradually fold the flour into the egg mixture, continuing to beat until smooth. Add the water. Spread the batter evenly over the prepared tin and bake for 10–12 minutes until golden brown. Sprinkle a clean dish towel with the remaining sugar.

4 To make the chocolate buttercream filling, cream the butter and icing sugar in a large bowl until light and fluffy.

5 Stir in the egg yolk until blended, add the cocoa and mix thoroughly.

GRANDMOTHER'S TIP
Don't let the cake cool flat, otherwise it will crack and break when you roll it.

6 Turn the cooked cake out on to the prepared towel, remove the parchment, and trim the edges. While still warm, roll the cake, then leave to cool slightly.

7 When the cake is almost cool, unroll it, spread with buttercream and roll up again. Dust with icing sugar and cocoa powder, and serve.

Energy 196kcal/826kJ; Protein 2.8g; Carbohydrate 35.1g, of which sugars 29.7g; Fat 5.9g, of which saturates 3g; Cholesterol 73mg; Calcium 34mg; Fibre 0.4g; Sodium 70mg.

BREAD PUDDING

COOKS HAVE ALWAYS BEEN INCREDIBLY INVENTIVE WHEN IT COMES TO USING UP LEFTOVERS.
THIS SPECIAL PUDDING MADE OF STALE BREAD CAN BE SERVED AS A CAKE OR AS A DESSERT WITH
CREAM. IT NEEDS PLENTY OF DRIED FRUIT AND GRATED CITRUS RIND TO SHARPEN THE FLAVOUR.

MAKES 9 SQUARES

INGREDIENTS
    225g/8oz/4 cups stale bread,
      weighed after removing crusts
    300ml/½ pint/1¼ cups milk
    butter, for greasing
    50g/1¾oz/4 tbsp dark muscovado
      (molasses) sugar
    85g/3oz/½ cup shredded suet
      (US chilled, grated shortening) or
      chilled, grated butter
    225g/8oz/1⅓ cups mixed dried fruit,
      including currants, sultanas (golden
      raisins) and chopped citrus peel
    15ml/1 tbsp mixed (apple pie) spice
    2.5ml/½ tsp freshly grated nutmeg
    finely grated rind of 1 small orange
      and 1 small lemon, plus a little
      orange or lemon juice
    1 egg, lightly beaten
    caster (superfine) sugar for sprinkling

1 Break the bread into small pieces. Place the bread in a large mixing bowl, pour the milk over and leave for about 30 minutes.

2 Preheat the oven to 180°C/350°F/ Gas 4. Butter an 18cm/7in square and 5cm/2in deep ovenproof dish. Using a fork, break up the bread in the milk.

3 Stir the sugar, suet, dried fruit, spices and citrus rinds into the bread and milk mixture.

4 Beat in the egg, adding some orange or lemon juice to make a soft mixture.

GRANDMOTHER'S TIP
Although suet is the traditional ingredient in this recipe, you may prefer to use grated chilled butter.

5 Spread the pudding mixture into the prepared dish and level the surface. Put into the hot oven and cook for about 1¼ hours or until the top is brown and firm to the touch.

6 Sprinkle caster sugar over the surface while still warm, then cool slightly before cutting into squares and removing from the dish.

Energy 254kcal/1072kJ; Protein 4.3g; Carbohydrate 39.7g, of which sugars 27g; Fat 10.2g, of which saturates 5.3g; Cholesterol 31mg; Calcium 103mg; Fibre 1.4g; Sodium 147mg.

WALNUT AND DATE CAKE

THIS IS A WONDERFULLY RICH AND MOIST CAKE. IT IS PERFECT FOR AFTERNOON TEA. THE DATES ARE FIRST SOAKED BRIEFLY IN HOT WATER BEFORE ADDING THEM TO THE MIXTURE, WHICH MAKES A SOFT DROPPING BATTER AND GIVES THE CAKE A LOVELY SOFT TEXTURE.

MAKES 18–24 SQUARES

INGREDIENTS
    225g/8oz/1⅓ cups chopped dates
    250ml/8fl oz/1 cup boiling water
    5ml/1 tsp bicarbonate of soda
       (baking soda)
    225g/8oz/generous 1 cup caster
       (superfine) sugar
    1 egg, beaten
    275g/10oz/2¼ cups plain (all-
       purpose) flour
    2.5ml/½ tsp salt
    75g/3oz/6 tbsp butter, softened
    5ml/1 tsp vanilla extract
    5ml/1 tsp baking powder
    50g/2oz/½ cup chopped walnuts

GRANDMOTHER'S TIP
This cake keeps well but if you want it to last a little longer, only cut what you need and store the rest in an airtight container.

1 Put the chopped dates into a warm, dry bowl and pour the boiling water over the top; it should just cover the dates. Add the bicarbonate of soda and mix in thoroughly. Leave to stand for 5–10 minutes.

2 Preheat the oven to 180°C/350°F/ Gas 4. Lightly grease a rectangular 23 x 30cm/9 x 12in cake tin (pan) and line with baking parchment.

3 In a separate mixing bowl, combine all the remaining ingredients for the cake. Then mix in the dates, along with the soaking water until you have a thick batter. You may find it necessary to add a little more boiling water to help the consistency.

4 Pour or spoon the batter into the tin and bake in the oven for 45 minutes. Cut into squares, when cool.

Energy 749kcal/3155kJ; Protein 10.5g; Carbohydrate 125.5g, of which sugars 77.8g; Fat 26.2g, of which saturates 11g; Cholesterol 88mg; Calcium 153mg; Fibre 3.4g; Sodium 141mg.

BANANA BREAD

THE IMPORTANT TRICK IN THIS TRADITIONAL CAKE IS TO USE BANANAS THAT ARE REALLY SOFT AND RIPE — THE BLACKER THE BETTER. IT IS A THRIFTY RECIPE, USING UP OVER-RIPE BANANAS THAT MIGHT OTHERWISE HAVE BEEN DISCARDED. MAKE THEM INTO THIS DELICIOUS SWEET CAKE INSTEAD.

2 Peel the bananas and slice them into a bowl. Mash them well, then stir them into the cake mixture. Add enough milk to give a dropping consistency.

3 Spoon the mixture into the loaf tin and level the surface. Bake for 1¼ hours or until a skewer inserted in the centre comes out clean. Cool on a wire rack.

MAKES 1 LOAF

INGREDIENTS
  115g/4oz/½ cup butter, plus extra for greasing
  5ml/1 tsp bicarbonate of soda (baking soda)
  225g/8oz/2 cups wholemeal (wholewheat) flour
  2 eggs, beaten
  3 very ripe bananas
  30–45ml/2–3 tbsp milk

VARIATION
Sunflower seeds make a good addition to banana cake. Add about 50g/2oz/½ cup to the mixture just before baking.

1 Preheat the oven to 180°C/350°F/Gas 4. Grease and base line a 23 x 13cm/ 9 x 5in loaf tin (pan). Cream the butter in a bowl until it is fluffy. Sift the bicarbonate of soda with the flour, then add to the creamed butter, alternately with the eggs.

Per loaf: Energy 1616kcals/5090kJ Fat, total 66g saturated fat 17.5g; polyunsaturated fat 15.2g; monounsaturated fat 26.5g; Carbohydrate 215g; sugar, total 70g; starch 145g; Fibre 23.5g; Sodium 2320mg

MARMALADE TEABREAD

THIS IS A CAKE THAT IS JUST PERFECT FOR SERVING WITH A CUP OF TEA. THE MARMALADE GIVES IT A LOVELY ORANGEY FLAVOUR AND AT THE SAME TIME KEEPS THE MIXTURE MOIST. IF YOU PREFER NOT TO ICE OR DECORATE THIS CAKE IT WOULD BE JUST AS DELICIOUS SERVED SLICED AND BUTTERED.

MAKES 8–10 SLICES

INGREDIENTS
200g/7oz/1¾ cups plain
(all-purpose) flour
5ml/1 tsp baking powder
6.25ml/1¼ tsp ground cinnamon
100g/3½oz/7 tbsp butter, cut into
small pieces
55g/2oz/3 tbsp soft light
brown sugar
1 egg
60ml/4 tbsp chunky orange
marmalade
about 45ml/3 tbsp milk
For the icing
juice of ½ lemon
115g/4oz/1 cup icing (confectioners')
sugar
shreds of orange and lemon rind,
to decorate

1 Preheat the oven to 160°C/325°F/ Gas 3. Grease a 450g/1lb loaf tin (pan), and line with baking parchment.

2 Sift the flour, baking powder and cinnamon together, then add the butter and rub in with the fingertips until the mixture resembles fine crumbs. Stir in the sugar.

3 Beat the egg lightly in a small bowl and mix it with the marmalade and most of the milk.

4 Mix the milk mixture into the flour mixture, adding more milk if necessary to give a soft dropping consistency.

5 Transfer the mixture to the prepared tin, put into the hot oven and cook for about 1¼ hours, until the cake is firm to the touch and cooked through.

6 Leave the cake to cool for 5 minutes, then turn on to a wire rack. Peel off the lining paper and leave the cake to cool.

7 Combine the icing sugar and lemon juice to make the icing, and spoon over the top of the cake. Decorate with shreds of orange and lemon rind.

Energy 250kcal/1049kJ; Protein 3.5g; Carbohydrate 38g, of which sugars 19g; Fat 10.4g, of which saturates 6.2g; Cholesterol 48mg; Calcium 56mg; Fibre 0.8g; Sodium 86mg.

CURRANT BREAD

THIS IS A SPECIAL LOAF PACKED TO BURSTING WITH DRIED FRUIT AND SPICES, ALL ROLLED UP IN SWEET YEAST DOUGH. THE FRUIT IS PLUMPED UP BY SIMMERING IT GENTLY IN HOT WATER WHILE THE DOUGH RISES. IT NEEDS NO MORE ADORNMENT THAN BUTTER AND MAYBE A SPOONFUL OF JAM.

MAKES 1 LOAF

INGREDIENTS
  500g/1¼lb/generous 4 cups strong
    white bread flour, plus extra
    for dusting
  2 sachets easy-blend (rapid-rise)
    dried yeast
  250ml/8fl oz/1 cup lukewarm milk
  50g/2oz/¼ cup white caster
    (superfine) sugar
  pinch of ground cinnamon
  pinch of ground nutmeg
  pinch of powdered saffron
  1 egg yolk, lightly beaten
  50g/2oz/¼ cup butter, softened, plus
    extra for greasing
  10ml/2 tsp salt
For the filling
  150g/5oz/⅔ cup currants
  150g/5oz/1 cup raisins
  50g/2oz/⅓ cup finely diced
    glacé (candied) citron peel
  50g/2oz/⅓ cup glacé (candied)
    orange peel

GRANDMOTHER'S TIP
Before rolling up the dough at the end of step 6, shape 200g/7oz almond paste into a roll, place on the dough rectangle, roll up and continue as above.

1 Sift the flour into a bowl and make a well in the centre. Add the yeast and a little of the milk to the well and mix together, incorporating some of the flour. Add 5ml/1 tsp of the sugar, cover the bowl with a clean dish towel and leave to stand for 10 minutes.

2 Add the cinnamon, nutmeg and saffron to the remaining milk, add to the bowl and mix well. Add the egg yolk, the remaining sugar and the butter and knead briefly, then add the salt.

3 Turn out the dough on to a lightly floured surface and knead vigorously for at least 15 minutes, until the dough is no longer sticky and is full of bubbles, add a little extra milk if necessary.

4 Shape the dough into a ball, return to a clean bowl and cover with a dampened dish towel. Leave at room temperature for 1 hour, until it has doubled in bulk.

5 To make the filling, poach the currants with the raisins in plenty of simmering water for 10 minutes. Drain well and pat dry in a cloth.

6 Turn out the dough and knead in the dried fruit and both types of glacé fruit peel. Dust both the dough and the work surface with flour and roll into a rectangle 30cm/12in wide. Brush the flour away on both sides. Roll up the rectangle, starting at the top or bottom, wherever the filling is most sparse.

7 Grease a 30 x 10 x 10-cm/12 x 10 x 10-in loaf tin (pan) with butter. Place the dough roll in the tin, with the final fold underneath. Cover with a damp dish towel and leave at room temperature for about 1 hour, until the dough has just risen above the rim. Preheat the oven to 200°C/400°F/Gas 6.

8 Bake the loaf for 35 minutes, then brush the top with cold water and return to the oven for 1 minute. Turn out on to a wire rack and leave to cool.

Per loaf: Energy 3375kcal/14303kJ; Protein 57.3g; Carbohydrate 705.8g, of which sugars 324.8g; Fat 55.2g, of which saturates 28.6g; Cholesterol 308mg; Calcium 1098mg; Fibre 26.2g; Sodium 4651mg.

COTTAGE LOAF

NOTHING COULD BE MORE TRADITIONAL THAN A PLUMP, ROUND COTTAGE LOAF. THIS CLASSIC SHAPE WITH ITS SMALL LOAF SITTING ON TOP OF THE BIGGER BASE IS BOUND TO APPEAL TO CHILDREN. THE OLD TRICK OF SNIPPING THE DOUGH ROUND THE EDGES GIVES IT ROOM TO EXPAND IN THE OVEN.

MAKES 1 LARGE ROUND LOAF

INGREDIENTS
  675g/1½ lb/6 cups unbleached
    strong white bread flour
  10ml/2 tsp salt
  20g/¾ oz fresh yeast
  400ml/14fl oz/1⅔ cups lukewarm
    water

1 Lightly grease 2 baking sheets. Sift the flour and salt together into a large bowl and make a well in the centre.

2 Mix the yeast in 150ml/¼ pint/ ⅔ cup of the water until dissolved. Pour into the centre of the flour with the remaining water and mix to a firm dough.

3 Knead on a lightly floured surface for 10 minutes until smooth and elastic. Place in a lightly oiled bowl, cover with lightly oiled clear film (plastic wrap) and leave to rise, in a warm place, for about 1 hour, or until doubled in bulk.

4 Turn out on to a lightly floured surface and knock back (punch down). Knead for 2–3 minutes, then divide the dough into two-thirds and one-third; shape into balls.

5 Place the balls of dough on the prepared baking sheets. Cover with inverted bowls and leave to rise, in a warm place, for about 30 minutes (see Grandmother's Tips).

6 Gently flatten the top of the larger round of dough and, with a sharp knife, cut a cross in the centre, about 4cm/ 1½ in wide. Brush with a little water and place the smaller round on top.

7 Carefully press a hole through the middle of the top ball, down into the lower part, using your thumb and first two fingers of one hand.

8 Cover the loaf with lightly oiled clear film and leave to rest in a warm place for about 10 minutes.

9 After the dough has rested, turn the oven on to 220°C/ 425°F/Gas 7 and place the bread on the lower shelf. The loaf will finish expanding as the oven heats up.

10 Bake for 35–40 minutes, or until the loaf is golden brown and sounding hollow when tapped. Cool on a wire rack.

GRANDMOTHER'S TIPS
• To ensure a good-shaped cottage loaf the dough needs to be firm enough to support the weight of the top ball.
• Do not over-prove the dough on the second rising or the loaf may topple over – but it will still taste good.

Per loaf: Energy 2302Kcal/9788kJ; Protein 63.5g; Carbohydrate 524.5g, of which sugars 10.1g; Fat 8.8g, of which saturates 1.4g; Cholesterol 0mg; Calcium 946mg; Fibre 20.9g; Sodium 3950mg.

FARMHOUSE LOAF

IN BAKERIES THIS HOMELY LOAF IS CALLED A SPLIT TIN LOAF BECAUSE OF THE WAY THE CRUST IS SPLIT DOWN THE MIDDLE. YOU COULD TRY MAKING IT AS TRADITIONAL BAKERS USED TO DO, WITH TWO SEPARATE PIECES OF DOUGH IN ONE TIN, WHICH JOIN UP AND LEAVE A CRACK WHEN BAKED.

MAKES 1 LOAF

INGREDIENTS
 500g/1¼ lb/5 cups strong white
  bread flour, plus extra for dusting
 10ml/2 tsp salt
 15g/1/2 oz fresh yeast
 300ml/½ pint/1¼ cups lukewarm
  water
 60ml/4 tbsp lukewarm milk

1 Lightly grease a 900g/2lb loaf tin (pan) 18.5 x 11.5cm/7¼ x 4½in. Sift the flour and salt together into a large bowl and make a well in the centre. Mix the yeast with half the lukewarm water in a bowl, then stir in the remaining water.

2 Pour the yeast mixture into the centre of the flour, and using your fingers, mix in a little flour. Gradually mix in a little more of the flour from around the edge of the bowl to form a thick, smooth batter.

3 Sprinkle a little more flour from around the edge over the top of the batter, and then leave in a warm place to 'sponge'.

4 After about 20 minutes, bubbles will appear in the batter. At this stage, pour in the milk and then gradually combine the remaining flour into the batter, and mix to a firm dough.

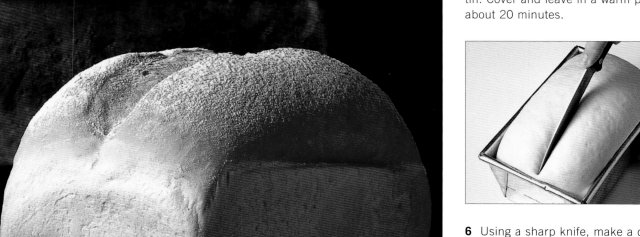

5 Place on a floured surface and knead for about 10 minutes until smooth and elastic. Place in a lightly oiled bowl, cover with lightly oiled clear film (plastic wrap) and leave to rise, in a warm place, for 1–1¼ hours, until doubled in size.

6 Knock back (punch down) the dough and turn out on to a floured surface. Shape into a rectangle, the length of the tin. Roll up lengthways, tuck the ends under and place seam side down in the tin. Cover and leave in a warm place for about 20 minutes.

6 Using a sharp knife, make a deep slash down the length of the bread; dust with flour. Leave for 10–15 minutes.

7 Meanwhile, preheat the oven to 230°C/450°F/Gas 8. Bake for 15 minutes, then reduce the oven temperature to 200°C/400°F/Gas 6. Bake for 20–25 minutes more, or until the bread is golden and sounds hollow when tapped on the base. Turn out on to a wire rack to cool.

Per loaf: Energy 1733kcal/7367kJ; Protein 49g; Carbohydrate 391.5g, of which sugars 10.5g; Fat 7.5g, of which saturates 1.6g; Cholesterol 4mg; Calcium 773mg; Fibre 15.5g; Sodium 3978mg.

BROWN SODA BREAD

THIS IRISH SPECIALITY IS BEST EATEN ON THE DAY OF BAKING SO THAT EVERYONE APPRECIATES ITS LOVELY RUSTIC FLAVOUR. IT IS ESPECIALLY GOOD WITH FRESH BUTTER, STRONG FARMHOUSE CHEESE AND SOME CRISP STICKS OF CELERY OR A BOWL OF HOME-MADE SOUP.

MAKES 1 LOAF

INGREDIENTS
  450g/1lb/4 cups wholemeal (whole-wheat) flour, plus extra for dusting
  175g/6oz/1½ cups plain (all-purpose) flour
  7.5ml/1½ tsp bicarbonate of soda (baking soda)
  5ml/1 tsp salt
  about 450ml/¾ pint/scant 2 cups buttermilk

GRANDMOTHER'S TIP
If you can't find buttermilk for this recipe, you can try mixing plain yogurt or lemon juice to fresh milk, this works in a similar way to buttermilk. Another way to provide the acid is to add 7.5ml/1½ tsp cream of tartar to the dry ingredients.

1 Preheat the oven to 200°C/400°F/Gas 6, and grease a baking sheet. Combine the dry ingredients in a mixing bowl and stir in enough buttermilk to make a fairly soft dough. Turn on to a work surface dusted with wholemeal flour and knead lightly until smooth. Form the dough into a circle, about 4cm/1½in thick.

2 Place on the baking sheet and mark a deep cross in the top with a knife.

3 Bake for about 45 minutes, or until the bread is browned and sounds hollow when tapped on the base. Cool on a wire rack. If a soft crust is preferred, wrap the loaf in a clean dish towel while cooling.

Per loaf: Energy 2262Kcal/9643kJ; Protein 88.5g; Carbohydrate 465.4g, of which sugars 31.4g; Fat 18.9g, of which saturates 6.5g; Cholesterol 27mg; Calcium 1.37g; Fibre 34.2g; Sodium 2.18g.

DROP SCONES

THESE LITTLE SCONES ARE KNOWN BY MANY DIFFERENT NAMES, SUCH AS GRIDDLE CAKES OR SCOTCH PANCAKES. THEY MAKE A QUICK AND EASY WARM BREAKFAST, OR A SPECIAL TREAT FOR ELEVENSES OR AT TEA TIME, TOPPED WITH BUTTER AND JAM OR DRIZZLED WITH HONEY.

2 Add the diced butter and rub it into the flour with your fingertips until the mixture resembles fine, evenly textured breadcrumbs.

3 Make a well in the centre of the flour mixture, then stir in the egg.

4 Add the milk a little at a time, stirring it in to check consistency. Add enough milk to give a lovely thick, creamy consistency.

5 Cook in batches. Drop 3 or 4 evenly sized spoonfuls of the mixture, spaced slightly apart, on the griddle or frying pan. Cook over a medium heat for 2–3 minutes, until bubbles rise to the surface and burst.

6 Turn the scones over and cook for a further 2–3 minutes, until golden underneath. Place the cooked scones between the folds of a clean dish towel while cooking the remaining batter. Serve warm, with butter and honey.

MAKES 8-10

INGREDIENTS
  115g/4oz/1 cup plain
  (all-purpose) flour
  5ml/1 tsp bicarbonate of soda
  (baking soda)
  5ml/1 tsp cream of tartar
  25g/1oz/2 tbsp butter, diced
  1 egg, beaten
  about 150ml/¼ pint/⅔ cup milk
  butter and honey, to serve

GRANDMOTHER'S TIP
Placing the cooked scones in a clean, folded dish towel keeps them soft and moist. Bring to the table like this and ask your guests to pull them out and serve themselves.

1 Lightly grease a griddle pan or heavy frying pan, then preheat it. Sift the flour, bicarbonate of soda and cream of tartar together into a mixing bowl.

Energy 90kcal/379kJ; Protein 2.8g; Carbohydrate 12.1g, of which sugars 1.1g; Fat 3.8g, of which saturates 2.1g; Cholesterol 32mg; Calcium 47mg; Fibre 0.5g; Sodium 36mg.

CRUMPETS

TOASTED CRUMPETS ARE A TREAT FOR ALL AGES, BUT ARE PARTICULARLY ASSOCIATED WITH NURSERY TEAS IN VICTORIAN TIMES, WHEN THEY WOULD HAVE BEEN BROWNED ON A FORK BY THE FIRE. THE YEAST BATTER IS FIRST COOKED IN METAL RINGS ON A GRIDDLE AND LEFT TO COOL BEFORE TOASTING.

MAKES ABOUT 10

INGREDIENTS
    225g/8oz/2 cups plain (all-purpose)
        flour
    2.5ml/½ tsp salt
    2.5ml/½ tsp bicarbonate of soda
        (baking soda)
    5ml/1 tsp easy-blend (rapid-rise)
        dried yeast
    150ml/¼ pint/⅔ cup milk
    oil, for greasing

1 Sift the flour, salt and bicarbonate of soda into a bowl and stir in the yeast. Make a well in the centre. Heat the milk with 200ml/7fl oz/scant 1 cup water until lukewarm, and pour slowly into the well.

2 Mix well with a whisk or wooden spoon, beating vigorously to make a thick, smooth batter. Cover and leave in a warm place for about 1 hour until the mixture has a spongy texture.

3 Heat a griddle or heavy frying pan. Lightly oil the hot surface and the inside of three or four metal rings, each measuring about 8cm/3½in in diameter. Place the oiled rings on the hot surface and leave for 1–2 minutes until hot.

4 Spoon the batter into the rings to a depth of about 1cm/½in. Cook over a medium-high heat for about 6 minutes, until the top surface is set and bubbles have burst open to make holes.

5 When set, carefully lift off the metal rings and flip the crumpets over, cooking the second side for just 1 minute until lightly browned.

6 Remove from the pan and leave to cool completely on a wire rack. Repeat with the remaining crumpet mixture.

7 Just before serving, toast the crumpets under a grill (broiler) on both sides, and butter generously.

Energy 93kcal/393kJ; Protein 3g; Carbohydrate 16.5g, of which sugars 1g; Fat 2.1g, of which saturates 1g; Cholesterol 21mg; Calcium 48mg; Fibre 0.6g; Sodium 21mg.

BAKES AND COOKIES

In this chapter you will find recipes for all kinds of individual small cakes, cookies and tray bakes that probably sum up the best of home baking. These delicious morsels make the most of store-cupboard ingredients and are ideal for filling the hunger gap between meals, serving with afternoon tea or for packing into a lunch box for a special treat.

GINGERBREAD

MAKING GINGERBREAD BRINGS BACK THE SCENTS AND TASTES OF CHILDHOOD TO THE KITCHEN, WITH THE AROMA OF WARM HONEY AND GINGER FILLING THE AIR. THIS VERSION ADDS CHOPPED TOASTED HAZELNUTS FOR A RUSTIC CRUNCH. IT IS VERY EASY TO MAKE AND WILL PROVE A REAL WINNER.

MAKES 30 SQUARES

INGREDIENTS
   300g/11oz/scant 3 cups hazelnuts
   300g/11oz/1½ cups soft dark
     brown sugar
   5 eggs
   150g/5oz/10 tbsp butter
   100g/3½oz/½ cup honey
   500g/1⅓lb/5 cups plain (all-purpose)
     flour
   25ml/5 tsp baking powder
   7.5ml/1½ tsp ground ginger

1 Preheat the oven to 160°C/325°F/ Gas 3 and line a 40 x 30cm/16 x 12in baking tray with baking parchment.

2 Toast the hazelnuts in a frying pan over medium heat, moving them around so they brown evenly. Cool, then chop.

3 Melt the butter in a small pan. Beat the sugar with the eggs until the mixture is light and thick.

4 Stir the melted butter, honey and hazelnuts into the egg mixture. Sift the flour with the baking powder and ground ginger and fold into the mixture. Pour the batter into the prepared tray. Bake for about 45 minutes. Cool in the tin before cutting into squares.

Energy 741kcal/3106kJ; Protein 14.1g; Carbohydrate 89.1g, of which sugars 45.4g; Fat 38.9g, of which saturates 11.5g; Cholesterol 144mg; Calcium 166mg; Fibre 3.8g; Sodium 171mg.

YORKSHIRE PARKIN

THIS MOIST GINGER CAKE IS TRADITIONALLY SERVED CUT INTO SQUARES, AS A FILLING TEATIME TREAT OR A DESSERT WITH APPLE SAUCE. IT IS BASED ON A NOURISHING OATMEAL AND FLOUR MIXTURE, WITH PLENTY OF DARK AND LIGHT SYRUP TO SWEETEN THE CAKE AND BLEND WITH THE GINGER.

MAKES 16–20 SQUARES

INGREDIENTS
    300ml/½ pint/1¼ cups milk
    225g/8oz/1 cup golden (corn) syrup
    225g/8oz/¾ cup treacle (molasses)
    115g/4oz/½ cup butter
    50g/2oz/scant ¼ cup soft dark
      brown sugar
    450g/1lb/4 cups plain (all-purpose)
      flour
    2.5ml/½ tsp bicarbonate of soda
      (baking soda)
    7.5ml/1½ tsp ground ginger
    350g/12oz/4 cups medium oatmeal
    1 egg, beaten
    icing (confectioner's) sugar, to dust

1 Preheat the oven to 180°C/350°F/
Gas 4. Grease a 20cm/8in square cake
tin (pan) and line the base and sides
with baking parchment.

2 Gently heat together the milk, syrup,
treacle, butter and sugar, stirring until
smooth; do not boil.

3 Sift the flour into a bowl, and add the
bicarbonate of soda, ginger and
oatmeal. Make a well in the centre of
the dry ingredients and add the egg.

4 Stir the egg into the flour and then
add the warmed milk and treacle
mixture, stirring well until you have a
smooth batter.

5 Pour the batter into the tin and bake
in the oven for about 45 minutes, until
the top is firm to the touch. Cool slightly
in the tin, then turn out onto a wire rack
to cool completely. Cut into squares and
dust with icing sugar.

Energy 273kcal/1152kJ; Protein 5.3g; Carbohydrate 50g, of which sugars 20.1g; Fat 7.1g, of which saturates 3.3g; Cholesterol 23mg; Calcium 127mg; Fibre 1.9g; Sodium 102mg.

COCONUT MACAROONS

THESE DELICATE, AROMATIC CAKES ARE SIMPLE FOR CHILDREN TO MAKE WITH A LITTLE SUPERVISION, AS JUST A FEW INGREDIENTS ARE NEEDED. THEY ARE BEST SERVED WARM, STRAIGHT FROM THE OVEN, BUT WILL KEEP REASONABLY WELL IN AN AIRTIGHT CONTAINER.

MAKES 15–20

INGREDIENTS
    1 vanilla pod (bean)
    120ml/4fl oz/½ cup double
      (heavy) cream
    200g/7oz desiccated (dry
      unsweetened shredded) coconut
    200g/4oz/1 cup caster (superfine)
      sugar
    1 egg

1 Put the vanilla pod in a pan with the cream. Bring to a simmer then turn off the heat and infuse for 20 minutes.

2 Preheat the oven to 200°C/400°F/ Gas 6. Line a baking sheet. Remove the pod from the cream and pour the cream into a large bowl. Mix in the coconut, sugar and egg.

3 Spoon the mixture in piles on to the prepared baking sheet. Bake for 12–15 minutes until golden brown. Leave the cakes to cool slightly before transferring to a cooling rack.

Energy 177kcal/740kJ; Protein 1.4g; Carbohydrate 14.9g, of which sugars 14.9g; Fat 13g, of which saturates 9.9g; Cholesterol 23.6mg; Calcium 16mg; Fibre 1.8g; Sodium 10.9mg.

HONEY AND SPICE CAKES

THESE GOLDEN CAKES FROM WALES ARE FRAGRANT WITH HONEY AND CINNAMON. THEY RISE QUITE SPECTACULARLY IN THE OVEN, SO LEAVE PLENTY OF ROOM IN EACH CAKE CASE. ONE OF THESE WOULD BE AN IDEAL ADDITION TO A CHILD'S LUNCH BOX OR AS A SWEET TREAT FOR ELEVENSES.

MAKES 18

INGREDIENTS
  250g/9oz/2 cups plain (all-purpose) flour
  5ml/1 tsp ground cinnamon
  5ml/1 tsp bicarbonate of soda (baking soda)
  125g/4½oz/½ cup butter, softened
  125g/4½oz/10 tbsp soft light brown sugar
  1 large (US extra large) egg, separated
  125g/4½oz clear honey
  about 60ml/4 tbsp milk
  caster (superfine) sugar for sprinkling

1 Preheat the oven to 200°C/400°F/ Gas 6. Butter the holes of a muffin tin (pan) or line them with paper cases.

2 Sift the flour, cinnamon and bicarbonate of soda into a large bowl.

3 Beat the butter with the sugar until light and fluffy. Beat in the egg yolk, then gradually add the honey.

4 With a large metal spoon and a cutting action, fold in the flour mixture plus sufficient milk to make a soft mixture that will just drop off the spoon.

5 In a separate bowl whisk the egg white until stiff peaks form. Using a large metal spoon, fold the egg white into the cake mixture.

6 Divide the mixture among the paper cases or the holes in the prepared tin. Put into the hot oven and cook for 15–20 minutes or until risen, firm to the touch and golden brown.

7 Sprinkle the tops lightly with caster sugar and leave to cool completely on a wire rack.

Energy 152kcal/639kJ; Protein 1.9g; Carbohydrate 23.6g, of which sugars 13g; Fat 6.3g, of which saturates 3.8g; Cholesterol 26mg; Calcium 30mg; Fibre 0.4g; Sodium 49mg.

CHOCOLATE CHIP CAKES

NOTHING COULD BE EASIER — OR NICER — THAN THESE CLASSIC MUFFINS. THE CAKE MIXTURE IS PLAIN, BUT HAS A SURPRISE LAYER OF CHOCOLATE CHIPS INSIDE THAT WILL PARTICULARLY APPEAL TO CHILDREN. SPRINKLE A FEW CHOCOLATE CHIPS ON TOP OF EACH CAKE TO MAKE THEM IRRESISTIBLE.

MAKES 10

INGREDIENTS
  115g/4oz/½ cup butter, softened
  75g/3oz/⅓ cup caster (superfine)
    sugar
  30ml/2 tbsp soft dark brown sugar
  2 eggs
  175g/6oz/1½ cups plain (all-purpose)
    flour
  5ml/1 tsp baking powder
  120ml/4fl oz/½ cup milk
  175g/6oz/1 cup plain (semisweet)
    chocolate chips

1 Preheat the oven to 190°C/375°F/ Gas 5. Arrange 10 paper cases in a muffin tin (pan).

2 In a large bowl, beat the butter until it is pale and light. Add the caster and dark brown sugars and beat until the mixture is light and fluffy. Beat in the eggs, one at a time, beating thoroughly after each addition.

3 Sift the flour and baking powder together twice. Fold into the butter mixture, alternating with the milk.

4 Divide half the mixture among the paper cases. Sprinkle with half the chocolate chips, cover with the rest of the mixture and the chocolate chips. Bake for about 25 minutes, until golden. Leave to stand for 5 minutes, then transfer to a wire rack to cool.

Energy 296kcal/1241kJ; Protein 4.2g; Carbohydrate 36.5g, of which sugars 22.3g; Fat 15.9g, of which saturates 9.5g; Cholesterol 67mg; Calcium 59mg; Fibre 0.5g; Sodium 110mg.

ORANGE CUPCAKES WITH ORANGE GLAZE

THESE DELICIOUS CAKES CONTAIN THE SHARP, FRUITY TANG OF OLD-FASHIONED MARMALADE, BOTH IN THE CAKE MIXTURE AND IN THE CITRUS-FLAVOURED GLAZE. THE BUTTERMILK IN THE SPONGE BASE ADDS TO THE PIQUANT FLAVOUR. THEY ARE IDEAL FOR SERVING WITH A CUP OF TEA OR COFFEE.

MAKES 9–10

INGREDIENTS
    75g/3oz/6 tbsp butter
    1 egg, lightly beaten
    175ml/6fl oz/¾ cup buttermilk
    juice of 1½ Seville (Temple) oranges,
        plus grated rind of 2 Seville oranges
    225g/8oz/2 cups plain (all-purpose)
        flour
    10ml/2 tsp baking powder
    150g/5oz/¾ golden caster (superfine)
        sugar
    15ml/1 tbsp Seville orange
        marmalade
For the orange glaze
    juice and finely grated rind of
        ½ Seville (Temple) orange
    75–90ml/5–6 tbsp icing
        (confectioners') sugar, sifted
    5ml/1 tsp Seville orange marmalade

VARIATION
If Seville oranges aren't in season, use sweet oranges instead.

1 Preheat the oven to 180°C/350°F/ Gas 4. Lightly grease a muffin tin (pan). Melt the butter in a pan over a low heat, set aside to cool slightly.

2 In a bowl, mix together the egg, buttermilk, orange juice and grated rind and the cooled, melted butter.

GRANDMOTHER'S TIP
If you don't have any homemade marmalade, make sure you buy good-quality roughly cut marmalade.

3 Add the flour, baking powder and sugar. Fold in gently, with the marmalade, until just blended.

4 Spoon the mixture into the tin, filling almost to the top. Bake for 25 minutes until golden. Leave to stand, then turn on to a wire rack to cool.

5 To make the orange glaze, put the juice in a bowl and beat in the sugar, grated rind and marmalade. The mixture should cover the back of a spoon, but be thin and fluid. Drizzle the glaze in a loose zigzag over the tops of the cakes just before serving.

Energy 242kcal/1020kJ; Protein 3.5g; Carbohydrate 43.9g, of which sugars 26.8g; Fat 7g, of which saturates 4.3g; Cholesterol 37mg; Calcium 70mg; Fibre 0.7g; Sodium 76mg.

RASPBERRY CRUMBLE BUNS

These fruity little cakes are best made in high summer, when raspberries are bursting with flavour. The nutty crumble topping contrasts beautifully with the soft fruit inside. These cakes can be served with raspberry jam and cream for a special treat.

MAKES 12

INGREDIENTS

    175g/6oz/1½ cups plain (all-purpose) flour
    10ml/2 tsp baking powder
    5ml/1 tsp ground cinnamon
    115g/4oz/½ cup butter, melted
    120ml/4fl oz/½ cup milk
    50g/2oz/¼ cup caster (superfine) sugar
    50g/2oz/¼ cup soft light brown sugar
    1 egg
    225g/8oz/1⅓ cups fresh raspberries
    grated rind of 1 lemon
For the crumble topping
    50g/2oz/½ cup pecan nuts, finely chopped
    50g/2oz/¼ cup soft dark brown sugar
    45ml/3 tbsp plain (all-purpose) flour
    5ml/1 tsp ground cinnamon
    40g/1½oz/3 tbsp butter, melted

1 Preheat the oven to 180°C/350°F/ Gas 4. Arrange 12 paper cases in a muffin tin (pan).

2 Sift the flour, baking powder and cinnamon into a large bowl. In another bowl, beat together the cooled, melted butter and milk.

3 Make a well in the centre of the flour and add the two types of sugar, then the egg. Add the melted butter and milk mixture and stir in gradually until just combined. Don't overmix, as this will make the buns heavier when cooked.

4 Stir the raspberries and lemon rind into the mixture, then spoon into the muffin cases, filling almost to the top.

5 To make the crumble topping, mix the chopped pecans, sugar, flour and cinnamon in a large mixing bowl. Stir in the melted butter to coat everything and create a crumbly texture.

6 Spoon a little of the crumble over the top of each bun. Bake for about 25 minutes until they are risen and golden.

7 Leave to stand for 5 minutes, then transfer to a wire rack to cool slightly. Serve while still warm.

Energy 251kcal/1051kJ; Protein 3.4g; Carbohydrate 28.9g, of which sugars 14.9g; Fat 14.4g, of which saturates 7.5g; Cholesterol 46mg; Calcium 56mg; Fibre 1.2g; Sodium 110mg.

MAIDS OF HONOUR

THESE LITTLE DELICACIES ARE SAID TO DATE FROM THE REIGN OF HENRY VIII. IN PAST TIMES THEY WOULD HAVE BEEN FILLED WITH STRAINED CURDS, BUT THESE DAYS THEY ARE MADE WITH A SHARP CURD CHEESE FILLING, WELL FLAVOURED WITH GROUND ALMONDS, LEMON AND SUGAR.

MAKES 12

INGREDIENTS
    250g/9oz ready-made puff pastry
    250g/9oz/1¼ cups curd (farmer's)
      cheese
    60ml/4 tbsp ground almonds
    45ml/3 tbsp caster (superfine) sugar
    finely grated rind of 1 small lemon
    2 eggs
    15g/½ oz/1 tbsp butter, melted
    icing (confectioner's) sugar, to dust

1 Preheat the oven to 200°C/400°F/ Gas 6. Butter a muffin tin (pan).

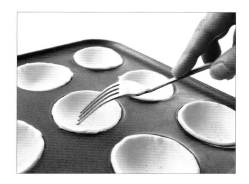

2 Roll out the puff pastry very thinly on a lightly floured surface and, using a 7.5/3in cutter, cut out 12 circles. Press the pastry circles into the prepared tray and prick well with a fork. Chill, while you make the filling.

3 Put the curd cheese into a bowl and add the almonds, sugar and lemon rind. Lightly beat the eggs with the butter and add to the cheese mixture. Mix well.

4 Spoon the mixture into the pastry cases. Bake for about 20 minutes, until the pastry is well risen and the filling is puffed up, golden brown and just firm to the touch.

5 Transfer to a wire rack (the filling will sink down as it cools). Serve warm or at room temperature, dusted with a little sifted icing sugar.

CUSTARD TARTS

THESE TARTS ARE AN INDULGENT TREAT, REDOLENT OF TEAS BY THE FIRE IN WINTER OR PICNICS ON THE LAWN IN SUMMER. THE SWEET PASTRY CONTAINS A DELICATELY FLAVOURED EGG CUSTARD, WITH NUTMEG LIBERALLY SPRINKLED ON TOP. USE UP THE LEFTOVER EGG WHITES TO MAKE MERINGUES.

MAKES ABOUT 8

INGREDIENTS
  175g/6oz/1½ cups plain
    (all-purpose) flour
  pinch of salt
  75g/3oz/6 tbsp unsalted butter, at
    room temperature
  75g/3oz/6 tbsp caster (superfine)
    sugar
  3 egg yolks, at room temperature
  a few drops vanilla extract
For the filling
  600ml/1 pint/2½ cups full cream
    (whole) milk
  6 egg yolks
  75g/3oz/6 tbsp caster (superfine)
    sugar
  freshly grated nutmeg

1 To make the pastry, sift the flour and salt into a bowl.

2 Put the butter, sugar, egg yolks and vanilla extract in a food processor and process until the mixture resembles scrambled eggs. Add the flour and blend briefly.

3 Transfer the dough to a lightly floured surface and knead gently until smooth. Form into a ball, flatten and wrap in clear film (plastic wrap). Chill for at least 30 minutes. Bring back to room temperature before rolling out.

4 Roll out the pastry and line eight individual 10cm/4in loose-bottomed tartlet tins (pans). Chill for 30 minutes.

5 Preheat the oven to 200°C/400°F/ Gas 6. To make the custard filling, gently heat the milk in a pan until just warmed but not yet boiling.

6 In a bowl, vigorously beat the egg yolks and sugar together until they become pale and creamy in texture.

7 Pour the milk on to the egg mixture and stir well with a wooden spoon to mix. Do not whisk as this will produce too many bubbles.

8 Strain the milk mixture into a jug (pitcher), then carefully pour the liquid into the tartlet cases. Grate fresh nutmeg over the surface of the tartlets.

9 Bake for about 10 minutes, then lower the heat to 180°C/350°F/Gas 4 and bake for another 10 minutes, or until the filling has set and is just turning golden. The tartlets should be a bit wobbly when they come out of the oven. Remove from the oven and lift the tarts out of the tins. Serve warm or cold.

Energy 336kcal/1409kJ; Protein 7.9g; Carbohydrate 40g, of which sugars 23.4g; Fat 17.1g, of which saturates 8.6g; Cholesterol 257mg; Calcium 157mg; Fibre 0.7g; Sodium 101mg.

ALMOND SHORTBREAD

THIS CLASSIC SCOTTISH RECIPE CAN BE MADE VERY QUICKLY AND EASILY IN A FOOD PROCESSOR, OR BY HAND IN THE TRADITIONAL WAY, WHICH TAKES SLIGHTLY LONGER. THE GROUND ALMONDS ADD TASTE AND CRUNCH AND THE RESULTING BUTTERY, CRUMBLY BISCUITS ARE DELIGHTFUL.

MAKES ABOUT 18 FINGERS

INGREDIENTS
- oil, for greasing
- 275g/10oz/2½ cups plain (all-purpose) flour
- 25g/1oz/¼ cup ground almonds
- 225g/8oz/1 cup butter, softened
- 75g/3oz/scant ½ cup caster (superfine) sugar
- grated rind of ½ lemon

VARIATION
You can replace the lemon rind with the grated rind of two oranges for a tangy orange flavour, if you prefer.

1 Preheat the oven to 180°C/350°F/ Gas 4 and oil a 28 x 18cm/11 x 7in shallow cake tin (pan).

2 Put all the ingredients into a blender or food processor and pulse until the mixture comes together.

3 Place the mixture on the oiled tray and flatten it out with a palette knife or metal spatula until evenly spread. Bake in the preheated oven for 20 minutes, or until pale golden brown.

4 Remove from the oven and immediately mark the shortbread into fingers or squares while the mixture is soft. Allow to cool a little, and then transfer to a wire rack and leave until cold. The shortbread should keep for up to two weeks in an airtight container.

GRANDMOTHER'S TIP
To make the shortbread by hand instead of using a food processor, sift the flour and almonds on to a pastry board or work surface. Cream together the butter and sugar in a mixing bowl and then turn the creamed mixture out on to the pastry board with the flour and almonds. Work the mixture together using your fingertips. It should come together to make a smooth dough. Continue to follow the recipe from Step 3.

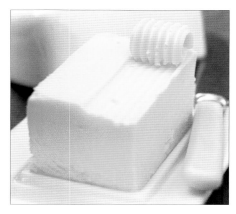

Energy 64kcal/266kJ; Protein 0.7g; Carbohydrate 6.1g, of which sugars 1.8g; Fat 4.2g, of which saturates 2.5g; Cholesterol 10mg; Calcium 11mg; Fibre 0.2g; Sodium 29mg.

GINGER BISCUITS

This recipe produces spicy biscuits that make the most of several different flavourings. A combination of traditional store-cupboard spices — ginger, cinnamon and cloves, with the surprise of a little cardamom and black pepper — gives them an unusual twist.

MAKES 24–28

INGREDIENTS

100ml/3½fl oz/scant ½ cup golden (light corn) syrup
5ml/1 tsp grated orange rind
5ml/1 tsp ground cinnamon
2.5ml/½ tsp ground pepper
2.5ml/½ tsp ground ginger
2.5ml/½ tsp ground cloves
5ml/1 tsp ground cardamom
10ml/2 tsp bicarbonate of soda (baking soda)
100ml/3½fl oz/scant ½ cup double (heavy) cream
200g/7oz/scant 1 cup unsalted butter, softened
100g/3¾oz/generous ½ cup caster (superfine) sugar
1 egg, beaten
400g/14oz/3½ cups plain (all-purpose) flour

GRANDMOTHER'S TIP
When spooning syrup from the tin, use a metal spoon, dipped in just boiled water. The hot metal will mean the syrup slips off it straight away. If possible, weigh it in the pan in which you intend to heat it.

1 Put the golden syrup, orange rind, cinnamon, pepper, ginger, cloves and cardamom in a pan and heat gently until warm. Remove from the heat.

2 Mix the bicarbonate of soda into the cream so that it is evenly distributed. Put the butter and sugar in a large bowl and whisk together until light and fluffy. Keep whisking as you add the beaten egg, and then the warm spiced syrup. Mix together well.

3 Add the flour to the bowl and mix together to form a dough. Wrap in clear film (plastic wrap) and leave to rest in the refrigerator for at least 1 hour.

4 Preheat the oven to 200°C/400°F/Gas 6. On a lightly floured surface, roll out the dough to a 3mm/⅛in thickness.

5 Using a cookie cutter or shapes, cut out the dough, re-rolling and cutting out the dough trimmings.

6 Place on a baking sheet and bake in the oven for 7–10 minutes, until light brown. Remove from the sheet and leave to cool on a wire tray.

Energy 1039kcal/4349kJ; Protein 12.4g; Carbohydrate 125.6g, of which sugars 48.1g; Fat 57.7g, of which saturates 35.1g; Cholesterol 188mg; Calcium 193mg; Fibre 3.1g; Sodium 399mg.

MELTING MOMENTS

AS THE NAME SUGGESTS, THESE CRISP BISCUITS REALLY DO MELT IN THE MOUTH. THEY HAVE A SHORTBREAD TEXTURE AND ARE ROLLED IN OATS FOR EXTRA CRUNCH. THEY ARE TRADITIONALLY TOPPED WITH A LITTLE PIECE OF GLACE CHERRY, WHICH MAKES THEM LOOK MOST ATTRACTIVE.

MAKES 16–20

INGREDIENTS
   40g/1½oz/3 tbsp soft butter
   65g/2½oz/5 tbsp lard or white
      cooking fat
   85g/3oz/6 tbsp caster (superfine)
      sugar
   1 egg yolk, beaten
   few drops of vanilla extract
   150g/5oz/1¼ cups self-raising (self-
      rising) flour
   rolled oats, for coating
   4–5 glacé (candied) cherries

VARIATION
If you wish, use almond extract instead of the vanilla extract, and place an almond on top in place of the cherry.

1 Preheat the oven to 180°C/350°F/ Gas 4. Beat together the butter, lard and sugar, then gradually beat in the egg yolk and vanilla extract.

2 Sift the flour over, and stir to make a soft dough. Roll into 16–20 small balls.

3 Spread rolled oats on a sheet of baking parchment and toss the balls in them until evenly coated.

4 Place the balls, spaced slightly apart so they have room to spread, on two baking sheets. Flatten each ball a little with your thumb.

5 Cut the cherries into quarters and place a quarter of cherry on top of each biscuit (cookie). Put the baking sheets into the hot oven and cook for 15–20 minutes, until they are lightly browned.

6 Allow the biscuits to cool for a few minutes on the baking sheets before transferring them to a wire rack to cool completely.

Energy 88kcal/370kJ; Protein 0.7g; Carbohydrate 10.9g, of which sugars 5.4g; Fat 5g, of which saturates 2.4g; Cholesterol 7mg; Calcium 30mg; Fibre 0.3g; Sodium 40mg.

ALMOND BISCUITS

THESE INTRIGUING ALMOND SHAPES ARE MADE WITH A SMOOTH DOUGH, WHICH IS ROLLED OUT THINLY AND SHAPED INTO A TWIST. CHILDREN WILL REALLY ENJOY THE ROLLING AND SHAPING PROCESS. THEY CAN BE SERVED WITH COFFEE OR ALONGSIDE A CREAMY FOOL OR ICE-CREAM DESSERT.

MAKES 20

INGREDIENTS
  200g/7oz/1 cup sugar
  150g/5oz/10 tbsp butter
  3 eggs
  350g/12oz/3 cups plain
    (all-purpose) flour, plus extra for
    dusting
  100g/3¾oz/scant 1 cup ground
    almonds
  caster (superfine) sugar, and chopped
    almonds, to decorate

GRANDMOTHER'S TIP
If you are making these with children, try shaping the biscuits into letters.

1 Preheat the oven to 180°C/350°F/ Gas 4. Put the sugar and butter in a large bowl and beat until light and fluffy. Add the eggs, one at a time, beating after each addition.

2 When all the eggs are incorporated, add the flour and almonds to the bowl and mix thoroughly to make a dough.

3 On a floured surface, roll out the dough quite thinly and cut into strips. Cut the strips into 4cm/1½in lengths.

4 Twist each strip into an S shape. Place on a baking tray. Sprinkle with sugar and chopped almonds. Bake for 10 minutes, until golden brown.

Energy 188kcal/788kJ; Protein 3.5g; Carbohydrate 22.5g, of which sugars 10.9g; Fat 10g, of which saturates 4.4g; Cholesterol 45mg; Calcium 44mg; Fibre 0.8g; Sodium 58mg.

BUTTER COOKIES

THESE CRUNCHY, BUTTERY COOKIES MAKE A DELICIOUS AFTER-SCHOOL TREAT SERVED WITH A GLASS OF MILK. THE CLEVER FEATURE OF THESE SWEET COOKIES IS THAT THE DOUGH CAN BE MADE WELL IN ADVANCE AND CHILLED UNTIL YOU ARE READY TO SLICE IT AND BAKE A FRESH BATCH.

MAKES 25–30

INGREDIENTS

  175g/6oz/¾ cup unsalted butter, at
    room temperature, diced
  90g/3½oz/½ cup golden caster
    (superfine) sugar
  250g/9oz/2¼ cups plain
    (all-purpose) flour
  demerara (raw) sugar, for coating

VARIATIONS

• To flavour the cookies, add ground cinnamon, grated lemon or orange rind, or vanilla or almond extract to the butter mixture. You can also try adding whole glacé (candied) cherries, or chocolate chips, chopped nuts or dried fruit such as chopped apricots to the dough when you add the flour.

• As an alternative, coat the outside in a mixture of sugar and chopped nuts.

1 Put the butter and sugar in a bowl and beat until light and fluffy. Add the flour and, using your hands, gradually work it in until the mixture forms a smooth dough.

2 Roll the dough into a sausage shape about 30cm/12in long, then pat to form either a square or triangular log.

3 Sprinkle a thick layer of demerara sugar on a piece of baking parchment paper. Press each side of the dough into the sugar to coat. Wrap and chill for about 30 minutes until firm. Meanwhile, preheat the oven to 160°C/ 325°F/Gas 3.

4 When ready to bake, remove the dough from the refrigerator and unwrap it. Cut into thick slices and place slightly apart on non-stick baking sheets. Bake for 20 minutes until just beginning to turn brown. Transfer to a wire rack to cool.

Energy 84Kcal/350kJ; Protein 0.8g; Carbohydrate 9.6g, of which sugars 3.3g; Fat 4.9g, of which saturates 3.1g; Cholesterol 12mg; Calcium 14mg; Fibre 0.3g; Sodium 36mg.

VIENNESE WHIRLS

KEEN COOKS CAN HAVE THE CHANCE TO SHOW OFF THEIR SKILLS WITH THESE COOKIES. THE MIXTURE IS PIPED IN ROSETTE SHAPES ON TO A BAKING SHEET, THEN EACH PIECE IS SANDWICHED TOGETHER WITH SWEET, COFFEE-FLAVOURED BUTTERCREAM ICING. SERVE WITH MORNING COFFEE.

2 Spoon the mixture into a piping bag fitted with a 1cm/½in fluted nozzle.

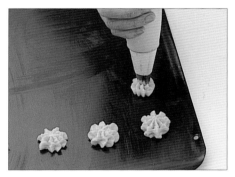

3 Pipe rosettes on greased baking sheets. Bake for 12–15 minutes until golden. Transfer to a wire rack to cool.

4 Put the coffee in a bowl. Heat the cream to near-boiling and pour it over. Infuse (steep) for 4 minutes, then strain.

MAKES 20

INGREDIENTS
   175g/6oz/12 tbsp butter
   50g/2oz/½ cup icing (confectioners')
    sugar
   2.5ml/½ tsp vanilla extract
   115g/4oz/1 cup plain (all-purpose)
    flour
   50g/2oz/½ cup cornflour (cornstarch)
   icing (confectioners') sugar and
    cocoa powder, to dust
For the filling
   15ml/1 tbsp ground coffee
   60ml/4 tbsp single (light) cream
   75g/3oz/6 tbsp butter, softened
   115g/4oz/1 cup icing (confectioners')
    sugar, sifted

1 Preheat the oven to 180°C/350°F/ Gas 4. Cream together the butter, icing sugar and vanilla extract until light. Sift in the flour and cornflour and mix together until smooth.

5 Beat together the butter, icing sugar and coffee cream. Use to sandwich the whirls in pairs. Dust with icing sugar and cocoa powder.

Energy 210Kcal/877kJ; Protein 2.2g; Carbohydrate 21.3g, of which sugars 11.2g; Fat 13.5g, of which saturates 7.6g; Cholesterol 22mg; Calcium 28mg; Fibre 0.8g; Sodium 64mg.

SUGAR COOKIES

THESE UNUSUAL LARGE COOKIES ARE MADE WITH A SWEETENED YEAST DOUGH SPICED WITH CINNAMON. THEY ARE EXTRA DELICIOUS SERVED WARM FROM THE OVEN, WITH THEIR CRUNCHY SUGAR COATING MELTING INTO THE FRAGRANT COOKIE DOUGH.

MAKES 5

INGREDIENTS

  250g/9oz/5 cups plain (all-purpose)
    flour, plus extra for dusting
  100g/3¾ oz/generous ½ cup sugar
  6ml/1¼ tsp easy-blend (rapid-rise)
    dried yeast
  pinch of salt
  5ml/1 tsp ground cinnamon
  30ml/2 tbsp full cream (whole) milk
  2 eggs, beaten
  100g/3¾oz/scant ½ cup unsalted
    butter, cubed and softened
  demerara (raw) sugar, for coating

1 Sift the flour into a large mixing bowl. Stir in the sugar, dried yeast, salt and cinnamon.

2 Whisk the milk and eggs together in a jug (pitcher). Make a well in the centre of the flour mixture and pour in the milk and eggs. Stir, incorporating the surrounding dry ingredients until the mixture holds together.

3 Add the softened butter, a few pieces at a time, and mix with your fingertips until all of it has been incorporated.

4 Shape the dough into a round and knead on a lightly floured surface for 10 minutes, until smooth.

5 Place the dough in a lightly oiled bowl, cover with clear film (plastic wrap) and leave to rest in the refrigerator for 1 hour.

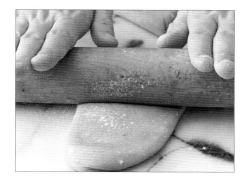

6 Divide the dough into five pieces and, with your hands, roll each piece into a long roll. With a rolling pin, flatten each roll to a rectangle.

7 Sprinkle the demerara sugar on a plate. Press each piece of dough in turn in the sugar until coated all over. Place on a baking sheet lined with baking parchment and leave to rest for 20–30 minutes.

8 Preheat the oven to 190°C/375°F/Gas 5. Bake the cookies for 20 minutes or until golden. Transfer to a wire rack. The cookies will harden as they cool. Break into pieces to serve.

GRANDMOTHER'S TIP
The cookies will keep for up to 1 week in an airtight container.

Energy 430kcal/1807kJ; Protein 7.6g; Carbohydrate 60.2g, of which sugars 22.1g; Fat 19.4g, of which saturates 11.2g; Cholesterol 119mg; Calcium 103mg; Fibre 1.6g; Sodium 154mg.

OAT BISCUITS

THESE CRISP AND CRUNCHY BISCUITS ARE WONDERFULLY QUICK AND EASY TO MAKE, AS WELL AS BEING UTTERLY DELICIOUS. THEY ARE HOMELY AND COMFORTING AT ANY TIME OF DAY, AND ARE FILLING ENOUGH TO KEEP HUNGER PANGS AT BAY.

MAKES ABOUT 18

INGREDIENTS
- 115g/4oz/½ cup butter
- 115g/4oz/½ cup soft light brown sugar
- 115g/4oz/½ cup golden (light corn) syrup
- 150g/5oz/1¼ cups self-raising (self-rising) flour
- 150g/5oz rolled oats

1 Preheat the oven to 180°C/350°F/Gas 4. Lightly grease or line two or three baking sheets with baking parchment.

2 Gently heat the butter, sugar and golden syrup in a heavy pan until the butter has melted and the sugar has dissolved, taking care not to let it burn.

3 Remove the syrup mixture from the heat and leave to cool, while you sift the flour. Stir in the flour to the butter, sugar and syrup mixture. Add the oats to the pan and mix together to make a soft dough.

4 Using your fingers, roll the dough into small balls and arrange them on the prepared baking sheets, leaving plenty of room for them to spread out.

5 Flatten each ball with a spatula. Bake for 12–15 minutes until golden brown, longer if more than one tray is in the oven.

6 Leave the biscuits to cool on the baking sheet briefly, then transfer to a wire rack to crisp up. Eat them warm, or cool completely before you store them.

VARIATION
Add 25g/1oz/¼ cup finely chopped toasted almonds, peanuts or walnuts, or a small handful of raisins, to the mixture in step 3.

Energy 151kcal/637kJ; Protein 1.8g; Carbohydrate 23.9g, of which sugars 11.9g; Fat 6g, of which saturates 3.3g; Cholesterol 14mg; Calcium 22mg; Fibre 0.8g; Sodium 59mg.

TOFFEE APPLE AND OAT CRUNCHIES

THESE SOFT COOKIES HAVE AN UNSOPHISTICATED APPEAL, WITH THEIR HOMELY ROUGH SHAPE. THE ADDICTIVE MIXTURE OF CHEWY OATS, SOFT APPLES AND CRUNCHY TOFFEE PIECES MEANS THEY ARE TOP OF THE CLASS FOR FLAVOUR. THEY COULD EASILY BECOME CHILDREN'S LUNCH-BOX FAVOURITE.

MAKES ABOUT 16

INGREDIENTS
- 150g/5oz/10 tbsp unsalted butter
- 175g/6oz/scant 1 cup light muscovado (brown) sugar
- 90g/3½oz/½ cup sugar
- 1 large (US extra large) egg, beaten
- 75g/3oz/⅔ cup plain (all-purpose) flour
- 2.5ml/½ tsp bicarbonate of soda (baking soda)
- pinch of salt
- 250g/9oz/2½ cups rolled oats
- 50g/2oz/scant ½ cup sultanas (golden raisins)
- 50g/2oz dried apple rings, coarsely chopped
- 50g/2oz chewy toffees, coarsely chopped

1 Preheat the oven to 180°C/350°F/ Gas 4. Line two or three baking sheets with baking parchment.

2 In a large bowl, beat together the butter and both sugars until creamy. Add the beaten egg and stir well until thoroughly combined.

3 Sift together the flour, bicarbonate of soda and salt. Add to the butter, sugar and egg mixture and mix in well.

4 Finally add the oats, sultanas, chopped apple rings and toffee pieces and stir gently until just combined.

5 Using a small ice-cream scoop or large tablespoon, place heaps of the mixture well apart on the prepared baking sheets. Bake for about 10–12 minutes, or until lightly set in the centre and just beginning to brown at the edges.

6 Remove from the oven and leave to cool on the baking sheets for a few minutes. Using a metal spatula, transfer the cookies to a wire rack to cool completely.

Energy 249Kcal/1047kJ; Protein 3.1g; Carbohydrate 38.8g, of which sugars 23.2g; Fat 10.1g, of which saturates 5.3g; Cholesterol 32mg; Calcium 34mg; Fibre 1.3g; Sodium 79mg.

HONEY CRUNCH CREAMS

GREEK HONEY WORKS WELL IN THIS RECIPE, AS IT HAS A STRONG FLAVOUR OF LIQUORICE AND ANISEED. IF YOU PREFER A MORE SUBTLE TASTE, USE HEATHER OR LAVENDER HONEY. WHICHEVER YOU PREFER, MAKING THESE COOKIES WILL BRING AN AROMA OF THE COUNTRYSIDE TO THE KITCHEN.

MAKES 20

INGREDIENTS
 250g/9oz/2¼ cups self-raising
  (self-rising) flour
 10ml/2 tsp bicarbonate of soda
  (baking soda)
 50g/2oz/¼ cup caster (superfine)
  sugar
 115g/4oz/½ cup unsalted butter,
  diced
 rind of 1 large orange,
  finely grated
 115g/4oz/½ cup honey
 25g/1oz/¼ cup pine nuts or
  chopped walnuts
For the filling
 50g/2oz/¼ cup unsalted butter, at
  room temperature, diced
 115g/4oz/1 cup icing (confectioners')
  sugar, sifted
 15ml/1 tbsp honey

GRANDMOTHER'S TIP
It is best to use a dark, heavy honey for this recipe, with as much flavour as possible, so that the cookies really taste like honey.

1 Preheat the oven to 200°C/400°F/ Gas 6. Line three or four baking sheets with baking parchment. Sift the flour, bicarbonate of soda and caster sugar into a bowl. Add the butter and rub in until the mixture resembles breadcrumbs. Stir in the orange rind.

2 Put the honey in a small pan and heat until just runny but not hot. Pour it over the flour and sugar mixture and mix to a firm dough.

3 Divide the dough in half and shape one half into 20 small balls about the size of a hazelnut in its shell. Place the balls on the baking sheets, spaced well apart, and gently flatten.

4 Bake for 6–8 minutes, until golden brown. Leave to cool and firm up on the baking sheets.

5 Use a metal spatula to transfer the cookies to a wire rack to allow them to cool completely.

6 Shape the remaining dough into 20 balls and dip one side of each one into the pine nuts or walnuts. Place the cookies, nut sides up, on the baking sheets, gently flatten and bake for 6–8 minutes, until golden brown.

7 Leave to cool and firm up slightly on the baking sheets before carefully transferring the cookies to a wire rack, still nut sides up, to cool completely.

8 To make the filling, put the butter, sugar and honey in a small bowl and beat together until light and fluffy.

9 When the cookies are completely cool, use the filling to sandwich the cookies together in pairs using a plain one for the bottome and a nut-coated one for the top.

VARIATION
You could use chopped peanuts instead of pine nuts or walnuts, and sandwich the cookies together with peanut butter mixed with honey.

Energy 164Kcal/688kJ; Protein 1.5g; Carbohydrate 23.4g, of which sugars 13.9g; Fat 7.8g, of which saturates 4.4g; Cholesterol 18mg; Calcium 24mg; Fibre 0.4g; Sodium 52mg.

SHREWSBURY CAKES

DESPITE BEING KNOWN AS CAKES, THESE ARE ACTUALLY CRISP, LEMONY SHORTBREAD BISCUITS WITH PRETTY FLUTED EDGES, WHICH HAVE BEEN MADE AND SOLD IN THE TOWN OF SHREWSBURY IN ENGLAND SINCE THE 17TH CENTURY. THEY ARE SIMPLE TO MAKE AND INCREDIBLY ADDICTIVE.

3 Add the egg yolks to the butter and sugar mixture, one at a time, beating thoroughly after each addition.

4 Sift the flour over the top and add the lemon rind. Stir in and then gather up the mixture to make a stiff dough. Knead the dough lightly on a floured surface then roll it out to about 5mm/¼in thick.

5 Using a 7.5cm/3in fluted biscuit (cookie) cutter, cut out circles and arrange on the baking sheets. Gather up the offcuts and roll out again to make more biscuits.

6 Put into the hot oven and cook for about 15 minutes, until firm to the touch and lightly browned. Transfer to a wire rack and leave to crisp up and cool completely.

VARIATION
Omit the lemon rind and sift 5ml/1 tsp mixed (apple pie) spice with the flour in step 3.

MAKES ABOUT 20

INGREDIENTS
   115g/4oz/½ cup soft butter
   140g/5oz/¾ cup caster (superfine)
   sugar
   2 egg yolks
   225g/8oz/2 cups plain (all-purpose)
   flour, plus extra for dusting
   finely grated rind of 1 lemon

1 Preheat the oven to 180°C/350°F/ Gas 4. Line two baking sheets with baking parchment.

2 In a mixing bowl, beat the softened butter with the sugar until pale, light and fluffy.

Energy 115kcal/482kJ; Protein 1.4g; Carbohydrate 16.1g, of which sugars 7.5g; Fat 5.4g, of which saturates 3.2g; Cholesterol 32mg; Calcium 23mg; Fibre 0.4g; Sodium 37mg.

CITRUS DROPS

THESE SOFT, CAKE-LIKE TREATS ARE DELICIOUSLY TANGY, WITH A CRUMBLY CITRUS-FLAVOURED BASE, FILLED WITH HALF A SPOONFUL OF LEMON OR ORANGE CURD BEFORE BAKING. THE CRUNCHY ALMOND TOPPING MAKES THE PERFECT FINISHING TOUCH. SERVE WITH A CUP OF COFFEE FOR ELEVENSES.

MAKES ABOUT 20

INGREDIENTS
    175g/6oz/¾ cup unsalted butter, at
      room temperature, diced
    150g/5oz/¾ cup caster (superfine)
      sugar
    finely grated rind of 1 large lemon
    finely grated rind of 1 orange
    2 egg yolks
    50g/2oz/½ cup ground almonds
    225g/8oz/2 cups self-raising (self-
      rising) flour
    90ml/6 tbsp lemon or orange curd
    milk, for brushing
    flaked (sliced) almonds, for
      sprinkling

1 Preheat the oven to 160°C/325°F/
Gas 3. Line two baking sheets with
baking parchment. Beat the butter and
sugar together until light and fluffy, then
stir in the citrus rinds.

2 Stir the egg yolks into the mixture,
then add the ground almonds and flour
and mix well.

3 Divide the mixture into 20 and shape
into balls. Place on the baking sheets.
Make a hole in each cookie with the
handle of a wooden spoon.

4 Put 2.5ml/½ tsp lemon or orange
curd into each hole and pinch the
opening to semi-enclose the curd.

5 Brush the tops with milk and sprinkle
with flaked almonds. Bake for about 20
minutes until pale golden brown. Cool
slightly on the baking sheets, then
transfer to a wire rack.

Energy 157Kcal/658kJ; Protein 2.1g; Carbohydrate 16.8g, of which sugars 8.2g; Fat 9.6g, of which saturates 4.9g; Cholesterol 39mg; Calcium 31mg; Fibre 0.6g; Sodium 55mg.

JAM TART BISCUITS

THESE SIMPLE BUTTERY BISCUITS FILLED WITH A SPOONFUL OF JAM ARE GIVEN AN EXTRA DIMENSION BY THE ADDITION OF THE SOUR CREAM TO THE MIXTURE. CHILDREN WILL LOVE TO HELP WITH THE CUTTING OUT OF THE DOUGH. MAKE PLENTY, AS THEY WILL BE POPULAR WITH ALL THE FAMILY.

MAKES 26–30

INGREDIENTS
  100g/3¾oz/generous ½ cup caster
    (superfine) sugar
  100g/3¾oz/scant ½ cup unsalted
    butter
  1 egg
  100ml/3½fl oz/scant ½ cup sour
    cream
  350g/12oz/3 cups plain (all-purpose)
    flour, plus extra for dusting
  5ml/1 tsp baking powder
  90ml/6 tbsp raspberry jam

1 Preheat the oven to 180°C/350°F/ Gas 4. Put the sugar and butter in a large bowl and beat together until light and fluffy. Beat in the egg, then mix in the sour cream.

2 Sift the flour and baking powder together, then incorporate into the sugar, butter and egg mixture, which will have a fairly wet consistency.

3 On a lightly floured surface, roll out the dough to 5mm/¼in thickness then, using a floured 5cm/2in round cutter, cut out rounds and place on a baking tray. Leave to rest for 15 minutes.

4 Press down the centre of each round with your thumb or the back of a teaspoon, then spoon a little raspberry jam into the indentation.

5 Bake the biscuits (cookies) in the oven for 12–15 minutes, until golden. Transfer to a wire rack and leave to cool before serving.

Energy 711kcal/2992kJ; Protein 10.9g; Carbohydrate 110.7g, of which sugars 44.1g; Fat 28.1g, of which saturates 16.7g; Cholesterol 116mg; Calcium 173mg; Fibre 2.7g; Sodium 190mg.

APPLE CRUMBLE AND CUSTARD SLICE

THESE TASTY SLICES CLEVERLY COMBINE ALL THE INGREDIENTS OF A VERY POPULAR DESSERT INTO A COOKIE. THEY ARE VERY QUICK TO MAKE IF YOU USE READY-MADE SWEET PASTRY, BUT OF COURSE YOU CAN MAKE YOUR OWN PASTRY FROM SCRATCH BY ADDING A LITTLE SUGAR TO ANY SHORTCRUST RECIPE.

MAKES 16

INGREDIENTS
   350g/12oz ready-made sweet pastry
   1 large cooking apple, about
     250g/9oz
   30ml/2 tbsp caster (superfine) sugar
   60ml/4 tbsp ready-made thick
     custard
For the crumble topping
   115g/4oz/1 cup plain (all-purpose)
     flour
   2.5ml/½ tsp ground cinnamon
   60ml/4 tbsp sugar
   90g/3½oz/7 tbsp unsalted butter,
     melted

1 Preheat the oven to 190°C/375°F/ Gas 5. Roll out the pastry and use to line the base of a 28 x 18cm/11 x 7in shallow cake tin (pan).

2 Prick the pastry with a fork, line with foil and baking beans and bake blind for about 10–15 minutes. Remove the foil and beans and return the pastry to the oven for a further 5 minutes until cooked and golden brown.

3 Meanwhile, peel, core and chop the apple evenly. Place in a pan with the caster sugar.

4 Heat gently until the sugar dissolves, then cover with a lid and cook gently for 5–7 minutes until a thick purée is formed. Beat with a wooden spoon and set aside to cool.

5 Mix the cold apple with the custard. Spread over the pastry.

6 To make the crumble topping, put the flour, cinnamon and sugar into a bowl and pour over the melted butter. Stir thoroughly until the mixture forms small clumps. Sprinkle the crumble over the filling.

7 Return to the oven and bake for about 10–15 minutes until the crumble topping is cooked and a golden brown. Leave to cool in the tin, then slice into bars to serve.

Energy 196Kcal/822kJ; Protein 2.1g; Carbohydrate 23.7g, of which sugars 8.1g; Fat 11g, of which saturates 4.9g; Cholesterol 15mg; Calcium 37mg; Fibre 0.9g; Sodium 124mg.

BRANDY SNAPS WITH CREAM

RECORDS SHOW THAT BRANDY SNAPS WERE SOLD AT FAIRS IN ENGLAND IN THE 1800S. THEY WERE CONSIDERED A SPECIAL TREAT FOR HIGH DAYS AND HOLIDAYS. EVERY KITCHEN HAD A LITTLE POT OF GROUND GINGER READY FOR ADDING TO CAKES, BISCUITS AND THESE LACY WAFER ROLLS.

MAKES ABOUT 12

INGREDIENTS
    50g/2oz/4 tbsp butter
    50g/2oz/¼ cup caster (superfine)
      sugar
    30ml/2 tbsp golden (light corn) syrup
    50g/2oz/½ cup plain (all-purpose)
      flour
    2.5ml/½ tsp ground ginger
    5ml/1 tsp brandy
    150ml/¼ pint/⅔ cup double (heavy)
      or whipping cream

1 Preheat the oven to 180°C/350°F/ Gas 4. Line two or three baking (cookie) sheets with baking parchment.

2 Gently heat the butter, sugar and golden syrup (in a pan on the stove or in the microwave on low power) until the butter has melted and the sugar has dissolved.

3 Remove the pan from the heat. Sift the flour and ginger, and stir into the mixture with the brandy.

4 Put small spoonfuls of the mixture on the lined baking sheets, spacing them about 10cm/4in apart to allow for spreading. Put into the hot oven and cook for 7–8 minutes or until bubbling and golden. Meanwhile, grease the handles of several wooden spoons.

5 Allow the wafers to cool on the tin for about 1 minute then loosen with a metal spatula and quickly roll around the spoon handles. Leave to set for 1 minute, before sliding them off and cooling completely on a wire rack.

6 Just before serving, whip the cream until soft peaks form, spoon into a piping bag and pipe a little into both ends of each brandy snap.

GRANDMOTHER'S TIP
Unfilled brandy snaps will keep for a week in an airtight container.

Energy 121kcal/505kJ; Protein 0.6g; Carbohydrate 11.7g, of which sugars 10g; Fat 7.9g, of which saturates 5g; Cholesterol 21mg; Calcium 16mg; Fibre 0.1g; Sodium 24mg..

STRAWBERRY CREAM SHORTBREADS

THESE PRETTY TREATS ARE ALWAYS POPULAR, ESPECIALLY SERVED WITH AFTERNOON TEA OR AS A QUICK AND EASY DESSERT. SERVE THEM AS SOON AS THEY ARE READY BECAUSE THE SHORTBREAD COOKIES WILL LOSE THEIR LOVELY CRISP TEXTURE IF LEFT TO STAND.

SERVES 3

INGREDIENTS
   150g/5oz/1¼ cups strawberries
   450ml/¾ pint/scant 2 cups double (heavy) cream
   6 round shortbread cookies

1 Reserve a few perfect and unblemished strawberries for decoration. Hull the remaining strawberries and cut them in half, discarding any bad parts.

2 Put the halved strawberries in a bowl and gently crush them using the back of a fork. Only crush the berries lightly; they should not be reduced to a purée. A few larger chunks should still be left whole to add to the texture.

3 Put the cream in a large, clean bowl and whip until softly peaking. Add the crushed strawberries and gently fold in to combine. (Do not overmix.)

4 Halve the reserved strawberries – you can choose whether to leave the stalks intact or to remove them.

5 Spoon the strawberry and cream mixture on top of the shortbread cookies. Decorate each one with half a strawberry and serve immediately.

VARIATIONS
• You can use any other berry you like for this dessert – try raspberries or blueberries.
• Two ripe, peeled peaches will also give great results.
• Instead of shortbread, you can use freshly baked scones.

Energy 976kcal/4035kJ; Protein 5.7g; Carbohydrate 34.6g, of which sugars 16.8g; Fat 90.8g, of which saturates 50.1g; Cholesterol 206mg; Calcium 122mg; Fibre 1.3g; Sodium 204mg.

HONEY AND ALMOND BISCUITS

THESE DELECTABLE SPICED HONEY COOKIES WERE ONCE TRADITIONALLY MADE AT CHRISTMAS AS A SPECIAL SPICY TREAT. THEY ARE DELICIOUS SERVED WITH COFFEE, BUT ALSO MAKE A VERY GOOD ACCOMPANIMENT TO ICE CREAM, SORBETS, OR POACHED FRUIT DESSERTS.

MAKES 20

INGREDIENTS
225g/8oz/1 cup clear honey
4 eggs, plus 2 egg whites
350g/12oz/3 cups plain
  (all-purpose) flour, plus extra for
  dusting
5ml/1 tsp bicarbonate of soda
  (baking soda)
2.5ml/½ tsp freshly grated nutmeg
2.5ml/½ tsp ground ginger
2.5ml/½ tsp ground cinnamon
2.5ml/½ tsp ground cloves
20 blanched almond halves

1 Beat together the honey and whole eggs until light and fluffy. Sift over the flour, bicarbonate of soda and spices, and beat to combine.

2 Gather the cookie dough into a ball, wrap in clear film (plastic wrap) and chill in the refrigerator for 1 hour or overnight.

3 Preheat the oven to 200°C/400°F/ Gas 6. Roll out the dough on a lightly floured surface to a thickness of 5mm/ ¼ in. Using a 4cm/1½ in cookie cutter, stamp out 20 rounds.

4 Transfer the rounds to two lightly greased baking trays. Beat the egg whites until soft peaks form. Brush the tops of the rounds with the egg white, then press an almond half into the centre of each one.

5 Place in the oven and bake for 15–20 minutes, or until they are a pale golden brown.

6 Remove from the oven and allow to cool slightly before transferring to a wire cooling rack. Leave to cool completely, then serve.

GRANDMOTHER'S TIPS
• In the days before sugar was widely available, honey was the only sweetener cooks had at their disposal. These little biscuits (cookies), sweetened only with honey, are a throw back to those far off days.
• Because there is no fat in the recipe, these biscuits will keep for up to 2 weeks in an airtight container.

Energy 112kcal/473kJ; Protein 3.4g; Carbohydrate 22.6g, of which sugars 8.9g; Fat 1.5g, of which saturates 0.4g; Cholesterol 38mg; Calcium 33mg; Fibre 0.5g; Sodium 22mg.

FRUIT TURNOVERS

BEFORE OVENS WERE INTRODUCED, TURNOVERS AND EVEN TARTS WERE COOKED ON THE GRIDDLE, AND IT MUST HAVE BEEN A SKILLED JOB TO GET THE TEMPERATURE JUST RIGHT AND TO FLIP THEM OVER WITHOUT LOSING THE FILLING. THIS RECIPE USES PLUMS, BUT YOU COULD USE APPLES OR JAM.

MAKES 8

INGREDIENTS
450g/1lb plums, stones (pits) removed and chopped
25–40g/1–1½oz/2–3 tbsp sugar
350g/12oz/3 cups plain (all-purpose) flour, plus extra for dusting
85g/3oz/6 tbsp lard or white cooking fat, cut into pieces
85g/3oz/6 tbsp butter, cut into pieces
milk and sugar for brushing and sprinkling
pinch of salt

VARIATION
These turnovers work well with puff pastry, too.

1 Bring the fruit and the sugar to the boil with 15ml/1 tbsp water, then cover and simmer for 5–10 minutes, stirring frequently, until the fruit is soft. You can reduce the liquid by bubbling uncovered and stirring until thick. Leave to cool.

2 Sift the flour and salt into a bowl, add the lard or cooking fat and butter, and rub them into the flour until the mixture resembles fine crumbs (alternatively, process in a food processor).

3 Gradually stir in cold water until the mixture forms clumps, then gather together to make a smooth dough. Wrap the pastry and chill for 20–30 minutes to allow it to relax.

4 Preheat the oven to 190°C/375°F/ Gas 5. Then line a baking sheet with baking parchment.

5 On a lightly floured surface, roll out the dough to 3–5mm/⅛–¼in thick. Using a small upturned bowl or plate as a guide, cut out eight 15cm/6in circles, re-rolling and cutting the pastry offcuts as necessary.

6 Place a spoonful of cooled fruit on to each pastry circle and brush the edges with water. Fold the pastry over the fruit, pinching the edges to seal them well. Arrange the pastries on the baking sheet, brush with milk, sprinkle some sugar over and make a small slit in each.

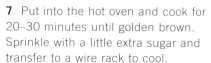

7 Put into the hot oven and cook for 20–30 minutes until golden brown. Sprinkle with a little extra sugar and transfer to a wire rack to cool.

Energy 340kcal/1420kJ; Protein 4.2g; Carbohydrate 38.5g, of which sugars 5.1g; Fat 19.8g, of which saturates 9.9g; Cholesterol 33mg; Calcium 66mg; Fibre 1.5g; Sodium 66mg

SUFFOLK BUNS

CARAWAY SEEDS WERE ONCE A POPULAR INGREDIENT OF BREADS, CAKES AND SWEET CONFECTIONS, AND WERE OFTEN CHEWED TO SWEETEN THE BREATH. ENGLISH FARMERS TRADITIONALLY GAVE SEED CAKES AND BUNS TO THEIR LABOURERS AT THE END OF WHEAT SOWING.

4 Lightly beat the eggs and stir them into the flour mixture, together with sufficient milk to enable you to gather the mixture into a ball of soft dough. Transfer to a lightly floured surface.

5 Roll out to about 2.5cm/1in thick. Using a 5cm/2in biscuit (cookie) cutter, cut into rounds, gathering up the offcuts and re-rolling to make more.

6 Arrange the rounds on the lined baking sheet, setting them quite close together so they support each other as they rise.

7 Put into the hot oven and cook for 15–20 minutes until risen and golden brown. Transfer to a wire rack and dust with caster sugar. Leave to cool.

GRANDMOTHER'S TIP
Replace the caraway seeds with 50g/2oz dried fruit, such as raisins or finely chopped apricots.

MAKES ABOUT 12

INGREDIENTS
350g/12 oz/3 cups plain (all-purpose) flour, plus extra for dusting
115g/4oz/²⁄₃ cup ground rice or semolina
10ml/2 tsp baking powder
115g/4oz/½ cup butter
75g/3oz/½ cup caster (superfine) sugar, plus extra for dusting
30ml/2 tbsp caraway seeds
2 eggs
about 75ml/5 tbsp milk

1 Preheat the oven to 200°C/400°F/ Gas 6. Line a baking sheet with baking parchment.

2 Sift the flour into a large mixing bowl, then add the ground rice and baking powder and mix to combine.

3 Add the butter to the flour mixture and, with your fingertips, rub it into the flour until the mixture resembles fine breadcrumbs. Stir the sugar and caraway seeds into the flour mixture.

Energy 244kcal/1026kJ; Protein 5.1g; Carbohydrate 36.9g, of which sugars 7.3g; Fat 9.5g, of which saturates 5.4g; Cholesterol 53mg; Calcium 60mg; Fibre 1.1g; Sodium 75mg.

WELSH CAKES

THESE CAKES WERE COOKED AT LEAST ONCE A WEEK IN KITCHENS TO ENJOY WITH A CUP OF TEA OR TO OFFER A TRADITIONAL WELCOME TO VISITORS. ORIGINALLY COOKED DIRECTLY ON THE SOLID PLATES OF RANGES, THERE ARE MANY VARIANTS OF THIS RECIPE. SERVE WARM, WITH BUTTER.

MAKES ABOUT 16

INGREDIENTS
- 250g/9oz/2 cups plain (all-purpose) flour, plus extra for dusting
- 7.5ml/1¼ tsp baking powder
- 125g/4½oz/½ cup butter, cut into small cubes
- 100g/3½oz/½ cup caster (superfine) sugar, plus extra for dusting
- 75g/3oz/½ cup currants
- 1 egg
- 45ml/3 tbsp milk

1 Heat a bakestone or a heavy frying pan over medium to low heat.

2 Sift the flour, baking powder and salt into a large mixing bowl.

3 Add the butter to the flour mixture and, with your fingertips, rub it into the flour until the it resembles fine breadcrumbs. Alternatively, you can process the ingredients in a food processor. Stir the sugar and the currants into the mixture.

4 Lightly beat the egg, and with a round-ended knife and a cutting action, stir the egg into the flour mixture with enough milk to gather the mixture into a ball of soft dough.

4 Transfer to a lightly floured surface and roll out to about 5mm/¼in thick. With a 6–7.5cm/2½–3in cutter, cut out rounds, gathering up the offcuts and re-rolling to make more.

5 Smear a little butter or oil over the hot bakestone or pan and cook the cakes, in small batches, for about 4–5 minutes on each side or until they are slightly risen, golden brown and cooked through.

6 Transfer to a wire rack, dust with caster sugar on both sides and leave to cool a little before serving with butter.

Energy 128kcal/540kJ; Protein 4.1g; Carbohydrate 22.8g, of which sugars 1.3g; Fat 2.9g, of which saturates 1.4g; Cholesterol 29mg; Calcium 66mg; Fibre 0.9g; Sodium 29mg.

CHEWY FLAPJACKS

FLAPJACKS ARE POPULAR WITH ADULTS AND CHILDREN ALIKE, AND THEY ARE SO QUICK AND EASY TO MAKE. ALL SORTS OF EXTRA INGREDIENTS CAN BE ADDED TO THE BASIC MIXTURE, DEPENDING ON INDIVIDUAL TASTES, FROM CHOPPED APRICOTS OR RAISINS TO CHOCOLATE CHIPS AND NUTS.

SERVES 4

INGREDIENTS
   175g/6oz/¾ cup unsalted butter
   50g/2oz/¼ cup caster (superfine)
   sugar
   150g/5oz/generous ⅓ cup golden
   (light corn) syrup
   250g/9oz/2¾ cups rolled oats

1 Preheat the oven to 180°C/ 350°F/Gas 4. Line the base and sides of a 20cm/8in square cake tin (pan) with baking parchment.

2 Mix the butter, sugar and syrup in a pan and heat gently until the butter has completely melted.

3 Add the oats to the pan and stir until combined. Turn the mixture into the tin and level the surface.

4 Bake the flapjacks for about 15–20 minutes, until just beginning to turn golden. Leave to cool slightly, then cut into fingers and remove from the tin. Store in an airtight container.

Energy 241Kcal/1008kJ; Protein 2.7g; Carbohydrate 29.5g, of which sugars 14.3g; Fat 13.2g, of which saturates 7.2g; Cholesterol 30mg; Calcium 18mg; Fibre 1.4g; Sodium 125mg.

CHOCOLATE BROWNIES

THIS IS A CLASSIC TRAY BAKE THAT NEEDS TO BE SERVED CUT INTO SMALL PIECES, AS IT IS SO RICH. THE END RESULT SHOULD BE MOIST, DARK IN COLOUR WITH A CRUSTY TOP, AND SOFT ENOUGH TO EAT WITH A FORK OR SPOON. THESE BROWNIES ARE IMPOSSIBLE TO RESIST AT ANY TIME OF DAY.

MAKES 16

INGREDIENTS
- 150g/5oz plain (unsweetened) chocolate, broken into squares
- 120ml/4fl oz/½ cup sunflower oil
- 215g/7½oz/1¼ cups light brown sugar
- 2 eggs
- 5ml/1 tsp vanilla extract
- 65g/2½oz/⅔ cup self-raising (all-purpose) flour
- 60ml/4 tbsp cocoa powder
- 75g/3oz/¾ cup chopped walnuts or pecan nuts
- 60ml/4 tbsp milk chocolate chips

1 Preheat the oven to 180°C/350°F/ Gas 4. Lightly grease a shallow 19cm/7½in square cake tin (pan). Melt the plain chocolate in a heatproof bowl over hot water.

2 Beat the oil, sugar, eggs and vanilla extract together in a large bowl.

3 Stir in the melted chocolate, then beat well until evenly mixed.

GRANDMOTHER'S TIP
For a delicious dessert, warm these brownies slightly and serve with vanilla ice cream.

4 Sift the flour and cocoa powder into the bowl and fold in thoroughly.

5 Stir in the chopped nuts and chocolate chips, pour into the prepared tin and spread evenly to the edges.

6 Bake for 30–35 minutes, or until the top is firm and crusty. Cool in the tin before cutting into squares.

Energy 235Kcal/983kJ; Protein 3.4g; Carbohydrate 25.9g, of which sugars 22.2g; Fat 13.9g, of which saturates 3.8g; Cholesterol 25mg; Calcium 37mg; Fibre 1g; Sodium 49mg.

TOFFEE BARS

THREE LAYERS MAKE UP THIS WONDERFULLY IMPRESSIVE TRAY BAKE. THE SWEET DOUGH BASE IS TOPPED WITH A CARAMEL MIXTURE MADE WITH CONDENSED MILK, A STAPLE KITCHEN INGREDIENT IN DAYS GONE BY. MELTED CHOCOLATE IN THREE COLOURS ADDS THE FINAL LAYER.

MAKES ABOUT 24

INGREDIENTS
For the shortbread base
  250g/9oz/2¼ cups plain (all-purpose)
    flour
  75g/3oz/scant ½ cup caster
    (superfine) sugar
  175g/6oz/¾ cup unsalted butter,
    softened
For the filling
  90g/3½oz/7 tbsp unsalted
    butter, diced
  90g/3½oz/scant ½ cup light
    muscovado (brown) sugar
  2 x 397g/14oz cans sweetened
    condensed milk
For the topping
  90g/3½oz plain (semisweet) chocolate
  90g/3½oz milk chocolate
  50g/2oz white chocolate

1 Preheat the oven to 180°C/350°F/ Gas 4. Line and lightly grease a 33 x 23cm/13 x 9in Swiss roll tin (jelly roll pan).

2 Put the flour and caster sugar in a bowl and rub in the butter until the mixture resembles fine breadcrumbs. Work with your hands until the mixture forms a dough.

3 Put the dough into the prepared tin and press it out with your hands to cover the base. Then use the back of a tablespoon to smooth it evenly into the tin.

4 Prick all over with a fork and bake for about 20 minutes, or until firm to the touch and very light brown. Set aside and leave in the tin to cool.

5 To make the filling, put the butter, muscovado sugar and condensed milk into a pan and heat gently, stirring, until the sugar has dissolved.

6 Stirring constantly, bring to the boil. Reduce the heat and simmer the mixture very gently, stirring or whisking constantly, to prevent it sticking for about 5–10 minutes.

7 When the toffee filling has thickened and has turned a pale caramel colour, remove the pan from the heat. Take care that the mixture does not burn on the base of the pan, as this will spoil the flavour.

8 Pour the toffee filling mixture over the shortbread base, spread it evenly, then leave until cold.

9 To make the topping, melt each type of chocolate separately in a microwave or in a heatproof bowl set over a pan of hot water. Spoon lines of plain and milk chocolate over the set caramel filling.

10 Add small spoonfuls of white chocolate. Use a skewer to form a marbled effect on the topping. Allow to set, before cutting into squares.

Energy 305Kcal/1381kJ; Protein 4.6g; Carbohydrate 39.6g, of which sugars 31.6g; Fat 15.4g, of which saturates 9.6g; Cholesterol 37mg; Calcium 132mg; Fibre 0.4g; Sodium 120mg.

PICKLES AND
PRESERVES

*Preserving fruit and vegetables from the garden
was not just a pleasure for previous generations,
it was a necessity, and is the perfect solution for
a glut of produce at any time of year. These
chutney and jelly recipes make splendid
accompaniments to a rustic meal of bread and
farmhouse cheese or cold meat, while the jams
need only a freshly baked scone or a slice of
toast to set the taste buds tingling.*

ONION PICKLE

THIS DELIGHTFUL MIXTURE OF SLICED ONIONS AND HERBS IS SIMMERED WITH BALSAMIC VINEGAR, RED WINE AND THE SECRET INGREDIENT, CHOPPED DRIED PRUNES. USE OLD-FASHIONED YELLOW ONIONS IF YOU CAN GET THEM, AS THEY WILL GIVE THE BEST SWEET FLAVOUR.

2 Season the onions with salt and ground black pepper, then add the thyme, bay leaf and sugar. Cook slowly, uncovered, for a further 15–20 minutes until the onions are very soft and dark. Stir the onions occasionally during cooking to prevent them sticking or burning.

3 Add the prunes, vinegar, wine and 60ml/4 tbsp water to the pan and cook over a low heat, stirring frequently, for 20 minutes, or until most of the liquid has evaporated. Add a little more water and reduce the heat if it looks dry. Remove from the heat.

4 Adjust the seasoning if necessary, adding more sugar or vinegar to taste. Leave the pickle to cool then stir in the remaining 5ml/1 tsp olive oil. Store in the refrigerator for up to 3 weeks.

VARIATION
If you have a glut of shallots or pickling (pearl) onions, use those instead. Brown 500g/1¼lb peeled pickling (pearl) onions or shallots in 60ml/4 tbsp olive oil. Sprinkle in 45ml/3 tbsp brown sugar and caramelize a little, then add 7.5ml/1½ tsp crushed coriander seeds, 250ml/8fl oz/1 cup red wine, 2 bay leaves, a few thyme sprigs, 3 strips orange rind, 45ml/3 tbsp tomato purée (paste) and the juice of 1 orange. Cook gently, covered, for 1 hour, stirring occasionally. Uncover for the last 20 minutes. Sharpen with 15–30ml/1–2 tbsp sherry vinegar and serve when cool.

MAKES ABOUT 500G/1¼LB

INGREDIENTS
  30ml/2 tbsp olive oil
  15g/½oz/1 tbsp butter
  500g/1¼lb onions, sliced
  3–5 fresh thyme sprigs
  1 fresh bay leaf
  30ml/2 tbsp light muscovado (brown)
    sugar, plus a little extra
  50g/2oz/¼ cup ready-to-eat prunes,
    chopped
  30ml/2 tbsp balsamic vinegar, plus
    a little extra
  120ml/4fl oz/½ cup red wine
  salt and ground black pepper

1 Reserve 5ml/1 tsp of the oil, then heat the remaining oil with the butter in a large pan. Add the onions, cover and cook gently over a low heat for about 15 minutes, stirring occasionally.

Per batch: Energy 678Kcal/2827kJ; Protein 7.5g; Carbohydrate 87.9g, of which sugars 76.4g; Fat 35.5g, of which saturates 11g; Cholesterol 32mg; Calcium 161mg; Fibre 9.8g; Sodium 113mg.

SPICED CHUTNEY

THIS IS A WONDERFUL WAY TO USE UP A GLUT OF EATING APPLES, OR EVEN WINDFALLS. THE CHOPPED APPLES ARE COMBINED WITH DATES, GINGER AND RAISINS FROM THE STORE CUPBOARD TO MAKE A LOVELY SOFT CHUTNEY, IDEAL FOR SERVING WITH SAUSAGES OR CHEESE.

MAKES ABOUT 2.75KG/6LB

INGREDIENTS
  1kg/2¼lb green eating apples
  15g/½oz garlic cloves
  1 litre/1¾ pints/4 cups malt vinegar
  450g/1lb dates
  115g/4oz preserved stem ginger
  450g/1lb/3 cups raisins
  450g/1lb/2 cups soft light brown sugar
  2.5ml/½ tsp cayenne pepper
  30ml/2 tbsp salt

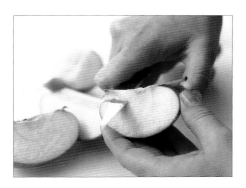

1 Quarter the apples, remove the cores but leave the peel on, and chop coarsely. Peel and chop the garlic.

2 Place the apple and garlic in a pan with enough vinegar to cover. Place on a high heat and bring to the boil, then boil for 10 minutes.

3 Chop the dates and ginger, and add them to the pan, together with the raisins, brown sugar, cayenne pepper and salt. Reduce the heat and cook the chutney gently for 45 minutes.

4 Leave the chutney to cool slightly and then spoon the mixture into warmed sterilized jars and seal immediately. Store in a cool dark place. Once opened, store in the refrigerator for up to 3 weeks.

GRANDMOTHER'S TIP
This sweet, chunky, spicy chutney is perfect served with cold meats for an informal buffet lunch. It also makes a lovely addition to cheese sandwiches.

Per batch: Energy 3920Kcal/16,737kJ; Protein 22.6g; Carbohydrate 1,014.4g, of which sugars 1,012.2g; Fat 3.3g, of which saturates 0g; Cholesterol 0mg; Calcium 599mg; Fibre 33.7g; Sodium 12,139mg.

PEAR AND WALNUT CHUTNEY

*THIS CHUTNEY RECIPE IS IDEAL FOR USING UP HARD PEARS THAT WILL NEVER RIPEN PROPERLY.
ITS MELLOW, SPICY FLAVOUR IS EXCELLENT SERVED WITH BREAD AND HAM OR A STRONG, MATURE
CHEESE SUCH AS CHEDDAR. IT WOULD ALSO GO WELL WITH SPICY RICE.*

MAKES ABOUT 1.8KG/4LB

INGREDIENTS
    1.2kg/2½lb firm pears
    225g/8oz tart cooking apples
    225g/8oz onions
    450ml/¾ pint/scant 2 cups cider
        vinegar
    175g/6oz/generous 1 cup sultanas
        (golden raisins)
    finely grated rind and juice of
        1 orange
    400g/14oz/2 cups sugar
    115g/4oz/1 cup walnuts, roughly
        chopped
    2.5ml/½ tsp ground cinnamon

1 Peel and core the fruit, then chop
into 2.5cm/1in chunks. Peel and
quarter the onions, then chop into
pieces the same size. Place in a
preserving pan with the vinegar.

2 Slowly bring to the boil, then reduce
the heat and simmer for 40 minutes,
stirring the mixture occasionally.

3 Meanwhile, put the sultanas in a
small bowl, pour over the orange juice
and leave to soak.

4 Add the sugar, sultanas, and orange
rind and juice to the pan. Gently heat
until the sugar has dissolved, then
simmer for 30–40 minutes, or until the
chutney is thick and no excess liquid
remains. Stir frequently towards the end
of cooking to prevent sticking.

5 Toast the walnuts in a non-stick pan
over a low heat for 5 minutes, stirring,
until lightly coloured. Stir the nuts into
the chutney with the cinnamon.

6 Spoon the chutney into warmed
sterilized jars, cover and seal. Store in a
cool, dark place and leave to mature for
at least 1 month. Use within 1 year.

Per batch: Energy 3501Kcal/14,797kJ; Protein 29.8g; Carbohydrate 705.3g, of which sugars 699.3g; Fat 81.4g, of which saturates 6.4g; Cholesterol 0mg; Calcium 603mg; Fibre 40.7g; Sodium 189mg.

BEETROOT AND ORANGE CHUTNEY

WITH ITS VIBRANT RED COLOUR AND RICH EARTHY FLAVOUR, THIS DISTINCTIVE CHUTNEY IS GOOD WITH SALADS AS WELL AS FULL-FLAVOURED CHEESES SUCH AS STILTON. IT WOULD ALSO MAKE A LOVELY CONTRAST TO A CREAM CHEESE TOPPING ON HOT, FLUFFY BAKED POTATOES.

MAKES ABOUT 1.4KG/3LB

INGREDIENTS
  350g/12oz raw beetroot (beets)
  350g/12oz eating apples
  300ml/½ pint/1¼ cups malt vinegar
  200g/7oz/1 cup sugar
  225g/8oz red onions, finely chopped
  1 garlic clove, crushed
  finely grated rind and juice of
   2 oranges
  5ml/1 tsp ground allspice
  5ml/1 tsp salt

1 Scrub or, if necessary, thinly peel the beetroot, then cut into 1cm/½in pieces. Peel, quarter and core the apples and cut into 1cm/½in pieces.

2 Put the vinegar and sugar in a preserving pan and heat gently, stirring occasionally, until the sugar dissolves.

3 Add the beetroot, apples, onions, garlic, orange rind and juice, ground allspice and salt to the pan. Bring to the boil, reduce the heat, then simmer for 40 minutes.

4 Increase the heat slightly and boil for 10 minutes, or until the chutney is thick and no excess liquid remains. Stir frequently to prevent it catching on the base of the pan.

5 Spoon the chutney into warmed sterilized jars, cover and seal. Store in a cool, dark place and allow to mature for at least 2 weeks before eating. Use within 6 months of making. Refrigerate once opened and use within 1 month.

GRANDMOTHER'S TIP
For a fine-textured chutney, put the peeled beetroot through the coarse grating blade of a food processor.

Per batch: Energy 1055Kcal/4506kJ; Protein 8.2g; Carbohydrate 271.1g, of which sugars 269g; Fat 0.8g, of which saturates 0g; Cholesterol 0mg; Calcium 195mg; Fibre 12.3g; Sodium 255mg.

SWEET PICCALILLI

Undoubtedly one of the most popular and traditional relishes, piccalilli can be eaten with meat or cheese. In some parts of England it was also eaten as an accompaniment to a meat and potato pie. Keep the pieces of vegetable quite large for an authentic look.

MAKES ABOUT 1.8KG/4LB

INGREDIENTS

1 large cauliflower
450g/1lb pickling (pearl) onions
900g/2lb mixed vegetables, such as
  marrow (large zucchini), cucumber,
  French (green) beans
225g/8oz/1 cup salt
2.4 litres/4 pints/10 cups cold water
200g/7oz/1 cup sugar
2 garlic cloves, peeled and crushed
10ml/2 tsp mustard powder
5ml/1 tsp ground ginger
1 litre/1¾ pints/4 cups distilled
  (white) vinegar
25g/1oz/¼ cup plain (all-purpose)
  flour
15ml/1 tbsp turmeric

1 Wash all the vegetables thoroughly. Divide the cauliflower into florets, discarding large pieces of stalk. Peel and quarter the pickling onions.

2 Seed and finely dice the marrow and cucumber. If the skin is tough you might want to peel them. Trim the French beans, then cut them into 2.5cm/1in lengths, smaller if you prefer.

3 Layer the vegetables in a large glass or stainless steel bowl, generously sprinkling each layer with salt. Pour the water over the vegetables, and cover the bowl with clear film (plastic wrap). Set aside and leave to soak for 24 hours.

4 Drain the vegetables, and discard the brine. Rinse well in several changes of cold water to remove as much salt as possible, then drain thoroughly.

5 Put the sugar, garlic, mustard, ginger and 900ml/1½ pints/3¾ cups of the vinegar in a preserving pan. Heat gently, stirring occasionally, until all the sugar has dissolved.

6 Add the vegetables to the pan, bring to the boil, reduce the heat and simmer for 10–15 minutes, until almost tender. Be careful not to overcook.

7 In a small bowl, mix the flour and turmeric with the remaining vinegar until combined. Then gradually stir the mixture into the vegetables. Bring to the boil, stirring, and simmer for 5 minutes, until the piccalilli is thick.

8 Spoon the piccalilli into warmed sterilized jars, cover and seal. Store in a cool, dark place for at least 2 weeks. Use within 1 year.

Per batch: Energy 1358Kcal/5757kJ; Protein 34.1g; Carbohydrate 300.8g, of which sugars 266g; Fat 12g, of which saturates 1.2g; Cholesterol 0g; Calcium 555mg; Fibre 20.6g; Sodium 4011mg.

TOMATO SAUCE AND MINT SAUCE

THESE TWO POPULAR CONDIMENTS MAY BE COMMERICIALLY AVAILABLE, BUT MAKING YOUR OWN IS DEEPLY SATISFYING. THE TOMATO SAUCE CAN BE USED TO LIVEN UP SAUSAGES OR BREAKFAST FRY-UPS, WHILE THE MOUTH-TINGLING MINT SAUCE IS A TRADITIONAL ACCOMPANIMENT TO ROAST LAMB.

TOMATO SAUCE

MAKES ABOUT 2.75KG/6LB

INGREDIENTS

    2.25kg/5lb very ripe tomatoes
    1 onion
    6 cloves
    4 allspice berries
    6 black peppercorns
    1 sprig fresh rosemary
    25g/1oz root ginger, sliced
    1 celery heart, chopped
    30ml/2 tbsp brown sugar
    65ml/4½ tbsp/⅓ cup white wine
       vinegar
    3 garlic cloves, peeled
    15ml/1 tbsp salt

1 Peel and seed the tomatoes, then chop and place in a large pan. Stud the onion with the cloves and add to the pan. In a double layer of cheesecloth, tie the allspice, peppercorns, rosemary and ginger and add to the pan.

2 Add the celery, plus the leaves, sugar, vinegar, garlic and salt to the pan and bring to the boil, stirring occasionally. Reduce the heat and simmer gently, uncovered, for 1–1½ hours, until thick and reduced by half.

3 Purée the mixture in a blender or food mill, sieve (strain) if you want a smooth sauce, then return to the pan. Bring to the boil and simmer for 15 minutes. Bottle in clean, sterilized jars and store in the refrigerator.

MINT SAUCE

MAKES ABOUT 250ML/8FL OZ/1 CUP

INGREDIENTS

    1 large bunch mint, finely chopped
    150ml/¼ pint/⅔ cup white wine
       vinegar
    30ml/2 tbsp sugar

1 Place the mint in a 600ml/1 pint/2½ cup jug (pitcher). Add 105ml/7 tbsp boiled water from the kettle and leave to steep. When the mint infusion has cooled down to lukewarm temperature, add the white wine vinegar and sugar.

2 Pour into a clean bottle and store in the refrigerator for up to six months, although it is best used within three.

Tomato sauce, per batch: Energy 543Kcal/2327kJ; Protein 18.1g; Carbohydrate 108.5g, of which sugars 107.2g; Fat 7.5g, of which saturates 2.3g; Cholesterol 0mg; Calcium 313mg; Fibre 26.6g, Sodium 6281mg.
Mint sauce, per batch: Energy 161Kcal/685kJ; Protein 3.9g; Carbohydrate 36.6g, of which sugars 31.3g; Fat 0.7g, of which saturates 0g; Cholesterol 0mg; Calcium 226mg; Fibre 0g; Sodium 17mg.

CRANBERRY AND RED ONION RELISH

THIS WINE-ENRICHED RELISH IS PERFECT FOR SERVING WITH HOT ROAST TURKEY AT CHRISTMAS. IT CAN ALSO BE STIRRED INTO A GAME CASSEROLE FOR EXTRA SWEETNESS, OR SERVED WITH COLD MEAT. IT LOOKS LOVELY GIVEN AS A HOME-MADE PRESENT IN A PRETTY GLASS JAR.

2 Meanwhile, put the cranberries in a pan with the remaining sugar, and the vinegar, red wine, mustard seeds and ginger. Heat gently until the sugar has dissolved, then cover the pan with its lid and bring to the boil.

3 Simmer the relish mixture for 12–15 minutes, until the berries have burst and are tender, then stir in the caramelized onions.

4 Increase the heat slightly and cook uncovered for a further 10 minutes, stirring the mixture frequently until it is well reduced and thickened. Remove the pan from the heat, then season with salt and pepper to taste.

MAKES ABOUT 900G/2LB

INGREDIENTS
    450g/1lb small red onions
    30ml/2 tbsp olive oil
    225g/8oz/1 cup soft light brown sugar
    450g/1lb/4 cups fresh or frozen
      cranberries
    120ml/4fl oz/½ cup red wine vinegar
    120ml/4fl oz/½ cup red wine
    15ml/1 tbsp mustard seeds
    2.5ml/½ tsp ground ginger
    30ml/2 tbsp port or orange liqueur
    salt and ground black pepper

VARIATION
Redcurrants make a very good substitute for cranberries in this recipe. They produce a relish with a lovely flavour and pretty colour.

1 Halve the red onions and slice them very thinly. Heat the oil in a large pan, add the onions and cook them over a very low heat for about 15 minutes, stirring occasionally until softened. Add 30ml/2 tbsp of the sugar and cook for a further 5 minutes, or until the onions are caramelized.

5 Transfer the relish to warmed sterilized jars. Spoon a little of the port or orange liqueur over the top of each, then cover and seal.

6 Store in a cool place for up to 6 months. Store in the refrigerator once opened and use within 1 month.

Per batch: Energy 1532Kcal/6486kJ; Protein 8g; Carbohydrate 314.6g, of which sugars 304.2g; Fat 23.3g, of which saturates 3.2g; Cholesterol 0mg; Calcium 259mg; Fibre 13.5g; Sodium 46mg.

CITRUS THYME JELLY

THE AROMATIC THYME ADDS A SPECIAL FLAVOUR TO THIS CLEAR CITRUS JELLY. YOU CAN VARY THE SHARPNESS BY ALTERING THE AMOUNT OF ORANGES, LEMONS AND LIMES — USE MORE ORANGES FOR A MILDER, SWEETER FLAVOUR. THIS WOULD MAKE A WONDERFUL SAUCE TO SERVE WITH ROAST PORK.

MAKES ABOUT 1.3KG/3LB

INGREDIENTS
   675g/1½lb lemons
   675g/1½lb limes
   450g/1lb oranges
   2 bay leaves
   2 litres/3½ pints/8¾ cups water
   about 800g/1¾lb/4 cups preserving
      or white granulated sugar
   60ml/4 tbsp fresh thyme leaves

VARIATION
For lavender jelly, replace the lemons, limes and oranges with apples, and the bay leaves and thyme with 90ml/6 tbsp of washed lavender flowers.

1 Wash all the fruit, then cut into small pieces. Place in a large heavy pan with the bay leaves and pour over the water.

2 Bring the mixture to the boil, then reduce the heat, cover and simmer for 1 hour, or until pulpy. Discard the bay leaves, then pour the fruit and juices into a sterilized jelly bag suspended over a large bowl. Leave to drain for 3 hours, or until the juices stop dripping.

3 Measure the juice into the cleaned pan, adding 450g/1lb/2¼ cups sugar for every 600ml/1 pint/2½ cups juice. Heat gently until the sugar has dissolved. Bring to the boil, then boil rapidly for about 10 minutes, or until setting point is reached (105°C/220°F). Remove the pan from the heat. Skim any scum off the surface.

4 Stir in the thyme leaves. Leave to cool for a few minutes until a thin skin forms, then gently stir again to make sure the thyme is evenly distributed.

5 Pour into warmed sterilized jars. Cover and seal when cold. Store in a cool, dark place and use within 1 year. Once opened, store in the refrigerator.

Per batch: Energy 3154Kcal/13,455kJ; Protein 4.2g; Carbohydrate 836.1g, of which sugars 836.1g; Fat 0.1g, of which saturates 0g; Cholesterol 0mg; Calcium 434mg; Fibre 0.2g; Sodium 50mg.

TOMATO AND HERB JELLY

*THIS DARK GOLDEN JELLY IS DELICIOUS SERVED WITH GRILLED AND ROASTED MEAT, ESPECIALLY LAMB.
IF YOU HAVE AN AUTUMN GLUT OF TOMATOES, THIS IS A GOOD WAY TO USE UP A WHOLE BASKETFUL.
A COUPLE OF TEASPOONS OF THE JELLY CAN ALSO ENLIVEN TOMATO-BASED SAUCES.*

MAKES ABOUT 1.3KG/3LB

INGREDIENTS
  1.8kg/4lb tomatoes
  2 lemons
  2 bay leaves
  300ml/½ pint/1¼ cups cold water
  250ml/8fl oz/1 cup malt vinegar
  bunch of fresh herbs such as
    rosemary, thyme, parsley and mint,
    plus a few extra sprigs for the jars
  about 900g/2lb/4½ cups preserving or
    granulated white sugar

1 Wash the tomatoes and lemons well, then cut the tomatoes into quarters and the lemons into small pieces. Put the chopped tomatoes and lemons in a large heavy pan with the bay leaves and pour over the water and vinegar.

2 Add the herbs, either one herb or a mixture if preferred. If you are using pungent woody herbs such as rosemary and thyme, use about six sprigs; if you are using milder leafy herbs such as parsley or mint, add about 12 large sprigs.

3 Bring the mixture to the boil, then reduce the heat. Cover the pan with a lid and simmer for about 40 minutes, or until the tomatoes are very soft.

4 Pour the tomato mixture into a sterilized jelly bag suspended over a large bowl. Leave to drain for about 3 hours, or until the juices stop dripping.

5 Measure the juice into the cleaned pan, adding 450g/1lb/2¼ cups sugar for every 600ml/1 pint/2½ cups juice. Heat gently, stirring, until the sugar dissolves. Boil rapidly for 10 minutes, to setting point (105°C/220°F), then remove from the heat. Skim off any scum.

6 Leave the jelly for a few minutes until a skin forms. Place a herb sprig in each warmed sterilized jar, then pour in the jelly. Cover and seal when cold. Store the jars in a cool, dark place and use within 1 year.

GRANDMOTHER'S TIP
Once you have opened a jar of this jelly, store it in the refrigerator and use within 3 months.

Per batch: Energy 3839Kcal/16,365kJ; Protein 11g; Carbohydrate 940g, of which sugars 920g; Fat 4g, of which saturates 1.5g; Cholesterol 0mg; Calcium 54mg; Fibre 14g; Sodium 184mg.

PICKLED ONIONS

SMALL PICKLED ONIONS ARE A TRADITIONAL FEATURE OF PUB LUNCHES ACROSS THE BRITISH ISLES. THEY ARE SERVED WITH COLD MEATS AND PIES, AND, MOST TYPICALLY, WITH FARMHOUSE BREAD AND CHEESE. STORE THEM FOR AT LEAST SIX WEEKS BEFORE EATING TO ALLOW THE FLAVOURS TO DEVELOP.

MAKES ABOUT 4 450G/1LB JARS

INGREDIENTS
   1kg/2¼lb pickling (pearl) onions
   115g/4oz/½ cup salt
   750ml/1¼ pints/3 cups
      malt vinegar
   15ml/1 tbsp sugar
   2–3 dried red chillies
   5ml/1 tsp brown mustard seeds
   15ml/1 tbsp coriander seeds
   5ml/1 tsp allspice berries
   5ml/1 tsp black peppercorns
   5cm/2in piece fresh root
      ginger, sliced
   2–3 blades of mace
   2–3 fresh bay leaves

1 To peel the onions, trim off the root end, but leave the onion layers attached. Cut a thin slice off the top (neck) end of the onion. Place the onions in a bowl, then cover with boiling water. Leave to stand for about 4 minutes, then drain. The skin should then be easier to peel with a small, sharp knife.

2 Place the peeled onions in a bowl and cover with cold water, then drain the water off and pour it into a large pan. Add the salt and heat slightly to dissolve it, then cool before pouring the brine over the onions.

3 Cover the bowl with a plate and weigh it down slightly so that it keeps all the onions submerged in the brine. Leave the onions to stand in the salted water for 24 hours.

4 Place the vinegar in a large pan. Wrap all the remaining ingredients, except the bay leaves, in a piece of cheesecloth, or sew into a coffee filter paper, and add to the vinegar with the bay leaves. Bring to the boil, simmer for 5 minutes, then remove from the heat. Set aside to cool and steep overnight.

VARIATION
To make sweet pickled onions, follow the same method, but add 50g/2oz/ 4 tbsp light muscovado (brown) sugar to the vinegar in step 4.

GRANDMOTHER'S TIP
For sterilizing, stand clean, rinsed jars upside down on a rack on a baking sheet and place in the oven at 180°C/350°F/ Gas 4 for 20 minutes.

5 Drain the onions, rinse and pat dry. Pack into sterilized jars. Add some or all of the spice from the vinegar, but not the ginger slices. The pickle will get hotter if you add the chillies. Pour the vinegar over the onions to cover, and add the bay leaves. Cover the jars with non-metallic lids. Store in a cool, dark place for at least 6 weeks before eating.

Per batch: Energy 109Kcal/454kJ; Protein 3.1g; Carbohydrate 24.5g, of which sugars 18.6g; Fat 0.5g, of which saturates 0g; Cholesterol 0mg; Calcium 67mg; Fibre 3.6g; Sodium 8mg.

APPLE, ORANGE AND CIDER JELLY

A SPOONFUL OR TWO OF THIS TANGY AMBER-COLOURED JELLY ADDS A REAL SPARKLE TO A PLATE OF COLD MEATS, ESPECIALLY HAM AND PORK, OR A RICH GAME PÂTÉ. TART COOKING APPLES SUCH AS BRAMLEYS MAKE THE BEST-FLAVOURED JELLY, WHILE THE CLOVES GIVE IT A SPICY AROMA.

MAKES ABOUT 1.8KG/4LB

INGREDIENTS
  1.3kg/3lb tart cooking apples
  4 oranges
  4 whole cloves
  1.2 litres/2 pints/5 cups sweet cider
  about 600ml/1 pint/2½ cups cold
    water
  about 800g/1¾lb/4 cups preserving
    or granulated white sugar

VARIATION
Replace some of the apples with crab apples for a more distinctive taste.

1 Wash and chop the apples and oranges, then put in a preserving pan with the cloves, cider and water to barely cover the fruit.

2 Bring the mixture to the boil, cover and simmer gently for 1 hour, stirring it occasionally.

3 Pour the fruit and juices into a sterilized jelly bag suspended over a large bowl. Leave to drain for at least 4 hours, or overnight, until the juices stop dripping.

4 Measure the juice into the cleaned preserving pan, adding 450g/1lb/ 2¼ cups sugar for every 600ml/1 pint/ 2½ cups juice.

5 Heat the mixture, gently stirring continuously, until the sugar has completely dissolved. Then boil the jelly rapidly for about 10 minutes until setting point is reached (105°C/220°F). Remove the pan from the heat.

6 Skim any scum off the surface, then pour the jelly into warmed sterilized jars. Cover and seal. Store the jelly in a cool, dark place and use within 18 months. Once opened, store in the refrigerator and eat within 3 months.

Per batch: Energy 3442Kcal/14,691kJ; Protein 10.4g; Carbohydrate 905.2g, of which sugars 905.2g; Fat 0.8g, of which saturates 0g; Cholesterol 0mg; Calcium 671mg; Fibre 13.3g; Sodium 79mg.

QUINCE AND ROSEMARY JELLY

FOR THIS RECIPE, HARD UNRIPE QUINCES, WHICH ARE FRUITS THAT RESEMBLE PEARS, SHOULD BE PICKED BEFORE THEY FALL FROM THE TREE, AS THEY CONTAIN THE MOST PECTIN AND THIS WILL HELP THE JELLY TO SET. A LITTLE LEMON JUICE WILL HELP IF THE QUINCES ARE RIPE.

MAKES ABOUT 900G/2LB

INGREDIENTS
   900g/2lb preferably unripe quinces,
      cut into small pieces,with bruised
      parts removed
   900ml–1.2 litres/1½–2 pints/
      3¾–5 cups water
   lemon juice (optional)
   4 large sprigs of fresh rosemary
   about 900g/2lb/4½ cups preserving
      or granulated white sugar

1 Put the chopped quinces in a large heavy pan with the water, using the smaller volume if the fruit is ripe, plus the lemon juice, and the larger volume, if the fruit is hard.

2 Reserve a few small sprigs of rosemary, then add the rest to the pan. Bring to the boil, reduce the heat, cover with a lid and simmer gently until the fruit becomes pulpy.

3 Remove and discard all the rosemary sprigs. (Don't worry about any of the tiny leaves that may have fallen off during cooking).

4 Pour the fruit and juices into a sterilized jelly bag suspended over a large bowl. Leave for 3 hours, or until the juices stop dripping.

GRANDMOTHER'S TIP
If you don't have a jelly bag, use a large square of cheesecloth tied to the legs of an upside down chair to strain the juice.

5 Measure the drained juice into the cleaned pan, adding 450g/1lb/2¼ cups sugar for every 600ml/1 pint/2½ cups juice. Heat the mixture gently over a low heat, stirring occasionally, until the sugar has dissolved completely.

6 Bring to the boil, then boil rapidly for about 10 minutes until the jelly reaches setting point (105°C/220°F). Remove the pan from the heat.

7 Skim any scum from the surface using a slotted spoon, then leave the jelly to cool for a few minutes until a thin skin begins to form on the surface.

8 Place a sprig of rosemary in each warmed sterilized jar, then pour in the jelly. Cover and seal when cold.

9 Store in a cool, dark place and use within 1 year. Once the jelly is opened, keep it in the refrigerator and use within 3 months.

Per batch: Energy 3666Kcal/15,636kJ; Protein 5.4g; Carbohydrate 970.5g, of which sugars 970.5g; Fat 0.3g, of which saturates 0g; Cholesterol 0mg; Calcium 510mg; Fibre 6.6g; Sodium 63mg.

BLACKBERRY AND SLOE GIN JELLY

THIS JELLY COMBINES TWO INGREDIENTS THAT ARE NATIVE TO THE BRITISH COUNTRYSIDE:
BLACKBERRIES AND SLOES. THE BLACKBERRIES ARE COOKED AND STRAINED TO GET RID OF THE SEEDS.
THE END RESULT IS A BEAUTIFUL DARK JELLY THAT MAKES THE VERY BEST OF A HEDGEROW HARVEST.

3 Bring the fruit mixture back to a simmer and cook gently for about 20 minutes, or until the sloes are tender and the blackberries very soft, stirring once or twice.

4 Pour the fruit and juices into a sterilized jelly bag suspended over a large bowl. Leave to drain for at least 4 hours or overnight, until the juices have stopped dripping.

5 Measure the fruit juice into the cleaned preserving pan, adding 450g/1lb/2¼ cups sugar for every 600ml/1 pint/2½ cups juice.

6 Heat the mixture gently, stirring occasionally, until the sugar has dissolved completely. Bring to the boil, then boil rapidly for about 10 minutes until the jelly reaches setting point (105°C/220°F). Remove the pan from the heat.

7 Skim off any scum from the surface of the jelly using a slotted spoon, then stir in the gin.

8 Pour the jelly into warmed sterilized jars, cover and seal. Store in a cool, dark place and use within 2 years. Once opened, keep the jar in the refrigerator.

MAKES ABOUT 1.3KG/3LB

INGREDIENTS
    450g/1lb sloes (black plums),
      washed
    600ml/1 pint/2½ cups cold water
    1.8kg/4lb/16 cups blackberries
    juice of 1 lemon
    about 900g/2lb/4½ cups preserving
      or granulated white sugar
    45ml/3 tbsp gin

GRANDMOTHER'S TIP
Sloes bring a good level of pectin to the jelly. If all blackberries are used without sloes, select some under-ripe fruit and use preserving sugar with added pectin for a good set.

1 Prick the sloes with a fine skewer and place in a large heavy pan with the water. Bring to the boil, reduce the heat, cover and simmer for 5 minutes.

2 Briefly rinse the blackberries in cold water and add them to the pan with the lemon juice.

GRANDMOTHER'S TIP
Sloes are harder to come by than blackberries but are ready around the same time. Don't be tempted to pick the berries too early – they will be too bitter.

Per batch: Energy 3750Kcal/15,985kJ; Protein 10.8g; Carbohydrate 984.3g, of which sugars 984.3g; Fat 1.4g, of which saturates 0g; Cholesterol 0mg; Calcium 743mg; Fibre 21g; Sodium 69mg.

BRAMBLE JAM

BLACKBERRYING IS A TRADITIONAL AUTUMN RECREATION AND LEADS TO A RANGE OF CULINARY DELIGHTS TOO, INCLUDING THIS JAM. SERVE WITH HOT BUTTERED TOAST, OR SCONES HOT FROM THE OVEN AND A DOLLOP OF THICK CLOTTED CREAM FOR A DELICIOUS TEATIME TREAT.

MAKES ABOUT 3.6KG/8LB

INGREDIENTS
  2.75kg/6lb/13¾ cups granulated
    white sugar
  2.75kg/6lb/16 cups
    blackberries
  juice of 2 lemons
  150ml/¼ pint/⅔ cup water

GRANDMOTHER'S TIP
The heating of the sugar in advance helps speed up the actual jam-making process and gives a brighter, more intense flavour.

1 Put the sugar to warm either in a low oven or in a pan over a low heat.

3 Stir in the sugar, bring to the boil and boil rapidly. Check for the setting point by placing a spoonful of jam on a plate, and allow to cool. If it wrinkles when pressed, it's ready. Ladle into warmed sterilized jam jars and seal. Store in a dark place and use within 2 years.

2 Rinse the blackberries and place in a large pan with the lemon juice and water. Bring to the boil and simmer for about 5 minutes.

Per batch: Energy 12570kcal/53550kJ; Protein 42g; Carbohydrate 3288g, of which sugars 3288g; Fat 6g, of which saturates 0g; Cholesterol 0mg; Calcium 2820mg; Fibre 93g; Sodium 240mg.

OXFORD MARMALADE

THE CHARACTERISTIC CARAMEL COLOUR AND RICH CITRUS FLAVOUR OF OXFORD MARMALADE IS OBTAINED BY CUTTING THE ORANGES COARSELY, AND THEN SIMMERING THEM FOR SEVERAL HOURS BEFORE ADDING THE SUGAR. THE RESULT IS A FULL-FLAVOURED PRESERVE.

2 Chop the fruit, reserving the pips (seeds), and add to the rind in the pan, along with the water. Tie the orange pips in a piece of muslin (cheesecloth) and add to the pan.

3 Bring to the boil, then cover and simmer for 2 hours. Add more water during cooking to maintain the same volume. Remove the pan from the heat and leave overnight.

4 The next day, remove the muslin bag from the oranges, squeezing it well to retain all the juice, and return the pan to the heat. Bring to the boil, then cover and simmer for 1 hour.

5 Add the warmed sugar to the pan, then slowly bring the mixture to the boil, stirring until the sugar has dissolved completely.

6 Increase the heat and boil rapidly for about 15 minutes, or until setting point is reached (105°C/220°F).

7 Remove the pan from the heat and skim off any scum from the surface.

8 Leave the marmalade to cool for about 5 minutes, stir through, then pour into warmed sterilized jars and seal. When cold, label, then store in a cool, dark place for up to one year.

MAKES ABOUT 2.25KG/5LB

INGREDIENTS
    900g/2lb Seville (Temple) oranges
    1.75 litres/3 pints/7½ cups water
    1.3kg/3lb/6½ cups sugar

GRANDMOTHER'S TIP
Traditionalists say that only bitter oranges such as Seville should be used to make marmalade. Although this isn't always true, it is most certainly the case when making Oxford marmalade.

1 Scrub the oranges, then remove the rind using a vegetable peeler. Thickly slice the rind and put in a large pan.

Per batch: Energy 5455Kcal/23,275kJ; Protein 16.4g; Carbohydrate 1435g, of which sugars 1435g; Fat 0.9g, of which saturates 0g; Cholesterol 0mg; Calcium 1112mg; Fibre 15.3g; Sodium 123mg.

LEMON CURD

THIS IS AN EXTREMELY POPULAR FAMILY RECIPE FOR A CLASSIC TANGY, CREAMY LEMON CURD. IT IS DELICIOUS SERVED AS A SPECIAL DESSERT SAUCE WITH A FRESH FRUIT TART, PANCAKES OR ICE CREAM, BUT MANY PEOPLE PREFER SIMPLY TO SPREAD IT ON BREAD AND BUTTER.

MAKES ABOUT 450G/1LB

INGREDIENTS
   3 lemons
   200g/7oz/1 cup caster (superfine)
      sugar
   115g/4oz/8 tbsp unsalted butter,
      diced
   2 large (US extra large) eggs
   2 large (US extra large) egg yolks

1 Wash the lemons, then finely grate the rind and place in a large heatproof bowl. Using a sharp knife, halve the lemons and squeeze all the juice into the bowl.

2 Set the bowl over a pan of gently simmering water and add the sugar and butter. Stir until the sugar has dissolved and the butter melted.

3 Put the eggs and yolks in a separate bowl and beat together with a fork. Pour the eggs through a sieve (strainer) into the lemon mixture, and whisk well until they are thoroughly combined.

4 Stir the mixture constantly over the heat until the curd thickens and lightly coats the back of a wooden spoon.

5 Remove the pan from the heat and pour the curd into small, warmed sterilized jars. Cover, seal and label.

6 Store in a cool, dark place, ideally in the refrigerator. Use within 3 months. (Once opened, store in the refrigerator.)

GRANDMOTHER'S TIP
If you are really impatient when it comes to cooking, it is possible to cook the curd in a heavy pan directly over a low heat rather than over a bowl of water. However, this can be risky, and you really need to watch the mixture like a hawk to avoid it curdling. If the curd looks as though it's beginning to curdle, quickly plunge the base of the pan in cold water and beat vigorously.

Per batch: Energy 1927Kcal/8056kJ; Protein 20.7g; Carbohydrate 212.1g, of which sugars 212.1g; Fat 116.8g, of which saturates 66.2g; Cholesterol 1029mg; Calcium 294mg; Fibre 0g; Sodium 871mg.

WILD STRAWBERRY AND ROSE PETAL JAM

HERE IS A PRESERVE THAT IS REDOLENT OF A SUMMER'S DAY. TINY WILD STRAWBERRIES GROW IN SUNNY SPOTS, OFTEN AMONG THE FLOWERS IN PEOPLE'S GARDENS, AND ALMOST UNNOTICED. THIS MAKES A FRAGRANT SPREAD TO SERVE AS PART OF A CREAM TEA WITH FRESHLY BAKED SCONES.

MAKES ABOUT 900G/2LB

INGREDIENTS
  900g/2lb/8 cups wild strawberries
  450g/1lb/4 cups strawberries, hulled
    and mashed
  2 dark pink rose buds, petals only
  juice of 2 lemons
  1.3kg/3lb/6½ cups sugar, warmed
  a few drops of rose water

VARIATION
To make plain strawberry jam, make in the same way but leave out the rose petals and rose water.

1 Put both the wild and cultivated strawberries into a non-metallic bowl together with the rose petals, lemon juice and warmed sugar. Cover and leave overnight.

2 The next day, transfer the fruit to a preserving pan and heat gently, stirring, until all the sugar has dissolved. Boil for 10–15 minutes, or to setting point (105°C/220°F).

3 Stir the rose water into the jam, then remove from the heat. Skim off any scum, leave to cool for 5 minutes, then stir and pour into warmed sterilized jars. Seal, label and store for up to one year.

GRANDMOTHER'S TIP
If you are unable to find wild berries, use the same weight in ordinary strawberries instead. Leave the smaller berries whole but mash any large ones.

Per batch: Energy 5487Kcal/23,379kJ; Protein 17.3g; Carbohydrate 1439.5g, of which sugars 1439.5g; Fat 1.4g, of which saturates 0g; Cholesterol 0mg; Calcium 905mg; Fibre 14.8g; Sodium 159mg.

BLACKCURRANT JAM

THIS JAM HAS A RICH, FRUITY FLAVOUR, ENHANCED BY THE ORANGE RIND AND JUICE AND LIFTED BY A COUPLE OF SPOONFULS OF CASSIS, A BLACKCURRANT LIQUEUR. ITS STRONG, DARK COLOUR REFLECTS THE SHINY TINTS OF THE FRUIT. IT IS DELICIOUS WITH SCONES OR TEACAKES FOR AFTERNOON TEA.

MAKES ABOUT 1.3KG/3LB

INGREDIENTS
  1.3kg/3lb/12 cups blackcurrants
  grated rind and juice of 1 orange
  475ml/16fl oz/2 cups water
  1.3kg/3lb/6½ cups sugar, warmed
  30ml/2 tbsp cassis (optional)

1 Wash the blackcurrants, removing the little stalks, then place in a large heavy pan with the orange rind and juice and water. Place on a medium heat and bring the liquid to the boil. Reduce the heat and simmer for 30 minutes.

2 Add the warmed sugar to the pan and stir over a low heat until the sugar has dissolved.

3 Bring the mixture to the boil and cook for about 8 minutes, or until the jam reaches setting point (105°C/220°F).

4 Remove the pan from the heat and skim off any scum from the surface using a slotted spoon.

5 Leave the jam to cool for 5 minutes, then stir in the cassis, if using.

6 Pour the jam into warmed sterilized jars and seal. Leave the jars to cool completely, then label and store in a cool, dark place for up to one year.

Per batch: Energy 5504Kcal/23,503kJ; Protein 18.4g; Carbohydrate 1448.7g, of which sugars 1448.7g; Fat 0.1g, of which saturates 0g; Cholesterol 0mg; Calcium 1474mg; Fibre 46.9g; Sodium 122mg.

RASPBERRY JAM

THIS IS A CLASSIC JAM THAT REQUIRES GOOD FIRM FRUIT, GATHERED AT ITS PEAK IN HIGH SUMMER. RASPBERRIES ARE LOW IN PECTIN, SO THE FRUIT TRADITIONALLY HAS SOME LEMON JUICE ADDED TO HELP IT SET INTO A WONDERFUL SOFT CONFECTION WITH A VIVID RED COLOUR.

MAKES ABOUT 3.1KG/7LB

INGREDIENTS
  1.8kg/4lb/10⅔ cups firm raspberries
  juice of 1 large lemon
  1.8kg/4lb/9 cups sugar, warmed

GRANDMOTHER'S TIP
To test if jam or jelly will set, put a spoonful of it on to a cold saucer. Allow it to cool slightly and then push the surface of the jam with your finger. Setting point has been reached if a skin has formed and it wrinkles. If not, boil for a little longer and keep testing regularly until it sets; the flavour will be better if the boiling time is short.

1 Put 175g/6oz/1 cup of the raspberries into a preserving pan and crush them. Add the rest of the fruit and the lemon juice, and simmer until soft and pulpy. Add the sugar and stir until dissolved, then bring back to the boil and boil hard until setting point is reached, testing after 3–4 minutes.

2 Pour into warmed, sterilized jars. When cold, cover, seal and store in a cool, dark place for up to 6 months.

VARIATION
For a slightly stronger flavour, 150ml/ ¼ pint/⅔ cup redcurrant juice can be used instead of the lemon juice.

Per batch: Energy 7542kcal/32,220kJ; Protein 34.2g; Carbohydrate 1963.8g, of which sugars 1963.8g; Fat 5.4g, of which saturates 1.8g; Cholesterol 0mg; Calcium 1.40g; Fibre 45g; Sodium 162mg.

PLUM JAM

THE FRUIT OF PLUM TREES RIPEN ALL AT ONCE SO USE THEM TO MAKE THIS QUEEN OF JAMS. IT'S LIKELY THAT YOU WILL HAVE MORE THAN 1KG/2LB OF PLUMS AT ONCE, SO JUST INCREASE THE QUANTITES OF WATER AND SUGAR ACCORDINGLY, AND ENJOY IT THROUGHOUT THE WINTER MONTHS.

MAKES ABOUT 2KG/4½LB

INGREDIENTS
1kg/2¼lb damsons or wild plums, washed, stalks removed
1.4 litres/2¼ pints/6 cups water
1kg/2¼lb/5 cups preserving or granulated white sugar, warmed

GRANDMOTHER'S TIP
It is important to seal the jars as soon as you have filled them to ensure the jam remains sterile. However, you should then leave the jars to cool completely before labelling and storing them, to avoid the risk of burns.

1 Put the plums in a preserving pan and pour in the water. Bring to the boil then reduce the heat and simmer gently until the damsons are soft. Add the sugar and stir it in thoroughly. Bring the mixture to the boil.

2 Skim off the stones (pits) as they rise to the surface. Boil to setting point (105°C/220°F). Remove from the heat, leave to cool for 10 minutes, then transfer to warmed sterilized jam jars. Seal immediately.

Per batch: Energy 4300kcal/18360kJ; Protein 11g; Carbohydrate 1133g, of which sugars 1133g; Fat 1g, of which saturates 0g; Cholesterol 0mg; Calcium 660mg; Fibre 16g; Sodium 80mg.

INDEX

ACKNOWLEDGEMENTS
Recipes supplied by Catherine Atkinson, Janez Bogataj, Judith Dern, Matthew Drennan, Brian Glover, Silvena Johan Lauta, Janet Lawrence, Elena Makhonko, Maggie Mayhew, Ewa Michalik, Janny de Moor, Anna Mosseson, Carol Pastor, Andy Parle, Mirko Trenkner, Jennie Shapter, Christopher Trotter, Biddy White Lennon, Annette Yates and Suzanne Vandyke.
Photography by Martin Brigdale, William Lingwood, Charlie Richards, Craig Robertson, Debi Treloar and Jon Whitaker.